MANAGING
PASSENGER
LOGISTICS

WEEK L

MANAGING PASSENGER LOGISTICS

The Comprehensive Guide to People and Transport

PAUL FAWCETT

The Institute of
Logistics and Transport

KOGAN
PAGE

First published in 2000

Kogan Page Limited
120 Pentonville Road
London N1 9JN

© Paul Fawcett, 2000

British Library Cataloguing in Publication Data
A CIP record for this book is available from the British Library.
ISBN 0 7494 3214 4

Typeset by Saxon Graphics Ltd, Derby
Printed and bound by Creative Print and Design (Wales)

Contents

Preface

The Road Freight Transport Industry has made great strides in the development and application of logistics techniques that have transformed its operations, delivered impressive productivity gains and improved customer responsiveness. This book suggests how these might transfer to road passenger operations.

The merger in 1999 of the Chartered Institute of Transport (CIT) and the Institute of Logistics (IoL) to form an Institute of Logistics and Transport has re-opened the debate about the precise nature of the science of logistics, and whether it truly embraces both freight and passenger operations. The new institute is developing a qualifying structure that no longer examines by way of modal papers (Road Passenger, Rail, Air, Sea, etc) but replaces these with just two papers: Movement of Passengers and Movement of Goods.

Managing Passenger Logistics has been written to cover the Movement of Passengers syllabus and will also meet the needs of Higher Diploma in Business Studies students and undergraduates at those UK and overseas universities that offer Transport Studies courses.

As a Management Studies textbook it deliberately follows closely the format of the Management Charter Initiative's identified Key Roles (eg Managing Human and Physical Resources, Finances, Information, etc). It will be invaluable to candidates preparing for the ILT's competence-based Certificates and Diplomas in Management

There are a number of well-respected texts on public transport operation (see Bibliography) but none of these are truly intermodal. *Managing Passenger Logistics* is intended to redress that deficiency. It has been written at a time of fundamental change as the government begins to implement the 'New Deal for Transport' White paper on its Integrated Transport Strategy. A Postscript has been added as the book went to print to examine and comment on the Transport Bill 2000.

If this book prompts future transport and logistics professional students to think and write holistically about both passenger and freight logistics, and to identify and emulate best practice in both, I will be well satisfied.

Paul Fawcett
April 2000

Managing Passengers

INTRODUCTION

Passengers are human cargo. From earliest times they have travelled with freight on cargo services; sailing ships, carriers' wagons, mail coaches, packet steamers and on the first railways (which were initially built as 'goods' lines). The separation of passenger and freight traffic and the dedication of specialized vehicles and infrastructure to each is a relatively new concept in historic terms. Moreover, there is considerable debate as to whether such separation will ever be complete or if it is desirable that it should be. The duplication of passenger and freight services over the same route or at the same times may well be uneconomic, inefficient, ineffective or environmentally unsustainable. There is a re-emergence of forms of hybrid transport (of which the rural post bus is an excellent example) and a re-awareness of their benefits.

Movement of passengers and goods

There is a tendency too for academics to study the movement of freight and passengers as if these were two discreet disciplines. In 1975, some members of the Chartered Institute of Transport (CIT) in the UK formed a breakaway Institute of Physical Distribution Management that later became the Institute of Logistics (ILog) because they felt that the CIT was becoming too 'passenger transport oriented'. CIT and ILog came together in 1999 to form an Institute of Logistics and Transport (ILT)! Actually, only the commercial movers of goods along the supply chain between producers and consumers defined logistics so narrowly.

Talk to any members of the armed services and they will confirm that the word logistics (which in any case had a military origin) always embraced the movement of both troops and supplies.

Logistics

The road freight transport industry has made great strides in the development and application techniques of logistics that have transformed its operations, delivered impressive productivity gains and improved customer service. Many of these techniques could be applied easily to the logistics of moving people with very little adaptation and the reverse is surely true. What, if it is not just-in-time delivery, is a dial-a-bus service? Is an airport departure lounge not a human warehouse? These and other significant analogies will be explored later in this book whose title, 'Managing Passenger Logistics', was deliberately chosen to highlight such congruencies.

Public v private transport

There are other similarities. Travel until the comparatively recent advent of the private car has always been a predominantly gregarious activity with groups of passengers travelling together either for security or because of economies of scale. For all but the very rich, a corollary of travel was enforced companionship. The operating costs of a private carriage were not much less than a stagecoach but the coach carried proportionally more passengers.

Schedule v charter

This distinction can be honed even further if comparisons are made between modes of passenger carriage that are truly public transport, usually operating to a published timetable and available to the general public on payment of a fare, and what might be described as private hire, where a vehicle is chartered for the exclusive use of a private party. However, similar distinctions have been commonplace in freight transport for centuries. One need only consider the differences between scheduled liner services carrying general cargo and vessels chartered for the exclusive transport of a single merchant's cargo (the so called 'charter party') or the differences between the distribution of a high-street retailer's product by a dedicated 'third party' operation and general haulage.

Travel purposes

Whether or not a passenger's mobility is shared with others, it is clear that, like different cargos, not all passengers are alike. Men and women in general have different travel needs as do, for example, children, pensioners and business travellers. The purposes for which passengers travel also vary and these create a demand for transport. However, the demand for transport, unlike the demand for other commodities and services, is derived from travel needs just as the demand for freight transport derives from commercial needs. Thus, economists explain that transport is generally a derived demand – the wish to travel for travel's sake is only manifest in leisure and tourism. Passenger transport moves people from where they are to where they need or wish to be whilst cargos are moved to where their economic utility is greatest, which is eventually the market where they are to be sold.

The military science of logistics saw this movement of troops and supplies (including ammunition) in strategic terms and even today some remote transport infrastructures still have greater strategic or defence than commercial purposes. However, the vast majority of commercial transport provision is for economic or social purposes such as employment, shopping, education, health and leisure.

Elements of transport

All transport systems are recognized as having a number of common components. There will always be a 'way' or infrastructure over which the vehicles will travel – a road, railway or canal for example. Even where the way is natural (eg, sea and air) or natural and artificially improved (such as a river navigation) the terminal (seaports and airports) will be man-made infrastructures and navigation systems will have to be provided (lighthouses, radar and air traffic control).

Likewise, there will be vehicles to carry passengers whether they are cars, taxis, buses, trams, trains, ferries or aircraft. Some of these will be self-propelled, others, such as the carriages of an intercity train, will be hauled by a locomotive. In any event, there will have to be a form of motive power, whether a remote power station providing the current to an electrified railway line or an integral internal combustion (petrol) or compression ignition (diesel) engine.

The vehicles themselves may run on fixed track or be more flexible road vehicles but they will generally have to be driven, unless they are remote controlled like the Docklands Light Railway in London. In addition, the system itself will need to have an operator responsible for resourcing, licensing and planning the operation. Every passenger transport system, then, to a greater or lesser extent, depends on there being a:

- way;
- vehicle;
- motive power;
- operator and driver;

and, ultimately, on there being passengers whose fares, or subsidies on their behalf, can finance the operation. It is therefore paramount in any passenger transport operation that operators and their staff understand the passengers they are carrying.

UNDERSTANDING PASSENGERS

No two persons and thus no two passengers are alike. However, passengers do have much in common. They have a common purpose of safe arrival at their destination. They want too to travel in comfort and to arrive on time. Nevertheless, passengers, even car drivers, are not in full control of their journey. Bad weather, congestion, mechanical breakdown and many other unpredictable events can disrupt this. Therefore, a fundamental attribute of all passengers, even though they will generally do their best to hide this, is their insecurity. This insecurity can be compounded in other ways:

- They may be confused by the operator's timetables or have been unable to obtain accurate information before commencing their journey.
- They may be confused by the fare structure, and possibly afraid to enquire for fear of appearing inadequate or foolish.
- They may be afraid of being late for an appointment, boarding the wrong vehicle or missing a connection.
- They may have young, elderly or disabled dependants in tow, and not wish to appear confused themselves in front of their charges.
- They may be young, elderly or disabled themselves. In some cases, the disability itself, such as deafness, may not be immediately apparent, or it may be transient, such as the mobility impairment of a parent accompanied by toddlers in a folding buggy or an otherwise fit person with a broken limb.
- They may be foreign and possibly not speak English.
- They may have difficulty spotting, reading or interpreting signage or hearing announcements. Bus and rail stations, airports and seaports are confusing places, scenes of hectic activity, and passengers can easily become confused.
- They may not be able to access 'real-time' information, or there may very probably be no such information, about the actual running of their transport or connections, and staff may appear to be too busy or unapproachable to help them.

Even if staff who meet passengers on the vehicles, at terminals or booking offices or on the telephone actually recognize this incipient insecurity, either they are unable to help or passengers become frustrated or disorientated. In all probability, they may then seek to avoid using the operator's service again or may even in the long run be lost to public transport and acquire or use their own private transport.

This message has not been lost on some of the better private operators who have entered the public transport arena since bus deregulation in 1986 or rail privatization in 1993 and they have made considerable investment in customer care training for their staff. However, in many cases it has proved difficult to motivate staff whose wages have been depressed by the resulting competition between operators.

TRANSPORT NEEDS ANALYSIS

'Need' is subjective, implying a desire for transport both embracing and exceeding mere requirement or demand. The Transport Act 1968 placed a duty on Passenger Transport Authorities to provide services to meet the needs of their area whilst the Transport Act 1985, which deregulated bus services, only required them and County Councils to meet those 'requirements which the market did not provide'. This last phrase assumes the market will have met demands that economists define as needs backed by an ability to pay.

Need and demand

Merseytravel's community transport officer once made a very succinct distinction between need and demand at a conference in 1985, sponsored by his employer the Merseyside Passenger Transport Executive (PTE) (attended by the author). He gave two homely examples:

> 'Two business men queuing for a taxi at Lime Street station to take them to Pier Head – that's demand... Two nurses waiting for a bus at six o'clock in the morning to take them on duty – that's need.'

Need, therefore, has a social dimension. Establishing the transport needs of a community, however, is far from simple. The demographic profile of an area can be illuminating and is not hard to access via census data, which Local Authorities hold. It provides general answers to questions such as:

- What is the total population of the area?
- What is its population density?
- What proportion is old-age pensioners (OAPs), children of school age and post-16-year-old students ('scholars' in the jargon of travel surveys)?
- What proportion of households has no car available to them?

The higher the population density of an area the easier, in general, it will be served by public transport. However, this generalization is affected by other criteria such as the level of car or multi-car ownership, the general prosperity of the area and the proportion of inhabitants of pensionable age. Nor are the multi-variable relationships between these factors as simple as they might appear. In rural areas for example, car ownership is often higher than in quite prosperous parts of London but this is not because it is more affordable but simply because it is essential where public transport is inadequate or non-existent. This rural phenomenon is often referred to as 'unwanted car ownership'. In addition, a high level of car ownership per household is not the same as individual car ownership because typically the breadwinner uses the family car to commute, leaving the rest of the family car-less whilst it is parked at the workplace.

All these factors must also be balanced against what is known about the actual level of public transport serving the area. In order to complete anything like an adequate transport needs analysis it is often necessary to conduct a survey. This will usually be of a sample of a population although small communities like a single village or parish council can sometimes find the time and resources to conduct an actual travel census. In some cases, it can be useful to ask respondents to complete a travel diary for a period, typically one month, preceding the survey.

Transport needs surveys

It is usual to commence a survey with questions about trips that are currently being made as these indicate travel decisions already taken (ie, revealed preferences) where choice exists, albeit this may have been a journey by private car. Such revealed preferences can be used to predict the needs of people without any form of transport. This can then be followed by questions about travel decisions not yet taken (ie, stated preferences) because these are currently prevented by a perceived lack of transport. It is far too often the case that some form of transport does operate but is not being used to satisfy a travel need because of ignorance of its existence, timetable or route.

The survey should reveal what are sometimes described as the five 'W's:[1]

- Who wants to go?
- What form of transport do people use or would like to use?
- When do they want to go?
- Where do they want to go?
- Why do they want to go?

Any assessment of need involves identifying trip origins, destinations and times. As with any market survey questionnaire design is crucial (see, for example, Figure 1.1). Leading questions such as 'if a service were provided between X and Y would you use this?' should be avoided since the respondents' preferences (both as revealed and stated) should make the answer to such a question obvious. Thought needs to be given as to how the survey will be designed and delivered. The sample frame should be as representative of the population as possible if the survey is to be based on a sample rather than a census. For example, if there is a high proportion of pensioners in the area there should be a similar proportion in the sample frame. It is also important that questionnaires are not delivered only to existing public transport users. Collection points like libraries, post offices and town halls can be used and respondents can be encouraged to return their forms there, or, if funds permit, be given a freepost envelope.

Community impact evaluation

There are a number of ways of modelling transport needs. One of the crudest is to apply a simple subsidy per passenger cut-off so that inordinately expensive transport needs are ignored. Inevitably, these will include some of the needs of mobility-impaired passengers. Another is by means of a technique known as community impact evaluation, developed in 1984.[2] The method enables the relative efficiency of options to be considered and for trade-offs to be made between the most efficient option and options delivering more equitable distributions of costs and social benefits.

Benchmarking

Yet another powerful tool is benchmarking, a system that applies a 'benchmark' level of service to every community dependent on its characteristics. In 1998, Lancashire County Council, with the help of consultants,[3] tried to determine where to spend the government's new Rural Bus Services Grant by benchmarking all communities in the county with a population of 10,000 or less. These were areas designated as 'rural' on maps prepared by the Department of the Environment, Transport and the Regions (DETR) for deciding where the grant could be spent (see Figure 1.2).

The DETR's guidelines[4] had stated that the criteria to be applied should be needs based and the county's existing criteria are based on subsidy per passenger and cost-to-revenue quotients. The initial benchmarking is against population only but this is being refined to take into account relative age profiles, levels of car (and two car) ownership, unemployment levels and other appropriate data.

A typical benchmark might be that for settlements with a population of 150 or more, services should be suitably timed to allow for a 9.00 am to 5.30 pm working day in the nearest major town with employment

TRANSPORT SURVEY

ANY TRAVEL PROBLEMS

Can you tell us about any local (less than 15 miles) journeys which members of your household would like to make but which you are currently unable to through lack of services, non availability of car or similar difficulty?

	Where would you like to travel from?	Where would you like to travel to?	General Purpose (eg Shopping)	Which day and at what time would you like to travel?	Why couldn't you make this journey?			
					No car available	No bus service	Too far to travel	Other (please explain in comments below)
EXAMPLE	HOME	CASTLE STEWART	CLINIC	THURSDAY, OUT AT 10.00 AM BACK AT 4.00 PM				
PERSON No								
PERSON No								
PERSON No								
PERSON No								
PERSON No								
PERSON No								

Are there any local (within 15 miles) journeys which you do not make as often as you would like, because of the cost of travel?

	Where would you like to travel from?	Where would you like to travel to?	General Purpose (eg Shopping)	Estimated cost of the journey
EXAMPLE	HOME	STIRLING	SHOPPING	£3.50
PERSON No				
PERSON No				
PERSON No				
PERSON No				
PERSON No				
PERSON No				

OTHER COMMENTS

NOTES

You may not be able to make journeys that you would like to make through not having access to a car, through there being no suitable bus services, or through the cost of travel being too expensive.
Please complete the sections overleaf if you are not able to travel because of any practical difficulty (the top section) or because of the cost (the bottom section).
There is also space for you to make any comments about difficulties encountered. You may continue these comments on a plain sheet of paper if you wish.
If you do not experience any problems please write 'NONE' along the top of the page.

Figure 1.1 Typical extract from a transport needs analysis   *Source:*   Scottish Office Rural Transport Survey

opportunities and that for settlements with over 1,000 inhabitants there should be provision to cater for a secondary 8.00 am to 4.30 pm working day. Similar benchmarks were developed for shopping, health and leisure trips but not for education. The latter is catered for at a statutory minimalist level by the provisions on school transport in the Education Act 1996 and the requirement in the Transport Act 1985[5] for Local Education Authorities (LEAs) and transport authorities (PTEs, county and unitary councils) to cooperate in the provision of public transport services. They are required to obtain 'best value for money' – hardly a needs-based criterion. In fact, the greatest unmet need arises in connection with access to further education and employment training.

JOURNEY PURPOSE

A passenger's journey may be essential or discretionary; it may be routine or unique. At the same time, there may be more than one purpose behind the journey. In today's hectic environment, more and more journeys are 'chained', with a person going perhaps to work, shopping and calling at a hostelry on the way home or maybe taking in an evening class or visit to a leisure centre. The more essential the journey the more price inelastic the fare will be because passengers, in the short run at least, have no alternative means of accessing, for example, their place of work. This accounts for the tendency of operators to try to raise commuter fares more than leisure fares – a topic returned to when competition, regulation and pricing are discussed.

Employment

Many transport commentators and textbooks give the impression that the journey to work is the dominant transport demand, the major cause of congestion and overcrowding, and the single most pressing transport problem. The reality is that other journeys account for more passengers/km than commuting but these are spread over longer periods and tend to be to more disparate destinations. Depending on how some forms of retailing such as visits to large out of town shopping developments are classified, leisure travel is more dominant than commuting. In 1996, for example, only 18 per cent of bus journeys were for commuting against 36 per cent for retail purposes and 46 per cent for 'other purposes'.[6]

Employment related journeys are often described as commuting, however this word perhaps more accurately describes mass movements of employees working conventional hours and taking place along radial corridors connecting suburbs and their town or city. Mass commuting is

LANCASHIRE COUNTY COUNCIL – BENCHMARK CRITERIA FOR SUPPORTED BUS SERVICES

Settlement Population	Category	No. of (return) trips to a designated centre for:			
		Employment/Training	Shopping	Healthcare/Hospital	Evening/weekend/leisure
10,000–2,500	A	Min. 2-hourly service 7.00–5.00 Mon–Sat		4 per day + daily visiting including evenings	4 per evening + 4 per Sunday
2,499–1,000	B	2 per day Mon–Sat	3 per day Mon–Sat	2 per day + 2 evenings visiting	2 per evening + 3 per Sunday
999–450	C	1 per day Mon–Sat	2 per day Mon–Sat	1 per day	3 evenings per week + 2 per Sunday
449–150	D	1 per day Mon–Fri	2 per day on 2 days	1 per day on 2 days	1 evening per week
50–149	E	Nil	1 per week	1 per week	Nil

Figure 1.2 Benchmark criteria for supported services   *Source:* Lancashire County council, 1999

relatively easy to provide for by conventional public transport but it does create its own unique problem, that of the rush hour or 'peak hour travel'.

From the transport providers' point of view, this means providing extra capacity for a relatively short period, capacity that will be surplus to requirements for the rest of the day. Workers who choose to commute by private transport add to the congestion of the peak and themselves become part of their own problem. However, increasingly, public transport is not an option for many of today's employees. They may work flexible hours, shifts or part-time hours when public transport is not available, or they may work at locations not served by public transport. Ironically, this is often the case with public transport employees. They have to reach their depot before the first public transport services in order to provide those very services. The real problem, however, has much deeper origins and stems from the historic lack of coordination between land use planners and transport planners. This has resulted in the creation of out-of-town industrial estates, business parks, retail developments, hospitals, schools and leisure facilities that are rarely sited on busy radial routes and are often difficult to serve by public transport. The classic many (employees) to few (locations) commuting pattern is replaced by a large number of disparate 'many' (origins) to 'many' (destinations) employment related trips. The many origins also have their root in the dispersal of new low density housing developments on greenfield sites in preference to the redevelopment of inner city 'brownfield' sites for housing, and 'mixed developments' of housing with an appropriate scale of employment, schools, retailing, leisure and health facilities. The government has identified lack of good public transport access to employment opportunities from areas of high unemployment, such as much post-war social housing and some even apparently well-off rural areas, as a major contributor to social exclusion.

Retail

The journey to the shops, traditionally made by women in 'off-peak' hours, is also changing dramatically. There are now as many women as men in employment although the proportion of female part-time posts is still much higher than male part-time posts. The growth of supermarkets and hypermarkets at out of town sites with extended opening hours means that shopping can also be done in the evenings and on Sundays, when the family car is most likely to be available. Even the traditional town centre shop for non-grocery items such as electrical goods, furniture, toys, garden and DIY items can be done at retail parks on the edge of town. Large retail developments such as Lakeside and Bluewater Park off the M25, Merryhill in the West Midlands, Meadowhall at Sheffield, the Trafford Centre in the Northwest and the Metro Centre in the Northeast are all within a comfortable day's drive for most people. They have had a well-documented detrimental effect on the retail trade of neighbouring city centres. A family trip to these developments with their food halls, cinemas and shops might even be perceived by some as a leisure journey. Once again, however, the question of social exclusion arises. The car-less family living in social housing in a run-down, edge-of-town estate is not only deprived of access to these glitterati, but also finds either the corner shop closing because of competition from the multiples of retailers in the local shopping precinct re-branding themselves as 'open all hours' convenience stores.

Convenient they may be but with fewer economies of scale than the supermarkets they will inevitably be expensive, perhaps even unafford-able to the people living nearby. Inevitably, many have closed, creating 'food deserts' in urban areas where it is impossible to purchase fresh pro-visions. In rural areas, similar problems occur with the closure of village shops and post offices and the local convenience store being replaced by a retail outlet at the nearest petrol filling station. The chain of Shellshops and the deal between BP and Asda are evidence of this trend. In an attempt to tackle the problem of their inaccessibility to non-car owners, many supermarkets operate free bus services from outlying areas; in some cases, these have been sufficiently successful for the operator to agree to extend the service and register it for use by the general public. It is also noticeable how the taxi (once seen as the rich man's chariot), but in this case the private hire car, has become a convenience vehicle at supermar-kets, with freephones to local operators encouraging the use of a shared vehicle to bring the shopping home. Often the individual's share of the fare is less than the bus fare.

Leisure

Many leisure trips are car based, and the lack of a household car is usually associated (as the national travel census shows) with much lower mileage travelled by the occupants of the house. This is in general accounted for by fewer leisure trips. Car trips can and do lead to congestion at holiday times at tourist honeypots, along the 'holiday highways' to the coast, and result also in over-visiting of National Parks and areas of outstanding natural beauty (AONBs). Poor land use planning, once again, is culpable. How many local swimming pools have closed as a result of the opening of an expensive 'mega pool' or 'water world' complete with slides, saunas, sun beds, diving pool and wave machine? Again, there is social exclusion but also much longer journeys to access the facilities, journeys that once might have been made more sustainable on foot or by bike. A feature of urban areas was once the day coach excursion, bookable at the local corner shop, to a leisure destination like the coast or a theme park. However, since bus de-regulation the number of small coach proprietors with suitable and available private hire vehicles has shrunk, although the longer extended period (several to ten days) holiday excursion by premium coach operators has survived remarkably well, and there is a growth in air charter flights and sea cruises. Since rail privatization, however, the number of excursion trains has been drastically reduced.

Health

Access to good health care is a fundamental need of all. Large hospitals and health practices are significant traffic generators. Day care patients and visitors need access throughout the day and evening (especially with today's more relaxed attitude to visiting hours). However, many town centre infirmaries have closed in order to concentrate facilities at large new hospitals on greenfield sites more easily accessible to private cars than by public transport. Not only does this create more car journeys, it also creates longer journeys. For the Health Trusts' Patient Transfer Services (PTS) (sitting ambulances) there are also longer trips to be provided or procured since much of this work is subject to compulsory competitive tender. In some cases, local community transport operators with their dial-a-ride services have entered into service level agreements with Health Trusts but equally many are swamped with requests for hospital trips that are clinical rather than social in nature.

The provision of 'care in the community', with providers bidding to run day care centres for frail, elderly persons, has a serious transport dimension: the tender for this work nearly always stipulates the provision of transport to and from the centres, a provision often only faced up to after the award of the contract. Social service departments also often run their own vehicles to transport special needs clients to work or education centres or on outings. There can be a high degree of duplication between community transport, social services, PTS and indeed schools transport; a number of vehicle brokerage schemes[7] have evolved to tackle this by sharing and group hiring members' vehicles. The recent creation of Health Action Zones in some deprived areas is likely to focus attention on the problems of access to health care and may result in imaginative solutions embracing more than just clinical needs transport.

Social

An increasing number of journeys are for purely social purposes, what the travel trade describe as visiting friends and relatives (VFR). Many higher education students make impromptu VFR trips in term time and the VFR market swells at holiday times, bank holidays and Christmas. These trips have a high elasticity of demand, which means that a small drop in fare creates a disproportionate rise in demand. For some operators such as Cross Country Trains and National Express coaches, the VFR market can account for as much as 33 per cent of turnover. Many leisure trips are also made with friends and could as easily be classified as social as can trips to social and religious events like rallies and church services.

Educational

The education transport budget of an average county council can be as much as five times as great as its public transport budget. This is because of the provision in the Education Act 1996[8] that requires them to provide free school transport to pupils who live more than the statutory walking distance of three miles (two miles for primary pupils under eight years of age) from their nearest available or suitable school. In some cases the nearest available school may not be suitable because of the parents desire to educate their child in a school of a particular religious denomination. However, there is no entitlement to free school transport where the child does not attend the nearest available school because of parental choice (other than on religious grounds). This does not mean, however, that no school transport is provided. Sometimes the parents or parent teachers association (PTA) will procure and pay for the transport from an operator; in other cases, especially where numbers are large, an operator may decide to provide a registered fare paying service passing the school on a commercial basis. If such a service is entitled to participate in a transport authority's concessionary fare scheme and there is a child concession, then the transport authority effectively provides a hidden subsidy to the local education authority (LEA), which may, or may not, be the same council.

Some LEAs allow non-eligible pupils for whom there is room to ride on school buses either gratuitously or more usually on payment of a fare or purchase of a season ticket. There is even provision in the Public Passenger Vehicles Act 1981 section 46 for LEAs to use school buses belonging to them to carry members of the public as fare paying passengers at the same time as they are being used to provide free school transport. The Transport Act 1985 also allows them to register such journeys as local services, simultaneously claiming fuel duty rebate in the process. LEAs may also register local services without the need to hold a public service vehicle (PSV) operator's licence.

In 1976, the House of Lords defeated a private member's bill to introduce a national school transport fare of 5p that would have redressed the imbalance between entitled and unentitled pupils. They did so largely because of the intervention of the Lord Bishops who feared that church schools, the majority of whose pupils lived at some distance and therefore had entitlement, would loose out. However, the 1998 White Paper, a New Deal for Transport, in proposing a national concessionary fare scheme for pensioners, may well re-open this debate.

Despite the above, the current situation is that LEAs can secure free school transport either by issuing passes or season tickets for the pupils to use on mainstream public transport, by procuring by tender dedicated school buses, or by providing buses themselves. The latter option is common where special needs pupils who may need an escort are carried but some LEAs are currently looking at the costs of providing all their own statutory schools transport as an alternative to tendering. This commonly happens in the USA where there are dedicated school transport fleets. It is an option that could have attractions for an authority where work could be found for the vehicles between school runs under a transport coordination scheme.

The issue of passes is contentious where the service used is a 'tendered' service that the transport authority already subsidises since the operator could receive a double subsidy. Equally, tenders for school buses often stipulate that operators must register the service as a local service available to the public. This makes sense in two ways; there is often spare capacity at a time when no local service operates and the operator can claim fuel duty rebate for a registered local service thus reducing the amount of subsidy in the tender. From all of the above it is obvious why the Transport Act 1985 requires LEAs, social services and transport authorities to cooperate in order to obtain best value for money for their council tax payers. Nevertheless, not every authority has a fully coordinated public-schools-social transport function. LEAs are not required to provide free transport to pupils at private schools or for 'scholars' aged 16–19 in full-time education at sixth-form colleges or colleges of further education, although they do have powers (but not a duty) to assist 'scholars'.

Many private schools procure or provide their own transport, charging parents for doing so. Some even own their own fleets and in a few cases have a PSV operator's licence and register their services so that parents and the public can ride – and the school can get the fuel duty rebate.

Because funding for further education is linked to enrolments, retention and qualifications gained colleges employ proactive marketing to attract students and this frequently involves the provision of free transport to and from college. The funding for this must come out of the Further Education Funding Council's (FEFC's) grant to the college, sometimes at the expense of the teaching budgets. It is common for two vehicles serving different colleges to pass each other in opposite directions carrying roughly equal numbers of students from what were each other's catchment areas when the colleges were LEA owned. It is difficult to persuade colleges to allow the operator of 'their' bus to register the service even when there is spare capacity that could be sold as fares to offset the hired transport costs because of their fear of their competitor's students using their bus.

In some cases, that 'competitor' will be a private training provider funded by the local Training and Enterprise Council (TEC) providing industrial placements and training, perhaps under the government's new deal programme. The problems of providing transport for work experience and training are just as acute and difficult to reconcile as educational transport, especially as training contracts often require the provider to arrange transport for the trainees (like care in the community contracts).

PROPENSITY TO TRAVEL

There is a vast difference between the average distance travelled per annum by an average middle class professional owner-occupier and an unemployed person in rented social housing. Largely, this can be explained simply by differences in their disposable incomes but there are other underlying determinants such as cultural differences and lifestyles. Neither is there always a simple linear relationship between individual or even household, incomes and disposable income. Many young professionals are heavily mortgaged and struggling to afford an annual holiday whilst their artisan contemporaries may be able to save over the year for a cheap package holiday abroad. Many professionals nevertheless may travel much further over the year on business, perhaps abroad and frequently at their employers' expense. In society as a whole propensity to travel is very much a function of Gross Domestic Product, which explains why rich countries like Japan and the USA are net exporters of tourism, spending more abroad than is spent in their own country by incoming tourists. It explains why many tourist destinations are unsustained, as the local economy is not the immediate beneficiary of tourist spend (the usual textbook example of this is the McDonalds burger franchise in Red Square Moscow, the profit of which goes to the USA).

The other factors that determine the extent to which people will travel are demographic. Patently, the retired London commuter no longer catches the 8.18 to Charing Cross every morning but that person, whilst active and in good health, may take three or four short breaks and one continental holiday per annum, far more than when employed. Students have a low disposable income but a high propensity to travel and of course are prepared to accept quite basic travel and accommodation facilities – National Express and Youth Hostels Association (YHA) in preference to intercity and hotels or guest houses. The same students when young busy professionals or young parents may at that stage in their life have quite a low propensity to travel unless, as suggested earlier, as part of their employment and may confine their travel in the early years of marriage to VFR journeys and local attractions. At a later stage in their life cycle when their offspring are more independent and the household disposable income is greater and less stretched by housing and education costs, they may well attempt to travel widely in a bid to make up for these 'lost' years. Finally, in this consideration of travel habits, it should not be surprising that possession of and access to private transport is one of the greatest travel motivators. An examination of the government's national travel statistics clearly highlights all the above trends as well as many more interesting correlations between travel and other variables, such as gender, race, educational levels and social class, that are too numerous to explore here.

SPACIAL CRITERIA AND TRANSPORT

The UK has become a dispersed society in the 50 years since the end of the Second World War. The Barlow Report is less well known as the post-war Beveridge report (which created the National Health Service and delivered old age pensions) and the Butler Report (which delivered free universal secondary education). It concentrated on post-war redevelopment and was responsible for the designation of a raft of New Towns as well as a post-war house-building boom, including the creation of large overspill 'council estates' on the edges of our major towns and cities. Hospitals, schools and roads were also built as part of the post-war consensus to provide a 'land fit for heroes' but there was, it is now generally agreed, insufficient reinvestment in the UK's run down industrial infrastructure, including our railways.

Many towns created industrial estates on ring road or motorway accessible sites close to the 'green belt'. Although this planning device generally achieved its aim of containing urban sprawl and ribbon developments, it also had the unfortunate side effect of causing private dormitory housing developments to seek greenfield sites beyond the belt, through which commuters, often car borne, had to 'leap frog' to work. The average length of the journey to work increased. A planning system that was based on separate residential, business, leisure and employment zones had no place for traditional mixed-use developments. In the highly liberalized planning environment of the 1980s, there was a presumption in favour of the developer, and a wave of out-of-town developments, retail, health, leisure and education accentuated the dispersal of traffic generators away from their already dispersed origins.

As already explained, the 'many-to-many' trip, not easily accomplished by public transport, replaced the 'many-to-few' trips, which were much simpler to serve by public transport. There was an almost total lack of any coordination between transport and land use planning. In contrast, many continental European cities developed 'master plans', with both housing and employment encouraged along corridors well served by public transport, and low-density housing discouraged near to transport nodes where it was considered more efficient to plan for higher density residential developments that would feed the transport network. It was not until the publication of Policy Planning Guidance 13 (PPG13)[9] in 1993 that the government formally recognized that the policy could not be sustained and instructed local planning authorities to resist pressures for more out of town developments. It did so although the 1963 report 'Traffic in Towns'[10] did spell out the inevitable eventual consequences of continuing to try to accommodate a society dependant on the mobility that private transport seemingly promised. The new Labour government's White Paper 'A New Deal for Transport'[11] supports and extends the philosophy of PPG13, promising an even more radical re-write of planning guidelines to embrace a holistic transport and land use framework.

THE URBAN TRANSPORT PROBLEM

Towns and cities are places to which people wish to travel for employment, retailing, education, health and other services and recreation. In urban areas, space is at a premium. Land is a finite and non-renewable resource that must be shared by developers and users alike and transport is a land hungry activity.[12] The obviously predictable result is urban congestion. Even in urban areas with much high-density development, congestion is relative, being worst at certain times (the so called rush hours or peak travel times) and in certain locations. One of the most congesting features of urban living is the home-to-school car journey, which, even where parents share this task, creates bottlenecks in the vicinity of schools,[13] frequently delaying or obstructing the far more environmentally friendly school bus. In 1970 over 70 per cent of junior school children walked to school unsupervised; today that figure is less than 7 per cent.[14] Although parents cite safety and security as reasons for driving their offspring to school there are now more children injured in road accidents involving a car carrying children and a child pedestrian. The level of pollution experienced by car passengers is also three times as high as that by pedestrians on the same road.[15] Urban congestion in ancient Rome even led to a daytime ban on chariots in the streets and in Victorian times congestion around the new transport interchanges created at railheads was severe. Trams were misguidedly removed from most UK cities in the post-war years, partly because it was perceived that their fixed track impeded other traffic, although the greater flexibility of the bus and cheap oil imports had an equally important part to play in that decision.

Although the Greater London plan of 1947 acknowledged the desirability of funnelling traffic along key radial routes and away from residential areas (described rather optimistically as 'islands' of tranquillity in a sea of traffic), at least it realized that busy roads, themselves corridors of communication, can also be barriers to communication at a local level, especially on foot and by cycle.[16] The first real admission by government that there was a developing urban traffic problem came with the commissioning of the report 'Traffic in Towns' in 1963 by Professor Buchanon[17]. Since new inter-urban motorways and by-pass schemes were having an impact by removing bottlenecks on trunk routes, perhaps, the Minister for Transport[18] suggested, urban motorways could reduce congestion also.

Buchanon's report gave an interesting answer to this speculation. 'We are living,' he said, 'with a monster, and yet we love him dearly'. The monster to which he referred was the private car. In Buchanon's view there had to be clear 'grade separation' between traffic and pedestrians, who should each circulate at different levels. More traffic could be accommodated in towns by complex reconstruction but this would be expensive and society would have to 'will the means'. The rather more low-key alternative agenda he proposed was to fix the traffic capacity of towns at an environmentally acceptable level and this would require traffic restraint.

Whilst the report stopped short of promoting the alternative of increased investment in public transport, the Labour government that followed its publication proposed that solution. In the largest conurbations in the country, Passenger Transport Authorities (PTAs) were created by the Transport Act 1968 with a remit to provide public passenger transport services to meet the needs of their areas.[19] Through the mechanisms of Transport Policies and Programmes (TPPs) transport authorities could bid for additional funding (the Transport Supplementary Grant), which at that time embraced both highway and public transport spending so that a brake could be placed on the former in order to promote the latter.

Large scale post-war slum clearance, the building of satellite housing estates and new towns, and the restructuring of employment away from the old 'smokestack' industries around which many urban areas grew up towards the often more land hungry and out-of-town-sited service industries, meant that by the mid-1970s cities were losing people and jobs at a massive rate. The process has left a legacy of inner-city cores of deprivation arranged rather like a doughnut around still vibrant centres (the so-called central business districts). These are themselves surrounded by more affluent suburbs and semi-rural dormitory 'subtopias', neither town nor country, sometimes even located beyond the green belt designed to contain urban sprawl. The work of Urban Development Corporations (UDCs) has done much to revitalize large inner city tracts but often the jobs created are not taken by local residents who are instead either displaced or marginalized. At the same time city centres are facing the challenge of large out of town developments whilst suburbia is expanding and embracing supermarkets, industrial and business parks, large educational establishments and hospitals. As already explained, such developments are much more difficult to serve by public transport than the traditional commuting to an urban centre along well-defined travel corridors.

The problem of the peak

The demands on urban highway space and rail track capacity are greatest during the morning and evening peak hours when most employees are travelling to and from work, roughly 7.30 to 9.00 am and 4.30 to 6.00 pm (see Figure 1.3). At these times, not only is total vehicle capacity often inadequate with crush loading of standing passengers but also traffic congestion is at its zenith preventing further the efficient deployment of vehicles. In fact, buses are both part of the problem, in contributing to the congestion, and part of the solution in terms of the number of private cars that they have the potential to replace. This simple fact is the justification for public transport priorities like bus lanes and the proposed pricing of scarce road capacity.[20] Operators often have a peak vehicle requirement (PVR) of as much as 33 per cent or more vehicles than are required to run an off-peak or between peak service. Valuable capital is tied up in maintaining this PVR, the revenue potential of which can be realized for at most three hours per day.

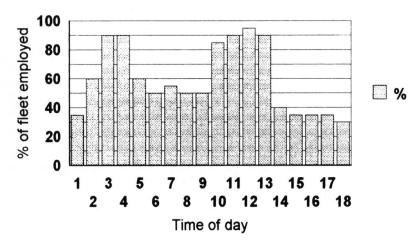

Figure 1.3   The problem of the peak – passenger transport vehicle requirements by time of day

Spreading the peak

Today's peak hour is thankfully less pronounced than during what many people saw as the golden days of public transport in the post-war years when car ownership was low and a much higher proportion of workers was employed in manufacturing and extractive industries. Then, however, the nominal working day, even discounting overtime hours, was longer and the workers' peak began before and finished after the school peak. Now the two coincide more but, at the same time, patterns of employment have changed. Fewer employees work fixed hours, flexitime is common and service industries replacing heavy industry have led to more shift work patterns and part-time employment. Operators can and do negotiate with major employers or large educational campuses to stagger starting and finishing times so as to obtain maximum productivity from their vehicles. Peak traffic builds up earlier now and abates later – in graphical terms it can be said that the peaks are more bell-shaped and have a much less severe 'shoulder', for another modern day reality is the excessive hours worked by UK employees despite nominally shorter hours in their contracts of employment. Time will tell if the EC Working Time Directive will overcome this so-called disease of 'presenteeism'.

Large operators often try to 'pass on' some of the high costs of peak hour operation and concentrate on core all-day services. One strategy for doing so is to decline to tender for work in the peak or to deregister such work so that it is put out to tender in the hope that a small competitor will take it on. Perversely, they then complain when the same operators use these often lower cost 'peak requirement' vehicles to compete with them at other times!

The urban transport problem, however, is much more than just a peak hour problem although this is inevitably when it is manifest. There are severe problems encountered in servicing industrial and retail premises by large goods vehicles, especially when the need to do so conflicts with, for example, pedestrianization or bus priority schemes. Difficulties are experienced in locating freight villages and rail freight terminals within reach of conurbations or siting 'parkway' stations or 'park and ride' (P+R) transfer points where there is easy access both from the trunk road network and, in the case of rail based P+R, to the rail network. Urban dwellers can experience problems in gaining access to the countryside, especially at times like Sundays or summer evenings when the level of public transport services is minimal or even non-existent.

Ultimately the urban transport problem (as well as the inter-urban problem) is dictated by an excess demand for a limited resource, road space or track capacity. The 1998 Integrated Transport White Paper – 'New Deal for Transport' – in suggesting rationing this by road pricing and 'hypothecating' the revenue stream to public transport, is an elegant potential solution (considered in more detail later in this book) long advocated by transport economists.

THE RURAL TRANSPORT PROBLEM

Ideally, each rural community would have access to all the services it needs but, in reality, people living in remote areas by default need mobility to access their needs. Car ownership in rural areas is higher than in urban areas. Although often unaffordable, the family car is essential, in some cases simply to stay in work. This 'unwanted car ownership' has given rise to the myth that in rural areas everyone has a car. A survey in 1990[21] found the following:

- 20–35% (depending on the county sampled) of rural households had no car;
- 45–65% of adults were without regular use of a car;
- 75% of households are deprived of the use of a car during the working day;
- 60% of women in rural areas had no driving licence nor do the young and many of the old and infirm population.

Rural dwellers actually walk less than 'urbanites' because their destinations are so dispersed, and ease of parking there, together with less congested roads, accentuates this disparity. Their transport expectations are low; parents are prepared to ferry children to school and recreation. Nevertheless, increased car usage denudes existing public transport (and local village services like shops, post offices and the 'pub'); low patronage and increased fares create a vicious spiral leading to inevitable de-registration of services. Passenger numbers have fallen by 70 per cent since the 1950s. Branch line closures dating from the Beeching Report (1963)[22] and commercialization of ferry services have had similar effects.

The newly privatized train operating companies (TOCs) have seen their inter-urban services as more lucrative than rural services and eliminated stops at rural stations. Arnside on Morecambe Bay now has fewer trains stopping there on their five-minute journeys across the bay to Grange-over-Sands although there are more trains on the line. The alternative road journey round the bay takes 30 minutes in a car and there is no direct bus service.[23] The countryside is a changing place and the needs of country people are continually changing. It has seen enormous demographic and structural changes. In 1997, 43 per cent of rural parishes had no post office, 42 per cent no shop, 83 per cent no general practitioner, 75 per cent no daily bus and 93 per cent no rail service at all.[24]

Rural depopulation is largely another myth. In many parts, it is apparent that for the majority the need to travel to services and facilities is not a problem but this majority is often composed of 'incomers', the retired, second homeowners and long-distance commuters. This drift from the urban areas can have a devastating effect on local property prices, forcing young people to relocate and creating an ageing rural population. The generation who are today's rural pensioners were brought up at a time when car ownership was the exception. Women in particular never learnt to drive and depended on their husbands so they are left isolated when widowed. The Rural White Paper of 1995[25] divulged that less than 30 per cent of rural parishes have a daily bus service. It explored the familiar reasons for the decline of public transport, including the relatively high levels of, in many cases unavoidable, car ownership in rural areas in response to the relentless centralization of educational, retail, health, employment and leisure facilities. It also made a number of recommendations that could have quite far-reaching consequences for public-transport operators, including giving parish councils powers to precept their council-tax payers to support local services.

Conventional public transport, it said, is not always the right answer to the transport needs of rural communities. Solutions, it suggested, must increasingly involve more flexible and innovative approaches drawing on the resources of the community. The theme of voluntary action runs right through the White Paper, covering everything from playgroups to car sharing, and there is no doubt that it is a marked feature of many rural communities. Social car schemes and 'section 22' community buses, all driven by volunteers, are found in many parishes.

Bus deregulation in 1986 had a devastating effect on rural services. Operators registered very few commercial rural services. These were mostly inter-urban, passing through rural areas on trunk roads only. County councils, which had a duty under the Transport Act 1985 to secure by tender those services that the market was unable to provide to meet the requirements of their area, were hard pressed even to restore the lost network to anything like its pre-1985 level let alone develop it. The Act created a Rural Transport Development Fund administered on behalf of the Department of Transport (now the DETR) by the Rural Development Commission (RDC). The fund was not intended to 'prop up de-regulation' (although it often did) but to encourage innovative rural transport services such as car sharing, taxi buses and dial-a-bus services as well as conventional registered local services. Whilst it was fully spent in the early years it was under spent in the early 1990s. In 1996, because of the Rural White Paper, it was extended to cover community transport initiatives. The new Labour government in 1998 provided local authorities with a three-year budget of £50 million per annum for rural transport. Much of this budget was allocated to a Rural Bus Services Grant, some to a Rural Challenge grant covering any local authority initiatives aimed at improving public transport patronage, and the rest to a Rural Partnership Grant (RPG) to be administered by the RDC.[26] The main objective of the RPG is to promote social inclusion in rural communities by securing a long-term improvement in their accessibility to jobs, services and social activities. Partners may include the local authority, local operators, rural community councils, health trusts and community transport projects. The partners will be expected to develop a strategy and draw up an action plan compatible with their Local Transport Plan to take action at local level to identify and meet needs and develop local solutions. At the time of writing, there are also proposals for a Millennium Minibus scheme to make a minibus available to communities having no public transport.

What is obvious is that rural transport problems have moved up the political agenda and more finance and resources are being devoted to them but eventually the success of these schemes is bound to depend on the enthusiasm of local communities to volunteer to run with them.

The rural transport problem – indicators

In 1997:[27]

- 75% of rural parishes had no daily bus (72% in 1991).
- Where services existed they were often limited; 44% of parishes had no service before 9.00 am and 77% no service after 7.00 pm.
- 93% of rural parishes had no rail service.
- Only 21% of parishes had any form of community transport and only 15% were included in a dial-a-ride scheme for mobility-impaired parishioners.
- Only 41% of pensioners in rural areas made use of concessionary travel schemes (compared to 82% in metropolitan areas).

Percentage of OAPs for whom:

	Rural	PTAs	Other Urban
Concessionary fares were available	93	100	93
Travel was free	5	67	13
Travel passes were free	62	96	51

- 84% of rural households had a car compared with 69% nationally; 38% had two or more cars (compared to 25% nationally).
- Twice as many low-income households (the bottom decile) in rural areas had a car than did those in urban areas.
- 80% of rural journeys to work were made by car (compared to 66% nationally).
- Average car trip lengths were 10 miles in rural areas compared to 8 miles in urban areas.

Key: Freight=lower case

After "Logistics Management" by Fawcett, McLeish & Ogden McDonald & Evans 1992

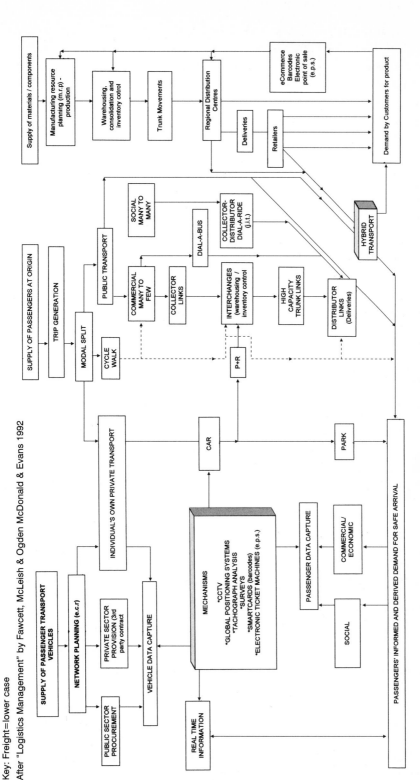

Figure 1.4 A comparison between passenger and freight logistics supply chains

Managing the Passenger Logistics Function

TYPES OF SERVICE

From the point of view of the passengers, as long as a service transports them safely and efficiently to their destinations, how it is provided is only of passing concern. One factor, however, that will concern prospective passengers is the general availability of the service since not all services are provided for the public. This is an important distinction from an operator's point of view since it can affect how the service is licensed, a topic that is dealt with in much greater detail in Chapter 8. There is an obvious difference between a passenger transport service for the exclusive use of one person or party (such as a taxicab or a privately hired coach) and a service to the public such as a timetabled railway service provided by a TOC under a franchise agreement with the Office of Passenger Rail Franchising Director (OPRAF).

However, simply distinguishing between what might loosely be described as private charters and public transport is insufficiently academically rigorous. This is because the term 'private transport' in the context of passenger transport has come to mean the private car, a very narrow and constricted meaning. Public transport is such a general term that, at least in the context of road passenger transport, it became necessary in 1985 to define it in legislation.[1]

To illustrate the difficulty of labelling services, consider the use of personnel carriers by employers to provide free transport to their employees either to and from work or to different work locations. These are not generally available to the public and are privately provided. However, similar vehicles owned by hoteliers to transport their guests to and from stations and airports might be described as 'own account' operation since they are provided privately and not by a public transport operator. Equally, however, they are available to those members of the public choosing to use the hotels – indeed the hotel booking fee will often confer a right to use the service. This then raises the question of whether a separate fare has been charged, an important consideration, since it affects how the service is licensed. The situation changes subtly if the hotelier hires the vehicle from a transport operator.

The following sections attempt to expand on some of the definitions and points made above. It should be remembered, however, that in reality there is an almost infinite number of service types and that these can often be described differently depending on from where they are viewed with passengers, operators and licensing authorities having quite different perspectives.

Public transport

The Transport Act 1985 placed a duty on PTAs and local authorities[2] to procure public transport services not already commercially provided to meet the requirements of their area and in so doing gave a robust definition of public transport. The Act said the public passenger transport services meant all those services on which the public rely for getting from place to place when not relying on their own private facilities. Certain caveats then followed. School services were included. However, it excluded services operated by community transport operators exclusively for their own clientele for social, educational, religious or other activities of benefit to the community except where these services provided for the elderly or disabled.[3] It also excluded excursions and tours, which could of course be defined as public transport since they are bookable by the general public. Although the definition was written in the context of local authority support for public passenger transport services (which included support for local rail services in the areas of PTAs it is wide enough to included ferry services, taxis and tramways and other developing light rapid transit services.[4]

Private transport

This term is now almost universally used to describe private motoring but it can be used in another context, that of own account operation.

Own account transport

The freight transport industry makes a very clear distinction between general haulage that any consignor can use and own account operation by traders' own vehicles used to carry their own goods. So too does legislation, in that own-account road transport operators, like hauliers, require an operator's licence. However, this is easier to obtain as, unlike hauliers, they are not required to furnish the Traffic Commissioners with proof of their professional competence to obtain a Standard Goods Vehicle Operator's licence; instead, they may obtain a Restricted Goods Vehicle Operator's licence.[5]

The equivalent for operators of road passenger transport is a restricted PSV operator's licence, granted to persons whose main occupation is not the operation of public service vehicles.[6] An obvious example is a post bus since Royal Mail's main occupation is the carriage of mail,[7] but restricted licences are held by hoteliers, travel agents, training centres and even taxi operators.

Scheduled and charter services

Another obvious distinction that can be made is between services that run to a timetable and can be boarded by the public, often without the need to pre-book, and charter services, which, whilst they may be timed, are provided by a vehicle chartered for the exclusive use of a private party.

Obviously there are scheduled bus, coach, rail, ferry and air services. All are available to the public at large, and many are 'walk on' services. Even operators like National Express and the airlines, who carry no standing passengers and traditionally required passengers to reserve a seat, operate some walk on services such as airline 'shuttle' services, some of National Expresses more rural routes where the driver will take fares, and high-frequency inter-urban express services. Since rail privatization in 1993, some TOCs have increased the range of discounted rail tickets that can be bought in advance with pre-booking and either reduced the availability or increased the relative price of their saver and standard fares.[8] This has prompted the Rail User Consultative Committees (RUCCs) to express fears that they are trying to remove the 'walk on' benefits of a railway network in order to manage their limited capacity and revenue yield. Paradoxically, in the airline industry the reverse trend can be detected, where operators, unable to obtain licences for popular routes, are entering into agreements with travel agents to charter planes for them to carry passengers booked by the agents. Thus, many 'charter flights' are really de facto scheduled services. This blurring of the distinction between public scheduled services and private charters is also complicated by arguments as to whether a separate fare has been paid for the journey taken and, if so, who made the arrangements for collecting this and to whom was it paid. These questions might appear irrelevant but in fact they have enormous relevance in terms of how the service is or can be licensed.

Separate fares

A group of four students may share a taxi from a city-centre club to their halls of residence. The fare as shown on the taxi meter may be £6, which the students share, paying £1.50 each. To all intents and purposes, it would seem that the students had paid separate fares but a strict interpretation of the relevant legislation would show that not to be the case. The taxi would probably be licensed by the local authority as a hackney carriage that (except in certain exceptional cases provided for in the Transport Act 1985[9]) would prohibit the carriage of passengers at separate fares, requiring the vehicle to be hired as a whole. This the students would have done by hailing the cab as it 'plied for hire' or by joining it at a taxi rank, and, crucially, the arrangements for bringing the party together or for payment of the fare would not have been made by the driver.[10]

Contrast this situation with a scenario where the students catch a bus and each pays his or her own fare to the driver. Clearly separate fares have been charged. However, what of the case of a guest who catches the hotel's free courtesy bus to the airport? In this case, the courts have held that where a payment in consideration of another matter (ie, accommodation at the hotel) confers a right to be carried (whether or not exercised) then separate fares exist.[11]

Why is this important? The answer lies in the definition[12] of a public service vehicle as a passenger carrying motor vehicle with nine or more seats (ie, a bus[13]) used for hire or reward. This covers its use either at separate fares or when privately hired as a whole. If, however, the vehicle has eight or fewer seats then it is only a PSV if used for hire or reward at separate fares.[10] These extremely complex legalities inform the licensing of taxis and PSV, the former by local authorities who issue hackney carriage and private hire car licences, and the latter by the Traffic Commissioners who issue PSV operator licences.[14] Since only the holder of a PSV operator licence may register a local bus service, the importance of separate fares becomes plain.

Similar distinctions are made in the rail and airline industries although without such licensing ramifications. It is still possible for promoters to arrange with a TOC or rail tour operator (and often too with the owner of an appropriate locomotive such as a rail heritage group or English, Welsh and Scottish Railways (EWS)[15]) to provide a rail tour for their clientele. From small beginnings in the 1950s, airline charter flights have grown to the point where their traffic now exceeds that on scheduled flights. Originally conceived as inclusive tours (ITs), where the flight plus accommodation was the minimum requirement to place the charter outside the remit of the International Air Transport Associations control over scheduled services' fares and tariffs, in recent years the IT principle has been relaxed to permit a growing number of seat-only charters, which now represent a significant market.

An interesting case study that illustrates the fine line between charter and separate fares is the creation from virtually nothing of one of the major trans-Pennine rail passenger flows, the so-called Roses line from Preston to Leeds. In the late 1980s, the portion of the route between Hebden Bridge and Burnley was used by freight traffic only. The Bradford and Bingley Building Society at that time merged with a smaller society on the other side of the Pennines and, having a requirement to move staff, papers and computer disks between their offices in Bradford and Burnley, they chartered a train to make two return trips per day. People seeing the train at Bradford and trying to book a journey on it were referred to the Building Society who eventually sold season tickets to some regular travellers. Regional Railways, the then operator of the service, approached the Building Society to discuss advertising the train in their timetable and selling tickets to the public. The demand for seats grew rapidly and, the capacity of the train quickly becoming insufficient, a two hourly service throughout the working day was introduced. Now there is an hourly Blackpool–Preston–Burnley–Bradford–Leeds–York–Scarborough service from early morning to late evening.

Demand responsive transport

London taxis are an excellent example of a transport system sufficiently flexible to be able to cater for anticipated demand. When a long distance express train (for example the heavily loaded Manchester Pullman at 10 am at Euston) is due at a rail terminal, the taxis begin building up on the rank. Even more demand responsive, by definition, are London minicabs that are not permitted to ply for hire but must respond to telephone or minicab office bookings.

The concept of 'hail and ride' is associated with hackney carriages and some rural bus services but the practice can also be seen on some rural railways. For example, on the Cumbria Coast line the only mandatory stops are at Grange-over-Sands, Ulverston, Barrow, Millom, Ravenglass, Sellafield, Whitehaven, Workington, Maryport, Wigton and Carlisle and any passenger wishing to board or alight at other stations must either indicate to the driver from the platform or to the guard on the train.

Duplication of vehicles to cater for exceptional numbers of passengers wishing to travel (perhaps because of a local event or just good weather) is also an example of demand response – airline shuttle services guarantee a flight to all walk-up passengers even if this means an additional plane being put into service,

The relaxation of PSV licensing in 1977[16] enabled organizations concerned with the social, educational, recreational, religious or other needs of the community to operate minibuses for hire or reward on a non-profit-making basis under a minibus permit scheme. This meant that their drivers do not need a vocational PSV driving entitlement and they do not need to obtain a PSV operator's licence. This freedom is used by community transport operators to provide demand responsive services for their members who might, for example, be elderly or disabled or belong to a youth group or sports team. The response may vary from group hire of a vehicle to take a team to a match, to meeting an individual's pre-booked journey need (on a 'ring and ride' basis). This latter kind of response is often on the basis of 'many-to-many' scheduling, where the vehicle will circulate in an area both picking up and setting down passengers from their journey's origin to their destination. Sophisticated computer scheduling models enable dispatchers to programme routes that optimize the utilization of the vehicle in the most effective and efficient ways.

Yet another type of demand responsive transport is the dial-a-ride concept, often so called to distinguish it from the many-to-many operation in that the vehicle will have a published timetable that is sufficiently flexible to enable diversions to be made within an 'envelope' describing a set distance either side of the route. Where such a service is provided by a commercial operator on a registered local service under a PSV operator's licence (rather than a community transport scheme under a minibus permit), it is usually referred to as a dial-a-bus service although the concept is identical other than that the commercial operator's service is available to the public. Not surprisingly, experience with commercial dial-a-bus services has shown that these are most successful in areas of high telephone connection, typically, but not exclusively, prosperous suburbs and rural dormitory commuter areas.

SERVICE SPECIFICATION

Many passenger transport services on which we rely today were first introduced many years ago. This is especially the case where they are confined to a fixed route like a train, tram or trolleybus. However, the original service could have been quite different in a number of specific ways:

- its timetable and in particular the frequency of operation;
- its speed and stopping pattern;
- the vehicles that were first used and their capabilities, especially their speed and capacity;
- the fares charged and the fare structure;
- onboard catering provided.

Services evolve over time, changes often lagging behind rather than anticipating new demand patterns. It was once said of the bus services that one

PTE inherited from a municipal operator in 1968 that they were guided by invisible tram track beneath the tarmac!

Some services, however, are quite new. One of the benefits of bus deregulation, the Rural Transport Development Fund and the more recent Rural Bus Services Grant (see Chapter 1) has been the encouragement of the introduction of innovative services. New services are more revolutionary than evolutionary (although they may be an extension of an existing service) and service planners will have a clean sheet of paper on which to devise them. How then should they proceed?

One answer to that question is to point to the distinction, often not made, or sometimes just implied, between the identification, specification and procurement of a service. The requirement for the service may be exactly known (for example the needs of individual pupils for statutory schools transport) or they may be formulated within parameters such as a county council's transport policy. These may be quite broad (for example the kind of benchmarks referred to earlier, which might dictate, say, a minimum of two return works journeys per day). In either case this can be translated into a specification that can be procured either by putting out a tender containing the specification or by negotiating additions or amendments to existing services that will meet the specification.

In the process of rail privatization, the train operating companies bidding for franchises were all given passenger service requirements (PSRs) in respect of the routes they intended to operate. PSRs oblige operators to include in their timetables certain minimum, passenger rail services. These must be 'broadly similar' to the services in the last British Rail timetable[17] but they are not, in rail jargon, 'hard wired' – in other words they are not exactly, as the Railways Act suggested, based on those actual times, but specify service characteristics that are important for passengers, including:[18]

- frequency of trains;
- stations to be served;
- maximum journey times;
- first and last trains;
- weekend services;
- through services;
- load factors and/or peak train capacity, where appropriate.

The question of frequency is fundamental to most service specifications. How often a service operates is usually expressed in terms of the number of journeys in a finite time span, thus we may talk of weekly or daily flights, hourly rail services or 'frequent' buses, when what we actually mean is one plane per week/day, a train each hour or perhaps six buses per hour. However, taking the last example, the fact that there are six departures in each hour does not necessarily mean that there is one vehicle every ten minutes. The departures could be at 00, 05, 10, 30, 35 and 40 minutes past each hour and still produce a frequency of six vehicles per hour. Therefore, another measure is needed, that of headway, or the time distance between successive vehicles. In the above example, the headways are 5, 5, 20, 5, 5 and 20 minutes respectively. If departures can be arranged at say 00, 20, 40 minutes past the hour this is often referred to as a 'clock face' headway and is obviously easily remembered and of most value to the passenger as vehicles are spaced evenly and waiting time is predictable.

There are many reasons why clock face headways cannot always be achieved. Commonly, vehicle arrivals at a bus or rail station all approach along the same corridor but have departed from outer termini at different distances away and so even when their departure times are clock faced the arrival times along the corridor and at the terminus are disparate. Because of the freedom to re-register bus timetables with only 42 days notice to the Traffic Commissioners given at bus deregulation in 1986, many operators deliberately registered services a few minutes ahead of their competitors only to find their competitors then re-registering their services ahead of them! Legislation in 1994 attempted to address this 'dancing round the clock', as it became known, by giving Traffic Commissioners powers to regulate the number and 'frequency' of vehicles along a route, but whilst this had some effect, the real power needed would have been to regulate headways![19]

Routing

Some services simply connect two places, making no intermediate stop. This may be by accident or design. Whilst there is really nowhere between Heathrow and New York for a transatlantic flight to stop, Eurostar services between London and Paris or Brussels can stop at Lille and Ashford although not all do so. However, the Eurostar route is fixed, the flight path is not and may be varied according to weather or air traffic conditions.

The UK has one of the densest road networks of any developed country, and bus and coach services can take an almost infinite variety of routes between their origin and destination. They may be routed via motorways or trunk roads, they may divert off their line of route to pick up or set down passengers or to avoid difficult terrain such as steep, narrow, high-altitude or exposed roads especially in winter.

It is often forgotten that the route chosen may well determine the vehicle used. This is true for all modes of transport. Short-haul aircraft cannot fly across large oceans, electric trains cannot use all railways, large double-decker buses cannot penetrate housing estates with narrow residential roads or go down country lanes with overhanging trees or pass under low bridges.

There is also the question of traffic generation. A service connecting two urban centres may lose passengers if the route chosen is too circuitous because the operator wishes to serve a number of towns or villages en route but necessitating diversions from the main inter-urban road or motorway. Services that run across a town rather than just into the centre can also generate traffic from passengers who dislike changing vehicles (for which there can also be a 'fares penalty' if the sum of the two individual fares exceeds the through fare). There can be a bonus in saving layover time at the town centre terminus by only making kerbside stops in the town but this can be countered by the lack of interchange opportunities that calling at the bus station can generate.

Thus, the actual route chosen for a service will depend on many factors such as:

- what is known of transport needs in the area (perhaps following a needs analysis);
- distances and attainable speeds by different roads or motorways;
- the known incidence of congestion;
- the existence of any bus priorities (such as bus lanes) along the line of route;
- the difficulty of the terrain;
- the sort of weather experienced.

One of the benefits of bus deregulation has been the ability for operators to experiment with new services by simply registering these and then giving 42 days notice of their intention to either re-register a variation or de-register altogether in the light of operating experience. The downside to this type of innovation has been the lack of stability in the network of registered local services.

Scheduling

Most passenger transport services run to a published timetable unless they are entirely demand responsive (like private hires, taxis and charter flights). Even many demand responsive services like charter flights and dial-a-bus are constrained to fairly tight time envelopes either because of terminal or line capacity problems or so as to give some degree of confidence to potential users that they will actually run. The timetable is the outcome of various service specification factors such as frequency, operating speeds, stops, platform, bay or terminal occupancy and 'layover' time, round trip running time and other variables, such as signalling, that may or may not apply to every type of service.

There is a fundamental relationship between round trip running time (RTRT – which includes any 'layover' time en route or at the termini) and the service headway (H) in that the number of vehicles required to operate the service (V) can be calculated using the formula:

$$V = RTRT/H$$

V may not always be an integer. For example, a service with a round trip running time of 80 minutes and a 15 minute headway would require a theoretical 5.33 vehicles whilst another service with a similar headway and 70 minute round trip running time would require 4.66 vehicles. In reality, of course, the first service would require six vehicles and the second five vehicles. However, suppose both these services meet at a common point – a bus or rail station perhaps – and could be joined to form a longer 15-minute service perhaps running across town rather than into town? The overall RTRT would now be 70 + 80 = 150 minutes and the vehicle requirement would be ten (150/15) vehicles. This example of interworking of two services shows a saving of one vehicle (5 + 6 – 10) and is an excellent example of a scheduler's skills in maximizing vehicle productivity. The product of such ingenuity is often a highly sophisticated working timetable that then has to be re-presented in a form that can be understood easily by the passenger (see Figure 2.1). The above interworking, for example, could be presented to passengers as two discreet timetables, one for each interworked service, although these might well be in the same booklet for the benefit of through passengers.

Optimal vehicle utilization, however, is only one part of service scheduling. Vehicles usually require drivers, and sometimes conductors or cabin and catering staff also, and this means preparing duties and rosters to ensure that every timetabled journey is staffed. Frequently, when calculated on an hourly basis, staff costs can be as high if not higher than vehicle operating costs so that achieving staffing economies can be as important as optimizing vehicle utility.

The conventional approach is to prepare a number of 'duties', linked portions of work making up a day's employment, and then to allocate these to staff on a rolling 'roster' designed to ensure that they have adequate breaks and rest days and work their fair share of early, late and 'split' duties (covering both peak hours). A common problem is that the more tightly the vehicle schedules are drawn, the less the opportunity to create productive duties that minimize the amount of non-productive time such as time spent walking or travelling to take over a vehicle or taking meal breaks. The latter is a good example, since either a driver is relieved at mealtime by another driver or the vehicle is laid up whilst the break is taken. If the vehicle is laid up and an even headway is to be maintained then another vehicle has to be slipped into the schedule. This is

Manchester — Hollinwood — Oldham — Grotton — Uppermill — Diggle   427
Manchester — Hollinwood — Oldham — Grotton — Greenfield   429

Sundays

Service No.	427 ▣	429 ▣	427 ▣	429 ▣	427 ▣	429 ▣	427 ▣	429 ▣	427	429	427	429	427	429	427	429	427	429
Manchester, Piccadilly Gardens							0916	0946	1016	1046	1116	1146	1216	1246	1316	1346	1416	1446
Newton Heath, Dean Lane							0926	0956	1026	1056	1126	1156	1226	1256	1326	1356	1426	1456
Hollinwood, Wickentree Lane	0622		0732		0832	0902	0932	1002	1032	1102	1132	1202	1232	1302	1332	1402	1432	1502
Garden Suburb	0628		0738		0838	0908	0938	1008	1038	1108	1138	1208	1238	1308	1338	1408	1438	1508
Oldham, West Street	0637	0717	0747	0817	0847	0917	0947	1017	1047	1117	1147	1217	1247	1317	1347	1417	1447	1517
Oldham, Mumps Bridge	0641	0721	0751	0821	0851	0921	0951	1021	1051	1121	1151	1221	1251	1321	1351	1421	1451	1521
Lees, County End	0649	0729	0759	0829	0859	0929	0959	1029	1059	1129	1159	1229	1259	1329	1359	1429	1459	1529
Grotton, Station Road	0652	0732	0802	0832	0902	0932	1002	1032	1102	1132	1202	1232	1302	1332	1402	1432	1502	1532
Grasscroft, Lovers Lane		0734	0804	0834	0904	0934	1004	1034	1104	1134	1204	1234	1304	1334	1404	1434	1504	1534
Greenfield, Clarence Hotel		0741		0841		0941		1041		1141		1241		1341		1441		1541
Uppermill, Commercial Hotel			0811		0911		1011		1111		1211		1311		1411		1511	

Service No.	427	429	427	429	427	429	427	429	427	429	427	429	427	429	427	429	427
Manchester, Piccadilly Gardens	1516	1546	1616	1646	1716	1746	1816	1846	1916	1946	2016	2046	2116	2146	2216	2246	2316
Newton Heath, Dean Lane	1526	1556	1626	1656	1726	1756	1826	1856	1926	1956	2026	2056	2126	2156	2226	2256	2326
Hollinwood, Wickentree Lane	1532	1602	1632	1702	1732	1802	1832	1902	1932	2002	2032	2102	2132	2202	2232	2302	2332
Garden Suburb	1538	1608	1638	1708	1738	1808	1838	1908	1938	2008	2038	2108	2138	2208	2238	2308	2338
Oldham, West Street	1547	1617	1647	1717	1747	1817	1847	1917	1947	2017	2047	2117	2147	2217	2247	2317	2347
Oldham, Mumps Bridge	1551	1621	1651	1721	1751	1821	1851	1921	1951	2021	2051	2121	2151	2221	2251	2321	2351
Lees, County End	1559	1629	1659	1729	1759	1829	1859	1929	1959	2029	2059	2129	2159	2229	2259		
Grotton, Station Road	1602	1632	1702	1732	1802	1832	1902	1932	2002	2032	2102	2132	2202	2232	2302		
Grasscroft, Lovers Lane	1604	1634	1704	1734	1804	1834	1904	1934	2004	2034	2104	2134	2204	2234	2304		
Greenfield, Clarence Hotel		1641		1741		1841		1941		2041		2141		2241			
Uppermill, Commercial Hotel	1611		1711		1811		1911		2011		2111		2211		2311		

▣ – Journey provided with the financial support of Greater Manchester Passenger Transport Authority.
Some service 429 journeys continue to Huddersfield via Holmfirth on Summer Sundays. Please see separate publication for full details.
Services 427 and 429 are operated by First Manchester.

Figure 2.1 Example of a published timetable

often referred to as a drop-back vehicle, a frequently resorted to scheduling device that is also used to compensate for delays caused by congestion in rush hours. Eventually the drop-back vehicle's timing will coincide with the time of the laid up or delayed vehicle and this or the drop-back will return to depot. The whole exercise will have increased the vehicle requirement by one but may have resulted in the saving of one duty and it is this kind of trade-off that schedulers must constantly evaluate. Although excellent scheduling software now exists, this tends to be either for timetabling or duty compilation with the integration of both programmes producing at best a sub-optimal solution. Computer-aided scheduling is however of enormous value in handling the 'donkey-work' of timetabling and duty compilation and enabling schedulers to test solutions and manually adjust these to improve their outcomes. Chapter 9 deals further with these.

Duties are usually numbered and a duty roster allocates a numbered duty to staff for every day on which they are scheduled to work. Rather like a football fixtures list, staff are rotated by moving their name down the list of numbered duties at fixed intervals, usually weekly. Rest days are allocated often and where working on that day would not infringe hours of work regulations. A common practice is to 'star' (*) these days on the roster and for starred days to be either allocated overtime (unless refused in advance) or afforded overtime opportunities (see Figure 2.2). Some duties are 'stand by' duties to cover for sickness and absenteeism and others are 'regular relief' to cover specific duties (earlies, lates, etc) of drivers or crew themselves on rest day. The total number of duties in a week (ie, five times the number of Monday to Friday duties, plus Saturday and Sunday duties) divided by the length of the working week (eg, five-day week) gives an indication of the length of the working roster or how many weeks a driver must work before encountering the same duty again. The formula is:

$$(5 \times (M - F) + Sat + Sun) / 5dw$$

The length of a roster can be reduced by splitting it (ie, allocating a group of staff to a single service or a number of interworked services). This has the advantage of ensuring that staff are familiar with the route, passengers, timetable and fares but it can affect job satisfaction. This may be because of the boredom factor or a feeling of unfairness as inevitably some rosters are easier to perform than others are. It can also inhibit flexibility if staff are not familiar with all routes that they may be required to operate.

To comply with legislation such as road vehicle drivers' hours regulations, and similar regulations affecting railway and airline workers[20] and trade union agreements, rosters are usually drawn up so that a long weekend is scheduled every month and no late duty is immediately followed by an early duty (see Figure 2.2).

Week Number	Monday	Tuesday	Wednesday	Thursday	Friday	Saturday	Sunday
1	L1	L1	L1	L1	L1	*	*
2	*	*	E1	E1	E1	E1	E1
3	E1	E1	*	R	S1	S1	*
4	M1	M1	R	*	*	L1	L1
5	L2	L2	L2	L2	L2	*	*
6	*	*	E2	E2	E2	E2	E2
7	E2	E2	*	R	S2	S2	*
8	M2	M2	R	*	*	L2	L2
9	L3	L3	L3	L3	L3	*	*
10	*	*	E3	E3	E3	E3	E3
11	E3	E3	*	R	S3	S3	*
12	M3	M3	R	*	*	L3	L3

Figure 2.2 Duty roster

Key:

* = rest day
L = late duty
E = early duty
S = split duty
M = middle duty
R = spare, relief for absent operatives

HYBRID TRANSPORT

There are no compelling reasons why passengers and freight should not share the same vehicle. However, because the specifications for each type of service vary fundamentally the practice of segregating traffic has become commonplace. Many, but by no means all, freight movements are less urgent or time constrained than passenger movements and such freight can be warehoused or consolidated into bulk consignments before despatch. Conversely, freight that is more urgent can often be of high value and low volume or weight such as courier or parcel traffic and easily accommodated on passenger vehicles.

The separation of passengers and freight on to different vehicles specifically designed for their own traffic is of relatively recent historic origin. The seagoing cargo passenger ship was common until the turn of the 19th century although the faster 'packet steamer' designed to carry mail became the forerunner of the passenger liner. Although the canals were built to carry freight, some canal companies in the 18th century did operate horse-drawn passenger barges until competition by the faster railways overtook these. The first railway (Stockton–Darlington, 1825) was built for freight although horse-drawn passenger trains were soon introduced and the Liverpool–Manchester Railway, 1830, was also built to carry freight, but the operator quickly discovered and met a demand for passenger travel.[21] From the 16th century, the operators of carters' wagons on the very inadequate road network of the British Isles were prepared to carry passengers amongst their consignments. The improvement of the road system with the advent of turnpike roads[22] and developments by the Royal Mail led to the creation of an incredibly efficient and dense network of mail coach services, the forerunners of both stage carriage buses and the modern post bus.

The practice of carrying mail and parcels in the 'guards van' of passenger trains is now far less common on today's privatized railways (much to the frustration of cyclists who are often prevented from travelling with their bikes). Ironically, the major rail freight operator in the UK, English, Welsh and Scottish Railways (EWS) who operate Rail Express Services on contract to Royal Mail to carry the post and who operate the travelling post offices (TPOs), also haul, on behalf of Scot Rail, the Scottish sleeper car services to London. It has been suggested that the attachment of sleeper coaches to mail trains would be possible!

Airlines nowadays carry heavy air cargo loads on commercial passenger flights. For more bulky, heavy or less time-constrained airfreight there are dedicated air cargo operations from most major airports. The Royal Mail has very intensive night movement of its own aircraft using both East Midland and Liverpool Airports as airmail hubs and commercial courier operators like DHL and TNT also have their own dedicated aircraft.

Freight traffic is often slower than passenger traffic and can impede this. At the time of writing, planning applications are being made to convert two redundant air force bases in the East and North East into freight-only airports and these are supported by airline operators anxious to free capacity at overcrowded airports in the South East. Rail freight traffic has grown significantly since rail privatization and the sale of the bulk of the rail freight operations to EWS. Although this growth is welcome for environmental reasons and could help reduce road congestion, the Rail User Consultative Committees are concerned that the overall capacity provided by Railtrack is already proving insufficient to accommodate this growth along with a corresponding growth in passenger traffic.

Public service vehicles are defined in law in the context of the number of seats available to carry passengers for hire or reward[23] but this does not prevent the carriage of parcels, newspapers and unaccompanied merchandise.

Many of the rural and inter-urban services of the National Bus Company (NBC) before bus deregulation (1986) had facilities for the carriage of light merchandise and parcels with an associated tariff and a network of parcels offices. The system survives today in the interworking arrangements between National Express coaches and TNT Parcels Express. The old British Rail Red Star parcels facility in conjunction with City Link collection and delivery services was also a similar concept.

In many instances, the amount of passenger or freight traffic offering on a route is insufficient to support a vehicle dedicated to the carriage of either type of traffic but a hybrid vehicle carrying both kinds of traffic may well be able to provide a viable service or at worse require a lower operating subsidy to continue. This is especially so of rural transport services where hybrid operations can often be the salvation of a 'thin' rural route. Not surprisingly, the following examples are exclusively rural.

The post bus is the archetypal hybrid vehicle (see Figure 2.3). There is a long tradition of combining the carriage of mail and passengers. In some continental European countries such as Switzerland and Germany, these vehicles are often given priority when they sound their 'post horns'. In the UK, the Royal Mail introduced the first four post-bus services in 1968 – in Scotland (Dunbar), Wales (Llanidloes) and England (Penrith and Honiton) – and by 1983 nearly 180 services were operating. Mail vans have to make early morning journeys into rural areas to deliver the post and afternoon journeys to collect mail from village post offices and letterboxes, and the logic of replacing these with minibuses equipped to carry mail is superficially attractive. The downside to this kind of operation has always been the priority given to the mail often requiring passengers to accept circuitous and prolonged journeys. However, it is recognized that a post-bus service is infinitely better than no service at all and following the demise of many rural bus services after deregulation in 1986 the Royal Mail and many 'shire' county councils promoted these, sometimes by offering *de minimis* postbus funding to services that were too marginal to attract bids when put out to tender. The Rural Development Commission also made grants from the Rural Transport Development Fund to support post buses. In response to these partnerships, the Royal Mail relaxed some of their strict criteria on the collection and delivery of mail to allow some post buses to make quicker or more direct journeys, sometimes returning in the middle of the day to 'sweep up' their unfinished tasks. However, it has to be remembered that the carriage of passengers is not the Royal Mail's core activity and whilst post buses are a welcome source of some, albeit minimal, revenue, the mail comes first. Post buses are usually operated on a restricted PSV operator's licence and where the vehicle has more than eight passenger seats the driver has to have passenger carrying vehicle (PCV) driving entitlement, thus creating both training and human resource operational constraints. Nevertheless there are now over 200 post-bus services in the UK

Figure 2.3 Post bus, Chester

and their success is indicative of the possible synergy that can be created between passenger and freight transport.

Another unusual but highly successful example of hybrid transport is the coast-to-coast Packhorse bus. The proprietor of the service, Mr John Bowman of Kirkby Stephen, originally offered a rucksack carriage service for walkers on A Wainwright's famous coast-to-coast walk between St Bees in Cumbria and Robin Hood's Bay in North Yorkshire. After being begged for lifts too often, he hit on the idea of replacing the 'packhorse' vehicles with minibuses and registered what is now the UK's longest registered local service!

Also in Cumbria, an enterprising private hire operator who had a contract with the local newspaper to carry their reporters' 'copy' and photographs from Workington to Carlisle two days per week, replaced his taxi with an eight-seater minibus operated under a special restricted PSV operator licence,[24] which he called the Town and Village Link (TVL). He then registered this as a local service carrying both the copy and passengers and serving a host of villages and hamlets on the Solway plain. Sadly the service terminated in 1998 when the newspaper group began using e-mail to replace hard copy.

In Lancashire an operator calling himself Linkline and who had a contract with the local health trust to collect samples from rural surgeries and take these to the main hospital in the area ran an eight-seater minibus as a PSV at separate fares in conjunction with this work. Whilst the

Coast-to-Coast Packhorse operation was commercial from its inception both TVL and Linkline were assisted by the Rural Transport Development Fund to acquire the right vehicle and begin their services.

Scotland has numerous examples of hybrid services. The Highlands and Islands Omnibus Company in Sutherland were running bus services with conventional single deck buses converted to have large goods compartments long before bus deregulation. An operator on the island of Arran has a midibus with a demountable passenger body that is used for school transport but which is replaced between times with a demountable goods body. Strathclyde Passenger Transport Authority, which, despite serving the Greater Glasgow conurbation also served a deeply rural hinterland before it was reduced in size as a result of local Government reorganization in 1997, supported two hybrid services, the Girvan 'Honey Bee' and the Biggar 'Gipsy' buses. Biggar is also served by a post bus.

The simultaneous carriage of passengers and freight is not a universal panacea; on high frequency and premium services, there is logic in separation but its widespread practice does support the hypothesis of this book that logistics is not purely the preserve of the freight transport operator.

PASSENGER HANDLING

Passengers have some similarity with freight. They may travel singly or in groups and may be consolidated on larger vehicles for the trunk portion of their journey, perhaps having been collected or brought to the 'trunk vehicle' by a smaller vehicle such as a taxi, bus or local train or even having walked, cycled or driven themselves. They differ from freight in that they are, in the main, self-loading although not every passenger can always 'walk on' and passengers with disabilities and mobility impairment require special handling. Passengers are also capable of complaining en route as well as subsequently whereas complaints from consignors are generally either retrospective or complaints of non-arrival of a consignment.

Operators have difficulty handling passengers where space is at a premium. Overcrowded vehicles and terminals with poor or non-existent passenger facilities create problems that can be avoided by sensible planning. Departure lounges at airports and large concourses at railway and bus stations where passengers can circulate and use retail, catering, toilet and booking facilities whilst waiting for their service to depart or interchanging are essential. They are effectively no more than passenger warehouses but adequate warehousing is none the less paramount in any logistic function although the need for it can be minimized by strategies such as 'just-in-time' delivery. In passenger terms, the provision of frequent and reliable services equally limits the build-up of passengers at a terminal but where interchange has to take place then it is sensible to provide as good a level of comfort, shelter and security as possible. In particular, the ability of passengers to access information about their service, not only the scheduled timings and ticket availability (which might have been accessed in advance of the journey) but also in real time via announcements and passenger information displays, is important.

Research has shown that many passengers are insecure and confused, even if they do not show or admit it, and the provision of comfort factors such as shelter, information, CCTV and primarily the visible presence of an operator's staff can do much to both reassure them and, by making their journey less stressful, retain their future patronage.[25] This is especially so where the passenger has any form of disability. Many operators make especial efforts to accommodate disabled passengers by the provision of more accessible vehicles (such as the current generation of low-floor buses) and the training of their staff in disability awareness. Some also instigate special procedures for handling disabled and mobility-impaired passengers, including encouraging them to pre-book assistance. The provision of recent legislation will be bound to accelerate this kind of provision in the next few years.[26]

THREE

Managing Transport Organizations

THE HISTORY OF PASSENGER TRANSPORT

Steam traction used on the first railways was the first agent to deliver what became the earliest form of power-assisted passenger movement. Before that, sailing vessels, horse drawn barges and wagons (primarily carrying freight) and the few canal-borne passenger vessels and many stagecoaches that succeeded them were the only alternatives to either walking or horse riding.

The Highways Act 1555 placed a duty on parishes to maintain their roads using statutory labour and, because of the manifest imperfections of this mechanism, the many trusts created by the Turnpike Acts of 1663 and later were able to charge tolls to finance and repair a network of primary local and strategic routes. The canals of the late 16th[1] and early-17th centuries were primarily built for freight traffic although some passenger movement took place along them. The opening of the Liverpool to Manchester railway in 1830 all but assured the success of steam locomotion[2] for rail passenger travel.[3] There followed from 1840 a burst of rail speculation culminating in some quite large consolidations of companies and legislation addressed to issues such as competition, running rights to other operators, common carrier obligations, gauge standardization, fares and even government powers (not exercised at the time) of nationalization.[4] The growth of rail traffic spelt the end not just of the canal traffic[5] of the day but also of the turnpike trusts as roads were 'de-turnpiked' to become the responsibility of the new local governments.[6] It also extinguished the national network of stagecoach services although local road passenger and freight traffic developed to feed the railheads.

In 1829 the first horse-drawn omnibus operated between Paddington and Bank in London[7] and by 1855 the French owned London General Omnibus Company (LGOC) had established itself as the principal bus operator in the capital with over 500 vehicles. However, it faced competition from small operators with one or two vehicles and from various associations of such operators, and by 1880 competition with the emergent London Road Car Company's vehicles had become intense. The opening of the first London Underground Railway in 1890 and the construction of horse tramways a decade later presaged the decline of the horse bus.

The Tramways Act of 1870 had influenced the development of tramways by empowering the local authorities to purchase those already constructed after 21 years and thereafter at seven-year intervals. (The disincentive for horse tramway operators to electrify their so amortized assets at the end of their 'franchises' is not dissimilar to the reluctance of train operating companies (TOCs) today to invest in new rolling stock within the short timescale of their franchise.)

Undoubtedly the most significant event in the development of land transport has been the rapid growth of motorized transport such as cars, buses, lorries and railway diesel locomotives and multiple units. The LGOC took up motorbus operation seriously early in the twentieth century. Despite a merger between them, their rival Road Car Company and another large competing operator,[8] and working agreements with other bus operators,[9] these amalgamations were not successful in preventing new entrants into what was still a deregulated market causing a resurgence of competition after the First World War.[10] So unbridled and wasteful was this competition that it provoked responses from both The General (as LGOC became known), who embarked on a fares war with its smaller competitors and a policy of attempting to buy them out, and the surviving competitors, who combined to defend themselves under common management as the London Public Omnibus Company. The government's initial response was to attempt a degree of regulation in the London Traffic Act 1924, but following the recommendations of the Royal Commission on Transport in 1928 and after:

- agreements by the 'General' and the 'Public' to coordinate their services;
- a revenue pooling agreement between the railway companies and the Underground; and
- attempts by the London County Council to promote 'coordination' Bills

the stage was set for complete unification of all public passenger transport in the metropolis. The London Passenger Transport Act 1933 transferred all these public passenger transport undertakings to a public authority.[11] The consequent monopoly created effectively marked the end of competition in London.[12]

During the 1920s, the railways gained a strong foothold in the bus industry. The Railways Act of 1921 had grouped the then existing 120 private railway companies into four large area monopolies, the London and North Eastern Railway (LNER), London Midland and Scottish (LMS), Great Western Railway (GWR) and Southern Railway (SR). Contained in a later Act[13] were powers for these companies to run their own road passenger transport services. These powers greatly concerned the territorial bus companies that had begun to dominate mainland Britain and they negotiated an agreement with the railways that they would only be able to hold up to 50 per cent of their shares, with the bus companies retaining overall control.

Outside London, by the turn of the 19th century many municipalities had exercised their powers under the Tramways Act 1870 to acquire their local tramways and many systems started this way were often the forerunners of municipal bus undertakings. However, not all private tramway companies were taken over in this way and many that survived gained strong footholds in urban areas and eventually diversified into bus operations. The British Electric Traction Company (BET) had many tramway subsidiaries and in time became one of the largest groupings of bus operators in the provinces. The other large group, Thomas Tilling, a pioneer of the London bus business, started provincial operations early in the 20th century and bought up many existing operators.

Apart from some ineffectual attempts by local authorities to license omnibuses as hackneys[14] the bus industry was essentially unregulated outside London before 1930. An Act was passed in that year[15] to regulate the industry in an attempt to prevent the sort of unbridled competition that had taken place in London, with 'pirate' operators running ahead of scheduled services to cream off their traffic.

The Road Traffic Act 1930 had a marked effect on the road-passenger transport industry, which then became highly regulated. In the first instance, it introduced quality controls in the form of PSV drivers' hours and driving licence regulations that significantly raised the 'barriers to entry' to the industry. More importantly, it instigated a system of quantity or economic control in the form of road service licensing (RSL) that effectively gave the operators of both stage carriage and express services a virtual monopoly on the routes for which they held a RSL. The number of contract carriage licences enabling operators to perform private hire work was not controlled. This new regulation of road passenger transport had the effect, outside London, of strengthening the position of the large provincial operators who were able to use their muscle to object to applications for road service licences from their smaller competitors. Most but not all of the large operators were associated with one of the three emergent oligopolies, Tilling, BET and in Scotland, Scottish Motor Traction (SMT).[16] They nearly all entered into area agreements not to compete in each other's territories. In 1942, a major policy disagreement resulted in a clear split between Tilling and BET[17] that was to have significant ramifications after the war.

As part of its commitment to the nationalization of transport, the post-war Labour government created a British Transport Commission (BTC) through the mechanism of the Transport Act 1947 to hold all the assets of the newly nationalized four major railway companies described earlier. In the following two years, both the Tilling Group and SMT (but not BET) sold out to the BTC recognizing that through their railway holdings they controlled up to 49 per cent of the shares of many of their constituent companies.

Outright nationalization of the bus industry was not in the 1945 manifesto although the government did have plans to create Area Boards. Many Labour controlled municipalities with their own passenger transport undertakings resisted these plans. Therefore, by the time the Conservatives took power in 1951, the only extensions of public ownership were the purchase of some private operators[18] and the incidental acquisition of some companies owned by electricity companies also being nationalized.[19]

The BTC was an unwieldy body composed of a number of executives for railways, London Transport, docks and waterways and road transport (including road haulage).[20] The new government's Transport Act 1953 reorganized this in a number of ways. It broke up the cumbersome and over centralized but still nationalized Railway Executive (British Rail) into six semi-autonomous operating areas. The same government then went further with the Transport Act 1962 in granting British Rail (BR) considerable commercial freedom, including freedom from the previous control of freight rates and passenger fares.[21] The 1962 Act created a Transport Holding Company (THC) to operate as a commercial company and hold the residual assets of the BTC after the privatization of road haulage and the 'hiving off' of the British Transport hotels and other activities. A consequence of this was the loss to BR of their shareholdings in the Tilling Company and SMT but a less expected outcome on the return of a Labour government in 1964 was the 'voluntary' sale by BET of all their bus assets to the THC.

The stage was thus set at the end of thirteen years of Conservative government, best described perhaps as a time of quasi-nationalization, denationalization and commercialization, for the emergence of a huge bus oligopoly, state owned and controlling over 90 per cent of bus services outside the not insignificant municipal transport empires. Two events of the 1960s shaped the thinking of the Labour government that crystallized in the Transport Act 1968. The first of these was the seminal report of Professor Buchanon, 'Traffic in Towns', which spelt out the consequences of increasing car dependency, and the second the massive programme of railway closures following Lord (then Dr) Beeching's report 'The Reshaping of British Railways'.

The 1968 Act created Passenger Transport Executives in the major conurbations[22] with a duty to create a properly coordinated and integrated public passenger transport system to meet the needs of their areas. The Executives were controlled by Passenger Transport Authorities comprising elected representatives of the Metropolitan Districts and in 1968 (or later in some cases) they took control of the assets of all the former municipal bus undertakings in their areas. They also had powers under section 20 of the Act to specify and purchase their rail service requirements from the British Railways Board (BRB). The bus assets of the Transport Holding Company[23] were transferred to a new state-owned National Bus Company that was also required to cooperate with the PTEs in their areas, a function the company willingly undertook since road services were not subject to RSLs in PTE areas but could only run with the PTE's agreement. The Act wound up the old BTC by creating a number of state owned Boards with commercial remits, prominent amongst which was the British Railways Board.[24]

Local government reorganization under a new Conservative government in 1974[25] created a two-tier system outside the metropolitan areas: top-tier 'shire' county councils having responsibility for highways and transportation, and the lower-tier district councils having very few transport functions.[26] Section 203 of the Local Government Act 1972 gave county councils similar powers to PTEs. Although there was another brief return of Labour to office at the end of the 1970s, the long period of Conservative rule begun in the 1980s saw a move away from the system of state control, even though this had by then allowed the public-owned transport undertakings considerable commercial freedom, towards an era of deregulation and privatization. First to be dismantled were the London County Council and the Metropolitan Counties. The existing London boroughs and metropolitan districts became new style unitary all-purpose authorities although the PTEs survived under the joint management of elected members of these authorities and, bizarrely, London Transport Executive became the nationalized and wholly state-owned London Regional Transport (LRT)!

The Transport Act 1985 completed the process of bus deregulation that had begun in 1980[27] with the removal of the need for express services to hold RSLs. The Act provided that outside London PTEs and county councils should secure by tender only those services that the market did not provide so as to meet the 'requirements' of their areas (a much less exacting criterion than that of the 1968 Act, which specified meeting 'needs'). Thus the industry was deregulated by legislating for the abolition of road service licensing and the substitution of a system whereby operators merely registered those services that they were prepared to provide either commercially or as a consequence of a service subsidy agreement entered into after a successful tender. In parallel, there were the necessary powers for the government to privatize the industry by the sale of the NBC and Scottish Transport Group (STG) bus operating companies and eventually[28] the operating divisions of the PTEs and all but thirteen municipal undertakings.

London Buses, the road passenger transport half of LRT,[29] was broken down into a number of subsidiary LRT owned companies that were then privatized. In the capital, however, the services were not deregulated; instead, the Transport London Act 1984 provided for LRT to specify and put out to tender a network comprising both commercial services and unremunerative but socially desirable services requiring subsidy.[30] This system of franchising in London has enabled the retention of such network benefits as the Travelcard and enabled LRT to retain and even grow slightly its bus market.

After bus deregulation and privatization, it was the turn of British Rail to face the uncertainties of the complete reorganization of their ownership and control. The whole process of rail privatization was carried out in unseemly haste in the months before the 1993 general election. Various ways were suggested of achieving this objective that the late Robert Adley, a conservative MP and rail 'buff', described as 'the poll tax on wheels'. The BRB favoured outright sale in much the same way as the disposal of British Gas and British Telecom; others suggested reverting to the old groupings model and selling off each regional railway rather like the sale of area companies of NBC and effectively recreating the old LMS, LNER, SR and GWR. However, in the end, the choice of model was heavily influenced by EC legislation that required the separation of the control and commercial operation (but not necessarily the ownership) of the track and the train operating units. The European Union (EU) Directive in fact merely required the 'normalization' of railway accounts so that track access charges could be disaggregated from other operating costs and the application of subsidies be transparent, something that the French state owned SNCF managed to do by creating a separate commercial arm to own and lease the track.

Accordingly, the Railways Act 1993 provided for the creation within BRB of 25 train operating units, separate freight and rolling stock companies (ROSCOs) and an infrastructure company that became called Railtrack to own the track and sell access to it. A Franchise Director was appointed to sell by tender the train operating units to Train Operating Companies (TOCs) who would bid for franchises of seven years or more on the basis of the amount of subsidy they would require over the franchise. In most cases the subsidy diminishes year by year over the life of the franchise and in a few cases actually becomes a premium payment to the Franchise Director in the final years of the franchise. In the event, 13 of the 25 TOCs were acquired by bus companies or groups and by the end of 1998 by a process of consolidation that figure had risen to 17. The big surprise in government thinking came with the disposal on the stock market of Railtrack, something not contemplated in the Railways Act and the legitimacy of which has been questioned often since, not least as the Act never actually mentions Railtrack by name! The Act also created the post of Rail Regulator to manage the licensing of the network (Railtrack, TOCs and freight operators) and oversee the Rail User Consultative Committees (RUCCs) that have a consumer protection role. The RUCCs also inherited from their predecessors, the TUCCs, the important duty of conducting inquiries into any closure proposals and for the first time have oversight of certain protected fares. The new Labour government inherited this privatized railway in 1998 and made it clear that although they could not afford to re-nationalize the system they would strengthen the Regulator's powers through the creation of a Strategic Rail Authority.

No account of the development of passenger transport could be complete without a reference to air transport, the fastest growing sector of that market (taking, that is, an international perspective). By 1929 the railways had acquired powers to operate not only buses (as referred to earlier) but also aircraft but they never used these until a developing network of domestic air transport services began to threaten their traffic,[31] whereupon their subsidiary Railway Air Services introduced flights on some important routes. However, these were operated on their behalf by Imperial Airways. By 1935 twelve companies operated 76 domestic services but these were on the whole very uneconomic and the largest of the companies merged to form British Airways, which became the government's chosen provider of internal flights. An Air Transport Licensing Authority (ATLA) was created in 1938 to control domestic services but international flights, for which Imperial Airways was the government's flag carrier, were subject to a different type of quantity control in the form of Air Service Agreements embodying bilateral and multilateral traffic rights to operate interstate scheduled services. These were brokered by the International Air Transport Association (IATA), a worldwide trade association playing a dominant role in setting fares and tariffs.

The Labour government's post-war nationalization extended to air as well as surface transport. In 1946 all British airlines (including the two major operators, British Airways and Imperial Airways) were taken into public ownership and grouped as either British Overseas Airways Corporation, providing long haul flights, or British European Airways providing mainly domestic and European flights, but also some middle Eastern flights. The post-war growth of air transport was rapid especially in the charter market for non-scheduled flights, including inclusive tours that developed outside these quantity controls and now account for more traffic than scheduled services! In 1960, the ATLA was reconstituted as the Air Transport Licensing Board (ATLB) and given a wider remit to control both entry to the market and fares. However, by 1969, the government had decided on a fundamental review of air transport and set up the Edwards Committee on 'British Air Transport in the 70's' that recommended that a 'second force' airline should be enabled to compete with the nationalized airlines. The result was the Civil Aviation Act of 1971, which created a Civil Aviation Authority to take over the ATLB's remit as well as the safety aspects of air transport licensing such as airworthiness certification and pilot licensing. It also decided on the merger of BOAC and BEA as a reconstituted British Airways (unconnected with the British Airways of the 1930s) and special provision for the encouragement of a second force that emerged as British Caledonian. In 1987, in common with other nationalized transport undertakings, British Airways was privatized since when British Caledonian has ceased to trade and other British airlines have been created including British Midland, Monarch, Manx Airways and Air 2000.

Airline deregulation in the United States[32] in 1978 ended 40 years of strict international quantity controls and destabilized the effects of the IATA cartel so that the trade association had to allow members to opt out if they wished. The advent of Computer Reservation Systems was also at the time another factor in favouring the consolidation of airlines then taking place, with 'hub and spoke' operations being developed at the 'home' airports of the major US airlines and competition resulting in a general lowering of fares.[33]

The European Community has been much slower than the US in liberalizing its air services although in the 1980s the UK, Eire and the 'Benelux' countries unilaterally did so. However, the process of creating 'open skies' within the Single European Market (SEM) now seems unstoppable although in practice it is subject to strict controls under EU competition legislation aimed at preventing the creation of dominant monopolies by mergers or alliances and the abuse of an airline's dominant position by predatory pricing strategies. An EU Directive of 1992 removed fares control and established the freedom to fly between any airports in the Community. This was followed in 1997 by the introduction of cabotage, the freedom of any European state's airline to carry another state's domestic traffic and a relaxation of capacity sharing regulations to allow member states to authorize more than one airline on any route.

OWNERSHIP AND CONTROL

Figure 3.1 presents a table that summarizes the changes in the ownership and control of public passenger transport described in the preceding section, beginning with the privately owned railways, through consolidation, nationalization and municipalization to 'quasi nationalization' with greater commercial freedom for public Boards with 'arms length control', public transport authorities and today's deregulation and privatization.

It is often argued that authorities such as PTEs or county councils can quite adequately coordinate public passenger transport within their areas (as indeed the Transport Acts of 1968 and 1972 required them to do) even though they are not any longer the owners of the transport undertakings providing their services. Simply having powers to procure (or secure by tender) services to meet the needs of their area should suffice. Whilst this is a persuasive argument, the reality is that funds were often insufficient to discharge their duty to meet needs. When this duty was diluted by the Transport Act 1985 to a duty to secure from the deregulated bus operators only those services that the market did not provide and then only to meet the areas' 'requirements' (as opposed to social needs), their powers of coordination were sadly depleted. In many cases this was compounded by the fact that the transport providers from whom services were to be procured were once owned by either the state (eg, NBC and BRB) or the local authority (in the form of municipal passenger transport undertakings) but have since been privatized (the NBC and most municipal undertakings[34] by the Transport Act 1985 and BRB by the Railways Act 1993).

The government's 1998 integrated transport White Paper ('A New Deal for Transport') suggests that transport policies should be integrated with other policies such as land use planning. Hitherto, 'transport integration' had a different meaning implying the common and almost invariably public ownership of the means of delivering the service. Thus, the Transport Act 1968 provided:

- for PTEs to own and operate all the previous municipal bus undertakings in their area;
- for the only other services to be allowed to operate to have to be provided with the 'consent' of the relevant PTE (which effectively made them their own licensing authority);
- for NBC to have a duty to cooperate with the PTEs in provision of joint services;
- for PTEs to secure from BRB the rail services needed in their area.[35]

Thus common ownership and control could be said to have delivered, in the words of the 1968 Act, 'a properly coordinated and integrated public passenger transport service'.

London bus services, as already explained, were never deregulated although London Regional Transport, the 'nationalized' passenger transport authority, was required to divest itself of its bus assets, which were privatized and passed into the hands, in the main, of the large bus

ACT	OWNERSHIP	CONTROL
Highways Act 1555	parish councils became highway authorities	provided for statutory labour
Turnpike Acts 1663	created turnpike trusts	authorized tolls
Railway Regulation Act 1840		Railway Inspectorate of Board of Trade
Railways Act 1844		'Parliamentary trains'
Railway and Canal Traffic Acts 1854/1873/1888/1894	Powers of nationalization (never used)	Railway Commission (1873) to supervise rates and charges; common carrier obligation
Tramways Act 1870	local authorities' powers to purchase after 21 years	
Local Government Act 1888	local government became highway authorities	highway funding from rates
Transport Act 1919		created MoT, which subsumed Roads Board
Railways Act 1921	grouping: LMS, LNER, SR, GWR	
London Traffic Act 1924		bus route licensing on designated streets
Railways (Road Transport) Act 1927		railways get bus and air operating powers
Road Traffic Act 1930		PSV regulation, road service licensing, driver licences, drivers' hours
London Passenger Transport Act 1933	London Passenger Transport Board	
Transport Act 1947	British Transport Commission created	road and rail transport nationalized (air was nationalized in 1946)
Civil Aviation Act 1947		BEA formed alongside existing BOAC
Transport Act 1953	BTC reorganized	denationalization – Road Haulage Disposals Board
Civil Aviation (Licensing) Act 1960		ATLB to succeed ATLA of 1938 (see CAA 71)
Transport Act 1962	Transport Holding Company and BRB established with Board for London Transport, waterways and docks. BTC abolished.	railway's bus shares passed to THC; commercial objectives for nationalized transport; rail closures reviewed by TUCC
Airports Authorities Act 1965		British Airports Authority created.
Transport Act 1968	five PTEs, NBC, STG established	BRB and PTEs enter 'section 20' agreements; road haulage deregulation

Figure 3.1 Table of transport legislation

ACT	OWNERSHIP	CONTROL
Transport (London) Act 1969	London Transport Executive of the London CC	LTE monopoly in London
Civil Aviation Act 1971		Civil Aviation Authority set up as licensing authority; BOAC and BEA merged as BA
Local Government Act 1972	S&W Yorks PTEs created	county councils get co-ordination role (s.203) but no 'section 20' powers
Railways Act 1974		public service obligations set for BRB
Transport Act 1978		permitted community transport and community buses; county councils to prepare Public Transport Plans (PTPs).
Transport Act 1980		'trial' deregulation areas and deregulation of long distance coach services; PSV O-licensing and car sharing at separate fares; control of bus fares ended
Civil Aviation Act 1980		by removing statutory preference allowed competition against British Airways (eventually privatized 1987)
Local Government (Planning and Land) Act 1980		abolition of metropolitan counties (but not PTEs)
Transport Act 1983		PTEs also to prepare PTPs and given protected expenditure limits (PELs)
Transport (London) Act 1984	created nationalized London Regional Transport	London bus franchising and eventual privatization
Transport Act 1985	privatization of NBC, STG, PTE bus operations and all but 13 municipalities	bus deregulation and competition
Railways Act 1993	separation of Railtrack from TOCs, ROSCOs and freight operators	Rail Regulator and OPRAF; TUCCs became RUCCs
Local Government Bill 1999		will replace compulsory competitive tendering with best value for money (BVM)
Transport Bill 2000		will create a Strategic Rail Authority from shadow SRA (old BRB) – see 'Postscript'

Figure 3.1 *continued*

operating groups. However, LRT retain the powers that the PTEs once had to specify services although the Traffic Commissioners can issue London local service licences (equivalent to road service licences) to other operators to whose proposed services LRT has refused consent. All the services specified by LRT, not just those that the market would be unwilling to provide, are then secured by tender, with the successful bidder being granted an exclusive contract to operate these.

The process is not unlike rail franchising in that tenders range from service subsidy bids (usually minimum cost tenders where LRT keep the fares but take the commercial risk) to franchises for which operators bid a price they are prepared to pay to operate a 'commercial' service. By this means, LRT is able to procure an integrated public passenger transport service with such benefits of integration as bus/rail/underground connections and through-ticketing, and London-wide concessionary fares and travelcard schemes.

Economists put yet another interpretation on the word integration. By reference to the processes that make up a product or service (for example a journey by public transport) they examine the extent to which the disaggregated parts of the service (for example bus/rail/metro) are 'aggregated' under common ownership or control. Taking the Greater Manchester Public Transport Executive (GMPTE) area as an example, the PTE's bus undertakings at deregulation in 1986 became a wholly owned (by the PTE) arms length bus operating company, GM Buses. Many smaller competing bus operators entered the market and eventually the Secretary of State for Transport required the PTE to dispose of its holdings. This was done by splitting GM Buses into a number of subsidiary companies, including GM South (eventually sold to Stagecoach) and GM North (eventually sold to First Bus, part of First Group). Later, with rail privatization, the train operating company NW Trains was eventually acquired by First Group to become First North Western Trains. This common ownership by First Group of both the trains and major bus operator in north Manchester is a good example of vertical integration. At the same time, however, some medium-sized competing bus operators in the north of the conurbation were also acquired by First Group, in one case (Pennine Motors) the acquisition had already been made by another First Group company, Potteries Motor Traction. The resultant area-wide concentration of ownership of one mode of transport (buses) to provide a network of bus services is an equally good example of what economists describe as horizontal integration.

The inevitable growth of oligopolies following bus deregulation and rail privatization has seen the acquisition by the big operating groups of neighbouring competitors to create large operating territories. For example, apart from the enclaves of GM North and Merseytravel, Stagecoach is now the predominant bus operator in the northwest of England. In this context the recent link between Stagecoach and Virgin trains providing bus/rail links between many points in Cumbria, Lancashire and Cheshire could, from the county councils' point of view as procurers (as opposed to the passengers' view as users), be viewed as horizontal (ie, spreading over an area) integration. Such wide-scale integration within the private sector does of course have implications in competition law that will be considered in Chapter 4. However, at this stage it is worth noting that changes to EU competition law are reflected in the UK's 1998 Competition Act and briefly, to put this and the issues of ownership and control into the context of the whole question of the EU's proposed liberalization of their Common Transport Policy.

Within the European Commission, there is constant debate about the nature of the Common Transport Policy and whether it should be prescriptive in attempting to create a 'level playing field' by 'harmonizing' the social, technical and fiscal legislation of the member states or whether it should seek to 'roll back intervention' by 'liberalization'. The three aspects of liberalization to which the UK and especially the Conservative government of 1980–98 has already responded more than most member states are:

- competition;
- deregulation;
- re-structuring.

Responses to the first two of these will be obvious to readers who have read this chapter so far. It is the question of restructuring that has produced a different response in the UK to that in other member states. EC Directives call for action such as the 'normalization of accounts' by the transparent separate identification of commercial and subsidized operations and the separation of rail operations into the provision of track and the running of trains. This has been achieved in other states without privatizing their nationalized railways but in the UK has involved privatization not only of the rail operating companies but also of Railtrack itself.[36] In France, by contrast, the separation of SNCF from RFF (the track authority) was achieved without privatizing the existing public/private SNCF. New Zealand however has gone furthest of all in actually privatizing their state highways.

LICENSING

All providers of public passenger transport are licensed to operate. Governments at every level (European, central and local) and of all persuasions have been convinced of the necessity to do so for good reasons.

These range from issues such as the protection of the environment, the safety and protection of passengers, the desire to control competition or even the need to raise government revenues either to finance the licensing system or to 'vire' to other expenditure that may or may not be transport related.

The degree to which licensing systems address the above issues varies between states (and may in future do so in the UK with Scottish and Welsh devolution), between transport modes and even (for example, in the case of taxis) between different local authorities. All licensing systems can be described either as quality or quantity licences or, in some cases, as both.

A quality licensing system generally addresses the issues of safety and the environment. Quality licences are usually granted 'as of right', unless combined with a quantity system (see below), provided the applicant can satisfy their licensing authority's criteria for issuing them. Thus in theory there should be no limit to the numbers of licences granted irrespective of whether demand for the applicant's services can be demonstrated. In practice the criteria may often be sufficiently demanding as to constitute a formidable 'barrier to entry' effectively limiting the number of applicants.

As an example, PSV operator licences granted by UK Traffic Commissioners under their powers in the Public Passenger Vehicles Act 1981 (as amended by the Deregulation and Contracting out Act 1994) are quality licences that take no account of the anticipated use of the buses specified on the licence. The Commissioners must grant a licence if the applicant can satisfy the criteria of the European Commission set out most recently in their 1998 Directive[37] on Access to the Occupation of PSV Operator, which requires them to demonstrate good repute, financial standing and professional competence. Although these appear to be straightforward quality controls, it should be noted that the 1998 Directive considerably raised the financial standing benchmarks and increased the difficulty of the examination for the Certificate needed to demonstrate Professional Competence. Thus in practice by raising the barriers to entry the quantity of applicants is guaranteed to be fewer!

A prime role of nearly every licensing authority is to ensure the safety of passengers and the means by which they each achieve this are discussed in Chapter 8. Safety is thus a sine qua non of nearly all licensing regimes. In goods vehicle operator licensing, which is beyond the scope of this book, strong environmental safeguards were introduced in 1984 but despite lobbying from local authorities for similar controls to be introduced to PSV operator licensing this has not happened, although an environmental challenge to a PSV operator's licence application was made by a local authority in 1986.[38] Thus, most licensing regimes have some kind of underpinning quality rationale whether or not they combine this with quantity controls.

Quantity controls are exercised where a licensing authority is given powers to do so for specific purposes. The system of road service licensing practised by the UK Traffic Commissioners between 1933 and 1985 (when buses were deregulated) and still practised as London Local Service Licensing by the Metropolitan Traffic Commissioner is a very clear illustration of what is meant by quantity licensing. Briefly, operators are required to have a licence to run their service thus bestowing on them a quasi-monopoly on the route. The Air Transport Licensing Board also has a similar quantity licensing remit that has been discussed earlier in this chapter.

The role of the Rail Regulator as set out in the Railways Act 1993 is to license Railtrack and train operating companies. Whilst safety and quality are paramount parts of his remit to license 'rail assets' the Regulator also has a quantity remit to control, in so far as they require his or her consent, access agreements. As part of his or her consumer protection role, the Regulator is also responsible for moderating competition to the franchised operator by way of open access proposals from a potential competitor. This last remit is not very different from the stated rationale for road service licensing which was to 'avoid wasteful competition'! The proposal for a Strategic Rail Authority in the government's integrated transport White Paper[39] will only see the new Authority take over the Regulator's consumer protection powers, not the licensing remit.

Deregulation is simply the removal of quantity licensing. Thus with bus deregulation in 1985, road service licensing was abolished outside London and replaced with a system whereby operators merely gave notice of any services they proposed operating and Traffic Commissioners are required to accept these 'registrations' provided only that they are made correctly. The 1998 government White Paper on integrated transport made no commitment to full scale re-regulation but did promise, and reinforced this promise in its later buses 'daughter document',[40] to give statutory force to two specific measures, which whilst their description uses the word 'quality' are in fact disguised quantity controls.

The first of these are quality partnerships between operator(s) and local authorities under which each invests in the necessary capital projects along a public transport corridor or less usually within an operating area, the operator usually in vehicles and the authority in infrastructure improvements. Thus, the operator may invest in low-floor buses, publicity and staff training and the authority in bus lanes, bus stops and real time information. Legislation would address the potential problem that operators who do not agree to raise their standards cannot, in a still deregulated situation, be excluded from using the new facilities. This avoids the danger of 'gate crasher' operators perhaps even resorting to predatory pricing or registering just in front of their 'quality' competitor.

The White Paper and daughter document, however, go further in saying that 'in some places strengthened quality partnerships may not be sufficient to guarantee necessary improvements'. Enabling powers to permit the establishment of 'quality contracts' similar, it says, to London franchising are proposed. These would work by giving local authorities powers to grant exclusive operating rights on defined routes or within specific operating areas. The enabling powers are to be subject to prior ministerial approval in England and the approval of the Scottish and Welsh National Assemblies. Bus franchising in its various forms is fairly common elsewhere in Europe, although subsidies and public ownership are both usually higher than in the UK, but there is no doubt that any return to regulation will be along such lines.

ROLE OF CENTRAL AND LOCAL GOVERNMENT

European Union

The UK is a member state of the Union and as such must observe its Regulations (eg, Drivers' Hours and Records Regulations) and enact its own legislation to implement its Directives (eg, the Working Time Directive). EU legislation is not made by the European Parliament (the legislature) but by its Commission (the administration) and ratified by its executive (the Council of Ministers) either by an absolute majority or in some instances a qualified majority (post-Maastricht Treaty 1992). In 1999, the Parliament showed that it did have more than just the power to agree the Commission's budget when it forced the resignation of all the Commissioners and it is likely that the new Commissioners will agree to a move towards co-determination (by Commission and Parliament) of new legislation.

In addition to its legislative powers, the EU has large budgets for economic regeneration (eg, the European Regional Development Fund – ERDF) that have been used by the UK to part fund capital transport projects (eg, Sheffield's super tram). Furthermore, some of the more high profile activities of the EU are having or are bound to have an inordinate effect on not only the UK transport industry but also the UK itself. Space does not permit a detailed examination of these activities but prominent amongst them are:

- the Single European Market adopted in 1992;
- The Social Contract and the European Convention on Human Rights, both of which the new Labour government of 1997 have adopted;
- the launch of the Euro currency throughout the larger continental states.

Central government

Westminster also comprises an executive (cabinet), administration (civil service) and legislature (Parliament). The cabinet determines its programme of legislation but because of the UK doctrine of collective responsibility individual ministers are not free agents. Thus the Secretary of State for Environment, Transport and the Regions, at the time of writing, is frustrated because his proposed Transport Act to implement his integrated transport White Paper ('A New Deal for Transport') is deemed by the Prime Minister and cabinet to have a lower priority than legislation on health, crime and social services. However, most legislation vests considerable powers in Secretaries of State who carry primary responsibility for the delivery of their policies (the doctrine of ministerial responsibility) by ministers, regional and local government and government agencies.

The previous government sought to 'roll back the frontiers of the state' by deregulation policies (for example the presumption in favour of the developer in planning legislation, which made any integration of transport and land use planning extremely difficult). Nevertheless, ministers can still use powers vested in them by the primary legislation to create subordinate legislation in the form of statutory instruments. In this way the Secretary of State at the Department of the Environment, Transport and the Regions (DETR) has been able to create a shadow Strategic Rail Authority (SRA) by using his powers to give 'objectives, instruction and guidance' to the residual BRB. In effect, this has made it the shadow SRA until primary legislation (a new Transport Act) can be passed to create a substantive SRA.

The major department of state with transport responsibilities is the DETR, which now embraces not only all forms of inland transport (road, rail and inland waterways) but also sea and air transport, once the responsibility of the Department of Trade and Industry. The DETR is also responsible for the work of a number of executive agencies with transport responsibilities:

- The Vehicle Inspectorate;
- The Driving Standards Agency;
- The Driver and Vehicle Licensing Agency at Swansea;
- The Vehicle Certification Agency;
- The Maritime and Coastguards Agency (safety at sea and coastguards);
- The Marine Accident Investigation Branch;
- The Highways Agency (HA).

A sixth agency, the Transport and Road Research Laboratory, has been privatized as the Transport Research Laboratory. The Department also sponsors a number of 'quangos' including the Standing Advisory Committee on Trunk Road Assessment (SACTRA), the Countryside Agency (CA), the Disabled Persons Transport Advisory Committee (DiPTAC) and the Rail User Consultative Committees (RUCCs, and their central committee, the CRUCC). It is the parent department for those parts of the transport industry that are still nationalized including:

- the Civil Aviation Authority (CAA);
- the residual British Railways Board (BRB – but see above);
- the British Waterways Board (BWB);
- the Port of London Authority (PLA);
- London Regional Transport (LRT) comprising London Underground and London Buses (until the creation of a Greater London Authority).

Other state departments impacting on the transport industry include the Department of Trade and Industry – DTI (competition law), the Treasury (funding and customs and excise), the Department for Education and Employment (training, health and safety and industrial relations) and the Home Office (police). The Secretaries of State for Northern Ireland, Wales and Scotland exercise similar powers to departmental Secretaries of State but many of the powers of the last two are now devolved to the new Scottish Parliament and Welsh Assembly.

Regional government

Nine new Regional Development Agencies (RDAs) were created on the 1st April 1999 as promised in the White Paper of December 1998.[41] Their proposed boundaries are shown in Figure 3.2. The Secretary of State sees these as 'bouncing alongside' Scottish and Welsh devolution and developing into regional assemblies appointed from elected members in their area and eventually, subject to referenda, becoming composed of directly elected members.

They are influential new bodies that will develop and promote economic strategies for their regions. London's new RDA, subject to a referendum in May 1999 and Parliamentary approval, will become a new metropolitan wide strategic authority led by an elected mayor. It will become responsible for London Regional Transport (LRT). From a transport perspective their main influence will be through the 15–20 years Regional Planning Guidance that they will develop and which will contain 10–15 year Regional Transport Strategies.

Local government

County councils in England (the so-called 'shire' counties) are 'top tier' authorities with responsibilities for transportation and highways. The district councils in these areas have few transport powers although they can determine their own concessionary fares schemes. In Scotland and Wales, strong unitary all-purpose (including transportation) authorities exist and

Figure 3.2 Proposed boundaries for Regional Development Agencies[41]

some unitary authorities have been created in England. The metropolitan counties and the Greater London Council were abolished in 1980[42] making the metropolitan districts and London boroughs unitary authorities but the Metropolitan Passenger Transport Authorities and London Regional Transport were retained as transport authorities as was Strathclyde PTA in Scotland. As mentioned above the new Greater London Authority when created in 2000 will take over responsibility for London Transport from the anomalously state-owned LRT.

The 'top tier' counties and strong unitary authorities are not only transport and highways supremos they also hold their own land-use planning briefs. However, local government can only do what it its statutory powers and financial resources can permit. The proportion of the local authorities' budgets that comes from local taxation (rates, poll tax and now council tax) is lower than ever and the authorities are hence heavily influenced by central government offices in their region (eg, Government Office North West (GONW)) that indirectly 'hold their purse strings'. The creation of RDAs and possible further regional devolution might affect this relationship but the extent to which local government will depend on central and European funding is unlikely to change radically in the near future.

Legislation that empowers local government including much transport legislation either gives them duties (eg, the duty to provide schools transport) or powers (eg, the power to determine concessionary fares schemes for their areas). The ways in which they use their enabling legislation can be challenged in the courts by way of judicial review on the grounds that they are acting 'ultra vires' or beyond their remits. This principle was graphically illustrated in 1981 when Ken Livingstone's newly elected Greater London Council (GLC) put into practice Labour's manifesto plan to cut back on highway spending (the election had largely been won by Labour's opposition to the plan for three motorway boxes around London). They also proposed to reduce London Transport's fares by 25 per cent[43] by levying a supplementary rate. Bromley Council sought to test the legality of this use by GLC of their discretionary powers. Their challenge was upheld by the Law Lords who ruled that the low fares were a gift to the travelling public at the ratepayer's expense for which the Transport London Act 1969 did not specifically provide. The Act required the then London Passenger Transport Executive, like its metropolitan cousins, to provide a properly integrated and coordinated system of public passenger transport with due regard to efficiency, economy and safety of operations. It was the word 'economy' (which does not appear in the 1968 Transport Act setting up the provincial PTAs) that led to the ruling that the GLC were in breach of their 'fiduciary' duty. After London Transport eventually carried out much more work on the economic effects of their proposals that demonstrated significant ratepayer benefits, they successfully introduced their immensely popular Travelcard. This multimodal ticket has done much to stem and even reverse in London the erosion of public passenger transport experienced elsewhere. To avoid similar costly challenges in the future, the Transport Act 1983 set protected expenditure limits (PELs) for PTEs and county councils within which their spending plans could not be legally challenged. Whilst helpful in avoiding uncertainty the PELs were just one more example of how central government can constrain local authority expenditure!

Highway provision has always been seen as a significant part of local authorities' expenditure. Whilst top tier authorities, as explained earlier, are highway and transportation authorities their highway remit is constrained by the fact that the Highways Agency (a DETR sponsored body) is responsible for motorways and trunk roads. Although these roads are only 4 per cent of the total road stock, they account for 32 per cent of all traffic and 56 per cent of all large goods vehicle (LGV) movements. The top tier authorities can also delegate (at their expense) to their districts the maintenance of restricted roads (with speed limits of 30 mph or less). What is perhaps of more interest to passenger transport providers is the extent to which these top tier authorities can 'vire' expenditure between highways and transportation. After the creation of PTEs in 1968 and local government re-organization in 1972, this was possible to an extent as the Transport Supplementary Grant (TSG) from central to local government covered both highways and transportation. However, after deregulation in 1985 the TSG became purely a highways grant, the rationale being that only where market forces did not provide for public transport should a local authority subsidize this, for which specific funding existed (described below). The integrated transport White Paper of 1998 makes it plain that the role of the Highways Agency is to change fundamentally – they are to become managers rather than providers of road space and no longer simply to 'predict (demand) and provide' (road space).[44] The HA has also recently 'de-trunked' many cross-urban former trunk roads whose traffic has been diverted to new bypasses and the motorway network.

A Local Government Act of 1980[45] introduced a new grant system for funding public transport. Local authorities were given block grants for heads of expenditure such as education, social services, housing and transport based on a formula that allocated to them a standard spending assessment (SSA) designed to provide a uniform level of provision across the UK. Any expenditure above the SSA could be bid for by way of an established process known as the annual Transport Policies and Programmes (TPPs). These TPPs might contain, for example, bids for 'section 56' (Transport Act 1968) infrastructure grants for interchanges or light rapid transit systems or for 'section 20' rail support grants in PTE areas.

The outcome of a TPP bid might be either funding or finance and it is useful to distinguish between the two. Finance is the provision of loan capital by either the treasury or private sector whilst funding is the provision of cash payments to enable a project to be procured or constructed. Manchester Metrolink, for example, was built partly by letting a Design, Build, Operate and Maintain (DBOM) franchise as a private finance initiative.

An important effect of local government re-organization in 1972 was the provision of section 203 of the Local Government Act of that year, which gave county councils the same kind of transport coordination powers as PTEs. This excluded powers to make section 20 rail support grants – although county councils are free to support their local rail networks but only a handful do so. The Transport Act 1978 also required them to prepare (with their TPPs) annual Public Transport Plans (PTPs) and this duty was extended by the 1983 Transport Act to PTEs also.

At the 1993/4 round of TPP bidding the then Department of Transport introduced a relaxation to the restrictive nature of TPPs as purely transport funding bids by inviting 'package bids' that would demonstrate the wider effects of authorities' transport plans. For example, the Greater Manchester package bid explored the savings in highway expenditure (especially the controversial, at that time, proposals for widening the Motorway Manchester Outer Ring Road) that might accrue from their Light Rapid Transit and Park and Ride proposals. The package bid process was also seen as a mechanism for including matching funding from new private finance initiatives (PFIs). Many of these, however, were simply disguised borrowing approvals where the private sector would invest (often at higher rates of return than the treasury borrowings they were intended to replace) against future revenue streams!

The integrated transport White Paper 1998[46] signalled the end of the TPP bidding system that it criticized for being too narrowly focused and only giving local authorities a one-year spending horizon. In 1999, transportation authorities were encouraged ahead of the necessary legislation to frame their annual TPPs as pilot new Local Transport Plans (LTPs) against which their regional government offices would give them an indicative spending 'steer'. LTPs will differ from TPPs in a number of important ways. They are longer term, intended to encompass a five-year planning horizon (2000–05). However, they are not a 'rolling plan' and consultation has already pinpointed concerns about the difficulty of amending plans once passed and getting consistency with Part I (strategic plans) of Planning Authorities' Unitary Development Plans (UDPs) and with the new 15–20 year horizons of Regional Planning Guidance and especially the Regional Transport Strategies that they contain.[47] However, the DETR have indicated that there will be scope to amend LTPs in certain circumstances. Being fixed five-year plans, LTPs have even been described as 'Stalinist'! This is unfair as they will be more flexible, strategic and discretional and give much greater emphasis to local consultation and be far more wide-ranging. It is intended that they should cover issues such as the social inclusion and health effects of transport strategies and that they will be more inclusive and focus more on sustainability.

The DETR's guidance on Regional Planning (PPG11) suggests some Local Transport Plan issues with land-use implications:

- Railtrack investment plans (eg, new station);
- proposals for road use charging and workplace parking charges;
- public transport interchange proposals;
- green transport plans;
- safe routes to schools;

- cycling and walking strategies;
- quality bus partnerships and contracts;
- surface access to airports;
- re-allocation of road space to cyclists, pedestrians and public transport.

Parish councils

The lowest level of local government is the parish council. Whilst some districts in urban conurbations have set up similar town councils, parish councils occur predominantly in rural areas. The 1996 Rural White Paper expressed the government's belief that parish councils should be able to take a more active role in the provision of transport for their communities and proposed they be given a number of additional functions, for which they duly legislated.[48] These include:

- conducting surveys to establish transport needs;
- providing revenue support for community minibuses (both section 19 community transport schemes and section 22 community buses, the latter providing registered local services);
- contracting with taxi operators to provide transport for the most needy members of their communities – those who are eligible for travel concessions under section 73 of the Transport Act 1968;
- organizing car-sharing schemes;
- with the agreement of their highway authority funding traffic calming schemes;
- providing information about local transport services (which they could purchase from providers if necessary).

None of the above are duties but they are useful powers for which, however, the parish council needs to set a precept on their council tax. For too long, too many parish councils have seen their primary statutory duty as being to comment on development plans that affect them, now the more forward looking councils will have the opportunity to take a holistic transport and land-use planning view in line with the thinking behind the integrated transport White Paper.[49]

The Economic Management of Financial Resources

ECONOMY, EFFICIENCY AND EFFECTIVENESS

Economists explain the production of a service in terms of its inputs, which they call factors of production. The simplest economic model identifies three 'M's – men, money and materials – and suggests that the wages, finance and purchase costs of these produce a service that can be sold with any surplus providing a profit to the entrepreneur.

This model however is over simple. It assumes that profit accrues only to the capitalists who invest in providing the service and takes no account of any distribution to other 'stakeholders' in the enterprise – eg, employees. Nor does it acknowledge other factors in the production of a transport service. Land obviously is a factor, especially as increasingly this or its proxy must be bought by the operator in terms of track access charges, vehicle excise duty and road tolls (and possible future road pricing), landing charges and port dues. The management of the undertaking is often seen as a fourth 'M' who, although not directly producing the service in the way drivers and fitters can be identified, are none the less an essential overhead to be rewarded out of income before profit. However, perhaps the most difficult factor of production to measure and appraise is information. Although information can be sold, the vendor is not thereby deprived of it! Hence the argument between the merits of free timetable booklets and the sale of comprehensive bound volumes as means of generating traffic, arguments that are becoming less and less meaningful as more and more operators are providing timetable information call centres and Internet Web pages. Operators with access to computerized ticketing and reservation systems have a competitive advantage as emerging airline 'alliances' (such as the One World alliance to which British Airways belong) demonstrate. In the early 1980s when the National Bus Company conducted one of the most comprehensive bus use surveys ever attempted[1] the Director General of a PTE heavily 'bussed' by NBC services made the wry remark 'He who holds the data runs the buses!'

Efficiency is the economic use of all the above factors to maximize production. Following deregulation, many bus-operating companies became very 'efficient' at submitting lowest-cost tenders for non-commercial services and as a result winning these and picking up lucrative service subsidy agreements. However, the successful tenderers were often low-cost units set up to compete 'off the road' for tenders using old, fully depreciated vehicles, cheap open-air depot facilities in industrial estates and new driver recruits paid minimum wages.

Tendering authorities also became adept at passing on commercial risk by asking for minimum subsidy tenders where operators were asked for a price that assumed that they would retain the fares collected rather than a full cost tender where the authority retains the fare revenue. The initial round of rail franchising was not much different in that many TOCs tendered on the assumption that they would grow the market with new trains and 'customer' services and thus require reducing levels of subsidy year on year. Some former intercity and Network South East services actually predicted paying the Office of Passenger Rail Franchising Director (OPRAF) a premium to operate in the final years of their franchise. A number of TOCs are now in severe financial difficulties as this rosy scenario refuses to unfold!

The effectiveness of the above examples is less easy to measure. Bus deregulation has caused a 33 per cent loss in patronage outside London[2] and rail privatization has swelled the RUCC's complaints postbag by 100 per cent. Thus, efficiency and effectiveness are not necessarily related although they can be and some would argue that they should be.

Effectiveness is perhaps best illustrated by the present government's move away from their predecessor's model of compulsory competitive tendering to a best value for money model (VFM) – what in the USA is described as 'getting more bangs per buck'. Thus where a tender that is not the lowest cost, or an in-house bid can be shown to deliver tangibly more benefits proportional to the cost quoted, then contracts should be awarded on that basis. The tendering regulation made pursuant to the Transport Act 1985[3] did in fact allow higher and 'non compliance' tenders to be accepted in certain heavily constrained cases provided that the reason was given when the tender prices were published but cash strapped local authorities all too often ignored this provision. Under the EU's Public Service Procurement Directive[4] large tenders[5] have now to be advertised throughout the community, a move that will enhance transparency and probably deliver even better VFM.

SUPPLY AND DEMAND

The demand for passenger transport is because of passengers travelling from where they are (their origin) to where they wish or have to be (their destination). It is thus in economic terms a derived demand, derived from a need to be somewhere rather than a need to travel. Sometimes of course, but considerably less frequently, it happens that, as with a steam trip on a preserved railway or an ocean cruise, the traveller is actually demanding the travel rather than the arrival.

The demand for transport is an objective measure of requirement. How much is demanded (ie, how many passengers travel) is a function of the price of the journey and the amount of transport supplied. High fares will suppress demand whilst frequent services will generate it. The willingness of passengers to pay high fares will also be influenced by the purpose of their journey. If this is essential, like commuting to work, fares increases will not deter travel to the extent they will if the journey is discretionary like a leisure trip.

Demand for travel is also influenced by the availability of substitutes. Thus a pensioner visiting friends and relatives (the classic VFR discretionary journey) may be deterred by high intercity rail fares but be prepared to take longer on a National Express coach because the fare is less. The business traveller with a meeting to attend will not be so easily influenced by a similar substitute alternative.

In economic terms, demand is said to have a measurable elasticity and cross elasticity. What that means is that if the percentage drop in demand is greater than the percentage increase in price, demand is said to be elastic, a typical attribute of discretionary travel. If an actual percentage increase in price produces a disproportionately smaller percentage decrease in travel, demand is said to be inelastic, a typical attribute of essential travel like commuting.

This theory of elasticity has important implications for operators' pricing policies for it can be shown that where demand is inelastic, increases in fares can result in revenue gains but where demand is elastic, increases in fares produce revenue losses. Thus in the short term an operator can increase fares in the peak hour and yet still maximize revenue, although in the long term passengers may find alternatives like another mode (train to coach) or even private transport. Similarly, low off-peak fares can be shown to generate traffic and maximize revenue.

Thus, demand when satisfied can produce profit. But equally there will be services, for example in rural areas or at times of low demand (Sundays, evenings), that will not be commercial in that there will be insufficient demand so that even if it can be satisfied it will not produce enough income to cover even their costs. The Transport Act 1985 recognizes this when it exhorts transport authorities to 'procure by tender those services which the market cannot provide... to meet the requirements of an area'. Contrast this with the duties of PTEs before deregulation spelt out in the Transport Act 1968 to provide 'a properly coordinated and integrated transport system to meet the needs of the area'.

Need is a more subjective measure of social exclusion than requirement (which implies willingness and ability to pay). Need often requires subsidy to be met effectively. The monetary school of economists argue for supply-side intervention, the deregulation of the supply of transport to allow the market to produce an efficient service. They argue that it is 'contestability', ie, the threat of additional supply (competition), that does this. [6] However, it has been observed in this context (see above) that markets are not guaranteed to maximize effectiveness. Keynesian economists argue that some markets (transport, education, health) are imperfect social markets where consumers do not have complete knowledge of competing products (they catch the 'first' bus) and are thus unable to make the rational choices of an 'economic man'. They propose demand-side intervention to produce a co-ordinated and integrated network that, whilst aiming for greater social inclusion, inevitably 'second guesses' the market. Thus, the objection operators usually make to network franchising is that they have a better knowledge of their operating area and its 'needs' (by which they really mean commercial viability) than the public servants charged with designing and procuring this. However, it is often overlooked that these same public servants are accountable to their elected representatives.

Factors affecting demand

It might be thought that the price of a journey was the overriding factor determining whether it is made but there is plenty of evidence that, whilst it is a significant factor, price is not always the major determinant of demand. In many cases, there is a clear alternative substitute, often private transport. In the case of private transport the cost of a journey is often perceived in terms of its marginal or avoidable cost, ie, the fuel costs, with no account being taken of other factors such as vehicle depreciation, tax and insurance. In addition, where, as demonstrated above, demand is inelastic higher prices will not proportionally suppress demand, as BRB discovered on some of its overcrowded intercity routes before rail privatization.

In the run up to bus deregulation, Dr Bob Tebb, working for West Yorkshire PTE, developed a demand forecasting model that he called Metrocast (see Figure 4.1). This was essentially a spreadsheet on which he rehearsed a number of 'what if' scenarios such as what would happen, both off peak (elastic demand) and peak (inelastic demand), if fares were raised/lowered or if frequencies were increased/decreased. Working on accepted industry average elasticities, he was able to show that a 10 per cent increase in fares suppressed demand by 3 per cent and a 10 per cent increase in the number of journeys provided (frequency) increased demand by 5 per cent. In other words, the elasticity of average fares of 0.3 is less than the elasticity of average supply of 0.5. Combining changes to service levels and fares and observing the resultant revenue effects showed clearly that high frequencies are more successful at generating traffic than low fares!

Other research at London Transport about this time also established that the punctuality and reliability of services is a prime consideration of passengers when selecting their mode of travel.[7] That frequency can

INELASTIC DEMAND

FARE pence	% FARE CHANGE	BUSES PER HOUR	% FREQUENCY CHANGE	PAXS	REVENUE £
100	0	10	0	1000	1000
110	10	10	0	970	1067
90	−10	10	0	1030	927
100	0	9	−10	950	950
100	0	11	10	1050	1050
110	10	9	−10	920	1012
110	10	11	10	1020	1122
90	−10	9	−10	980	882
90	−10	11	10	1080	972

ELASTIC DEMAND

FARE pence	% FARE CHANGE	BUSES PER HOUR	% FREQUENCY CHANGE	PAXS	REVENUE £
100	0	10	0	1000	1000
110	10	10	0	870	957
90	−10	10	0	1130	1017
100	0	9	−10	950	950
100	0	11	10	1050	1050
110	10	9	−10	820	902
110	10	11	10	920	1012
90	−10	9	−10	1080	972
90	−10	11	10	1180	1062

Key
PAXS = Number of passengers

Figure 4.1 METROCAST

generate traffic was clearly demonstrated by those bus operators (prior to deregulation) who, on routes that they felt would be vulnerable to competition, replaced large double-deck vehicles with fleets of minibuses, which operate a much higher frequency service (see, for example, Figure 4.2).[8] BRB Regional Railways in 1990 replaced their hourly loco-hauled eight coach trans-Pennine service with three DMU Sprinter services per hour and in so doing increased patronage from 2,000 passengers per day to 6,000 per day.

Frequency increase	Per cent passenger growth
x2	40
x3	80
x5	100

Figure 4.2   Minibus generation factors
Source: Fawcett, P (1989) *Minibus Services*, Croner Publications

Two other factors affecting demand are comfort and safety. Public passenger transport has an enviable safety record but even so, this is not always the rational perception of travellers after a high-profile coach, rail or aircraft accident even though the daily carnage on the roads far exceeds that of public transport. Ultimately, however, what passengers are buying for their fares is safe arrival. They also hope that they will have a pleasant, punctual, reliable and comfortable journey. Where services are unreliable or overcrowded, this can and does affect demand. Passengers dislike 'crush' seating and standing for long journeys. Observe seat occupancy on intercity trains where table seats fill up before the 'airline/cinema' style seating even though, ironically, there is more legroom in the latter! RUCCs' postbags are full of complaints of unreliability and overcrowding and OPRAF's Passenger Service Requirements (PSR) on some commuter routes set standards such as that no passenger should have to stand on a journey for more than 20 minutes.

On some quality partnership public transport corridors, the use of new easily accessible low-floor buses together with bus priority measures and good publicity have generated up to 25 per cent additional traffic. Operators are increasingly coming to appreciate the factors that affect demand for public transport and to realize that other operators are often not their main competitors but that private transport is!

COSTING PASSENGER SERVICES

In order to provide services operators have to buy in the factors of production. They must purchase vehicles and fuel, pay track access charges, employ and pay drivers and ancillary staff, and service the interest charges on any borrowings they have made. They thus incur capital cost in procuring the assets that they need and revenue costs in paying staff and dividends and track access charges.

Another way in which to view operators' cost structures is to divide their outgoings into fixed and variable costs. Fixed costs are sometimes called standing costs since they must be paid whether or not vehicles are standing or in revenue earning service. They include, for road transport operators, their vehicle excise duty (which is a track access tax), insurance, depreciation of their vehicle over time and other 'establishment' costs such as managers' salaries and depot overheads. The mnemonic TIDE (tax, insurance, depreciation and establishment costs) aptly describes operators' fixed costs since, like the sea's tides, they occur relentlessly.

Depreciation is a large part of operating costs. It represents the loss in value of a vehicle over its life and is catered for by accountants by 'writing down' the book value of the vehicle over time and allocating those monies to a replacement fund. The two most common methods of doing this are the straight line and the reducing balance methods (see Figure 4.3).

In the straight-line method, the estimated residual value of the vehicle is subtracted from the purchase price and this is then divided by the anticipated life of the vehicle in years to give an annual depreciation figure. The reducing-balance method subtracts a percentage amount at the end of the first year from the purchase price to arrive at a written-down value; it then repeats this process, subtracting the same percentage value from the written-down value to produce a new written-down value at the end of subsequent years. It has the advantage that it more accurately reflects real asset values in that depreciation is always greatest in absolute terms in early years and less in later years when, however, this lower depreciation is balanced by heavier repair and maintenance costs! Nowadays operators can use sophisticated computerized depreciation spreadsheets in which they can enter the actual retail value of their depreciating vehicles and their anticipated replacement costs.

Train Operating Companies on the other hand, because they lease their trains from Rolling Stock Companies (ROSCOs), see their leasing charges as semi-fixed costs related in the medium term to the level of service they provide. Many bus, and especially coach, operators are turning to leasing as an alternative to ownership. Leasing releases the capital tied up in assets since operators do not own 'their' leased vehicles (as they eventually do when they buy them even on hire purchase schemes). There are also tax advantages in leasing since although the assets appear on the operators' balance sheets, the leasing company can claim the capital tax allowances, thus reducing the leasing charges.[9] In addition, as the leasing charges appear additionally on the profit and loss account, they reduce the profit on which corporation tax is paid. Leasing companies can

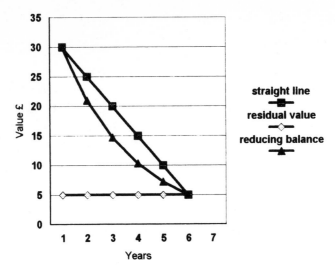

Figure 4.3   Straight line and reducing balancing methods of depreciation

arrange financial leases where they spread the vehicle cost over its full life. Operating leases are more commonly arranged through vehicle manufacturers and dealers and usually incorporate a maintenance contract. Although little different to a financial lease, they are effectively a contract hire arrangement since the vehicle is eventually disposed of back to the leesor either at its residual value or after an agreed leasing period. There is often the option (common with fleet cars) for the lessee to buy the vehicle after a fixed time at an agreed written-down value or trade it in for a new vehicle. These are often referred to as balloon leases since there is a large final payment unless the vehicle is returned or traded in against another lease – as happens with the increasingly popular car purchase 'option' schemes. Some of the rolling stock orders from TOCs for their 'millennium trains' are written as resource contracts where the manufacturer has agreed to provide a given level of seat miles per annum over the period of the contract, with penalty payments in default.

Thus whilst vehicle costs are fixed in the short to medium term, other operating costs vary with use of vehicles. Variable or 'running' costs obviously include fuel and tyre costs. Less obviously, they will include manpower costs, especially drivers' wages and the costs of other crew (such as conductors) needed to operate services. However, many drivers today are not hourly paid but are engaged on a fixed salary to work a negotiated annualized number of hours in which case the manpower costs can be regarded as semi-fixed apart from any necessary overtime payments. The bus industry has identified[10] a number of costs that are related to its 'peak vehicle requirements' such as ticket machines and vehicle licence discs as well as specific time-based costs such as vehicle maintenance, traffic supervision and revenue protection to help it in completing tenders.

It is important to separate out running costs since these are avoidable in economic terms and as such must be recovered from fares and/or subsidies. The cost of one additional unit of resource is known as the marginal cost of operation. The revenue generated by the additional unit can avoid an operating loss in the short term but the more that revenue can contribute to the operation's fixed costs over time the quicker an operation will break even.

The apportionment of an operator's overheads or establishment costs can be a difficult exercise. It can be done based on operating mileage, seating capacity or combinations of both. Variables such as the age of vehicles may also be factored into an apportionment formula. Some costs as already mentioned are attributable to an entire fleet but others are only incurred because of the necessity to have vehicles in the fleet to augment services in the peak hours. Thus, it is more realistic to allocate these fixed and semi-variable (ie, fixed in the short term) costs only to those vehicles (see Figure 4.4).

Cost heading	Basis of allocation
Variable costs	
Drivers' wages Vehicle servicing	Time
Fuel and oil Tyres Third party insurance	Mileage
Semi-variable costs	
Supervisory costs Revenue protection Vehicle maintenance Workshop expenses	Time
Ticket machines	
Publicity Vehicle licences/tax Vehicle depreciation Vehicle leasing/renting	Peak vehicles
Fixed costs	
Administrative and staff costs Training costs	Time
Establishment costs	Peak vehicles

Figure 4.4 Passenger vehicle costs, CIPFA 1983
Source: Fawcett, P (1984) *The Road to Transport Management,*
Fleetbooks

Variable costs such as drivers' pay (where this is not a fixed salary) and fuel costs are allocated on a time or mileage basis. In some cases, as with maintenance, there may be an element of each as when this is performed every so many thousand miles or so many months, whichever is first. Fuel costs of course are entirely mileage related as are tyre costs but in the latter case there is an accounting convention that subtracts tyre costs from vehicle acquisition cost before calculating depreciation.

The relative magnitude of different operators' costs is of interest. In the bus industry, it is usually reckoned that labour, fuel and overheads each account for approximately 20 per cent, 40 per cent and 40 per cent of costs respectively.[11] However, with train operating companies their track access and train-leasing charges can amount to nearly 75 per cent of their costs with fuel and labour accounting for only 25 per cent. This is why, faced with declining subsidies after privatization and franchising, their only strategy is to cut labour costs and grow revenue, a balancing act that it is feared will defeat some TOCs! With airlines, whilst landing and airport charges are a significant semi-variable cost (relating to the number of scheduled flights), fuel and flight staff costs are more significant but they do have a lucrative revenue source other than fares in the form of duty free in-flight sales. Airlines' direct or fixed costs in fact amount to 58 per cent of their total costs.[12] Also, there is no tax on aviation fuel.

FARES AND PRICING

In the long run, as economists are fond of pointing out, operators whose revenues are usually from fares and do not cover their costs eventually cease to trade. Operators must cover all their costs, both fixed/indirect/standing costs and variable/direct/running costs. It is generally agreed that there are five strategies by which operators can price their services to cover costs although how these are variously described differs enormously. For our purposes we will identify and explain the following strategies:

- cost-plus marginal;
- cost pricing;
- traffic pricing;
- competitive pricing;
- average pricing.

Pricing a service in terms of the cost of its provision plus a margin for profit is superficially the simplest strategy. This can be done quite easily with a job such as a private hire where operators can determine their time and mileage costs and seek to recover the total cost of the 'charter' plus a profit mark-up from the organizers of the trips who pay a composite charge for their transport. How the hirers then recover their charges from their clientele does not concern the operator although again this is often by a process of simple division of vehicle hire charge by numbers of passengers travelling. Where passengers are paying separate fares, as with a registered local bus service, a rail service or scheduled airline flight, then it is possible also to devise a fare scale that will produce an estimated revenue equal to the cost of operation plus a profit margin. However, doing so successfully relies on operators being able to predict demand accurately and requires a good understanding of demand elasticities (discussed earlier in this chapter when considering supply and demand factors).

Cost-plus pricing is thus a relatively simple strategy that works well where there is little evidence of aggressive competition. It is however inappropriate where competition arises from another operator having spare capacity on a route or at certain times. Consider for example a bus operator with a school contract from outlying villages to a comprehensive school in the local market town. First, the operator may register the service in order to be able to carry fare-paying passengers in spare seats that he is not contracted to provide (and thus incidentally claim fuel duty rebate). Secondly, he may decide, instead of bringing his vehicle back from the school empty at 9.00 am, to register an hourly service between the centre of the market town and one or more outlying villages to operate until 3.00 pm when he will pick up his (registered) school contract again.

Assuming that the price tendered for the school contract covered the vehicle's running and standing costs for the day, the only additional (or to use the economists' vocabulary) 'avoidable' cost attributable to the midday services will be fuel and tyre costs, some additional maintenance and possibly driver costs. Even so, in some cases the driver may have been 'paid through' to park up between school runs at the market town to save vehicle 'positioning' costs. With such low avoidable or marginal costs, the operator is in a strong position to compete with any existing operator already on the route. Providing that the fares charged produce a revenue that covers the marginal costs and ideally makes some contribution to overheads or standing costs, it is worth the while of the operator to run the service. The effects of competition from a marginal cost service are discussed below. A prime example of marginal costing is the use of post buses by the Royal Mail. In this case all the running and standing costs of a van are met by the mail, leaving only such marginal costs as driver training (to PCV driving entitlement) and the upgrading of the vehicle to carry passengers to be met from fares. This is just as well as by the very nature of the services post bus revenue is rarely very significant.

'Charging what the traffic will bear' is an old maxim with its origin in early railway rates and charging schemes. Freight traffic rates were much less per ton for aggregates such as coal and stone than for merchandise such as mail order consignments since the latter were more urgent and the consignors were willing to pay a higher charge. In the same way, British Rail developed market segmentation between business fares (first-class and full standard class) and leisure fares (saver and super saver) that relied on the high inelasticity of demand for business travel and the fact that frequently it was the passengers' employers who were paying, not the passengers themselves. Leisure passengers on the other hand tend to pay their own fare, their journeys are discretionary and demand from them is more elastic. They may indeed use substitute National Express coach services if priced off rail. In fact it was competition from National Express after express bus deregulation in 1980[13] that was the catalyst for BRB's successful market segmentation exercise! Airline pricing is heavily dependent on market segregation, with complex fare structures reflecting the degree of comfort on the aircraft, the demand for flights or willingness to commit in advance to certain flights on which operators know there is capacity. A final simple example of the principle of traffic charging might be the different prices quoted by a coach operator to a provincial football club supporters' group for two trips: the one to an away match with a London club and the other, obviously higher quote, to a Wembley cup tie at which the club was one of the teams.

There is little point in charging more than a competitor charges unless the difference can be perceived in terms of some clearly tangible benefit. Thus a coach operator with a very 'high spec' vehicle with toilets and servery might safely quote a higher price than his competitor with a ten-year old, second-hand vehicle. That kind of strategy works best where competition is 'off the road' although when it comes to tendering for service subsidies and school or social service contracts price alone is often the main or only determinant (and this for statutory reasons in some cases).[14]

Where competition is 'on the road' then it is known that unless an operator has managed to create a very strong 'brand loyalty', passengers will board the first bus to arrive at their stop. Indeed there are strong arguments that say that competition on a deregulated bus route is imperfect since perfect competition implies a transparent market. Thus, there is little point in offering lower fares than a competitor offers.[15] The fares of the biggest operator inevitably become the 'de facto' fares in an area. There has been little evidence of fare wars after bus deregulation despite the aggressive 'bus wars' fought in some areas with excessive competition resulting in unnecessarily high frequencies on routes where 'cherry picking' was possible. There have, however, been a number of cases of 'predatory pricing', considered below under 'Competition Law', where a larger incumbant's fares have been so low as obviously not to cover even their marginal costs in an attempt, since they would be able to bear the loss longest, to drive their smaller competitor off the road.

Fares regulation in the bus industry from 1930 to 1985, the airline industry under IATA rules, and on the railways before 1962 and to a smaller extent after 1993 by OPRAF, has led to a tradition of fares structures based largely on mileage travelled. Traffic Commissioners were given a duty in the 1930 Road Traffic Act to ensure that fares were reasonable, a duty they translated into a sophisticated system of fare control with hearings before them whenever operators wished to increase fares. The inevitable result was rigidity in bus fare structures generally based on tapering fare scales where the fare per mile reduced as the journey length increased. This suited very well the Commissioners' philosophy of the time that an affordable and certain fare was in the 'public interest', not least because it gave operators superprofits on good routes that they were then expected to use to subsidize unremunerative but socially desirable services. In reality, the grant of a road service licence for a profitable route was often a tacit reward for remaining on an unprofitable route!

Indeed, Mr Crosland Taylor, founder of Crossville Motor Services, in his well-known book *Sowing the Harvest*, boasted in 1948 that the company's network of rural services in north Wales was paid for out of the profits they made on the Wirral! Thus, the doctrine of cross subsidy delivered a system of average fares described by Professor John Hibbs as 'the dead hand of the Traffic Commissioners'. Certainly, it inhibited the sort of innovatory fare systems seen abroad and now illustrated.

There is no obvious reason why passengers cannot be charged by the time they spend on operator's vehicles rather than the distance they travel. Many continental operators sell tickets valid on their services for a fixed time, typically 90 minutes, after purchase. A season ticket on a fixed route valid for a week, month or year is a variation of time and mileage charging whilst area-wide travel cards like London Transport's or the Parisian Carte Orange, valid one, two or three days, a week or month are purely time-based within the network to which they relate. Flat fares giving a right to travel on a vehicle for any distance are another common variation, sometimes refined by making them applicable within zones, with a further flat fare being payable every time a zone boundary is crossed. The Dutch Strippenkarten, which can be bought at any station, tram or bus, is a 'clippercard' representing a number of prepaid fares that is clipped or decremented on boarding a vehicle and each time a zone is crossed and is valid throughout the Netherlands. Private operators traditionally dislike multi-modal and multi-operator ticketing of any kind since they claim they are only bought by passengers who perceive a discount relative to the sum of the individual tickets they would have bought and thus fail to maximize revenue. They also frequently dispute the revenue apportionment formulas underpinning such area-wide ticketing, especially where these attempt to capture a traffic generation factor! This blinkered view loses sight of the fact that such schemes are known to generate additional travel not least with accompanying passengers who will also pay fares, such as other family members, colleagues and friends. It is known that they can also affect the public/private transport modal split. In short, operators can easily lose sight of the fact that the real competitor is not the other public transport operator but the private car. The government's integrated transport White Paper 1998 and its buses 'daughter' document both make the point that modern fare collection methods such as electronic ticket machines and 'smartcards' will do a lot to make such schemes more attractive to operators, not least by guaranteeing a fair apportionment of the revenue generated.

REVENUE PROTECTION

The most sophisticated pricing strategy that can be devised will not yield maximum revenue if fares are not actually collected and passengers either ride free, override the destination to which they have paid a correct fare, or travel on an invalid ticket. The demise of bus conductors, bus inspectors and ticket barriers at stations, which began to happen well before bus deregulation or rail privatization, has made revenue protection even more difficult.

Some operators have carried out their own research into the trade-off between staff savings and fare evasion. Simply by a plain-clothes revenue inspector travelling on a vehicle and observing the fare paid and the actual alighting stop (the so-called silent check where passengers are not challenged) a good estimate of lost revenue can be made and a more vigorous ticket check by uniformed inspectors or train conductors can likewise give an approximation of fare avoidance. Understandably, operators are unwilling to divulge the results of such surveys especially where they operate under a tendered-for service subsidy agreement where fares accrue to the local authority or PTE. Anecdotal claims of losses ranging from 2 per cent to 15 per cent of revenue abound but even at the lower figure this can represent a significant absolute amount of cash. What is also not known is how such losses compare to the staff savings made in reducing revenue protection posts. South Yorkshire PTE, which had a low fares policy before bus deregulation that generated massive additional traffic, were known to be at the point of introducing free travel as the costs of fare collection were coming to exceed the value of the fares! Conversely, many PTEs and local authorities, worried about revenue loss on their supported services, have introduced data collection teams so that they can compare theoretical revenue from journeys taken with actual revenue declared by operators, and some have even introduced their own revenue protection officers.

The almost universal open station policy introduced by BRB and adopted enthusiastically by the TOCs means that the job of on-train conductors is in the front line of revenue protection. But conductors have other train crew duties, especially supervising departures at stations, and with current levels of overcrowding on many commuter trains often cannot physically sell and check tickets. Some TOCs have introduced a policy of random barrier checks at stations that have caught a number of offenders but many passengers, having made an assessment of the risk of being caught and charged the full or a penalty fare compared to the cost of buying a ticket, daily still persist in trying to avoid paying.

The question of penalty fares is also difficult. There are passengers who are genuinely confused by the validity of the variety of tickets on offer today and others who have been deterred by long ticket office queues but intend paying, even the full fare, on the train. The RUCCs, whilst supporting penalty fares regimes in principle, not least because of their perceived fairness to the fare-paying passenger and struggling TOCs, are none the less anxious that genuine mistakes should not be penalized. Much of course depends on the training and attitudes of the revenue protection staff applying the penalties.

Penalty fares charged on railways are underpinned by statute[16] but no such regulations apply to the bus industry. However, that has not prevented some large operators emulating a system first introduced in 1984 by GMPTE, then a bus operator, under which the PTE set a standard fare of £10 for all journeys except where the correct 'discounted' fare for the journey taken was paid. This latter then in effect became the de facto fare payable but allowed the standard (ie, penalty) fare to be charged to a passenger not paying the correct fare or overriding. There is some doubt as to whether such a high standard fare would pass muster under contract law[17] but this seems never to have been challenged effectively by a determined passenger. Doubtless, some reader will try this!

IMPARTIAL RETAILING

Wherever the possibility exists for passengers to complete their journey by using the services of more than one operator, there is always the risk that operators when asked for details of available services will attempt to promote their own services at the expense of their competitors. If operators deliberately exclude information about their competitors then in extreme cases this can amount to an anti-competitive practice. Such practices are defined and discussed in more detail under 'Competition Law' below.

Three of the consumer protection principles of the National Consumer Council are access to services, choice and information, all of which have direct relevance to passenger transport services and ticket retailing. Passengers who travel outward on one operator's service and pick up that operator's timetable can become very confused if other operator's services on the route are not shown. They may believe that the last journey operated is early in the evening when another operator is actually running a later trip, perhaps under a service subsidy agreement that they have won by tender in competition with the daytime operator. Shortly after rail privatization, timetables issued by Silverlink for their Northampton line trains did not show express Virgin Trains between Milton Keynes, Watford Junction and Euston.

In response to a Policy Statement by the Rail Regulator[18] issued in January 1997, the Association of TOCs (ATOC) issued a code of best practice to its members suggesting that in such cases the timetable should make clear that it excludes other operators' services. The Regulator also addressed such issues as ticket office windows, requiring that where these sold only the product of a single operator, they should be clearly signed as such and there should be adjacent windows selling the whole network's products.

Notwithstanding all this, there are clearly ways in which operators can, if allowed to do so, over-promote their own services. Airlines are adept at this, with their computerized reservation systems often being programmed so as to offer a prospective passenger a reservation on their own, or that of their operating alliance's, services before displaying competitors' services. The setting up after rail privatization of a National Rail telephone Enquiry Service was an attempt to create an impartial passenger information service but it was followed quickly by some TOCs, especially the old Inter-city railways, providing their own dedicated Telephone Enquiry Bureaux with added ticket booking facilities.

Railtrack have a duty to publish the Great Britain National Rail Timetable containing all operators' services (although the May 1999 timetable did not show their bus rail links). They also publish an electronic version on the Web,[19] and Virgin Trains have gone further with a Web site allowing timetable and fares enquiries and ticket purchases on their own and other TOCs trains.[20] Hopefully this will be incorporated into the work being done to establish a national passenger transport enquiry service by 2000 as promised in the integrated transport White Paper.[21]

In the days when the entire rail network was operated by BRB, a ticket between two stations was available by 'any reasonable route'. Today the revenue from every different passenger 'flow' is allocated to specific TOCs so it is obviously important to every TOC that passengers travel by routes on which they own the flow. Their trade association, ATCO, has produced a routing guide that purports to show which routes between origin and destination stations are permitted where the ticket issued is by 'any permitted' route rather than a specified route. The routing guide has been criticized by the passenger watchdogs[22] as complex, unnecessary and designed more to protect TOCs' revenue from abstraction by other TOCs than to provide, as ATOC insists is the case, certainty for passengers. There is a perception that the TOCs are creating more and more specific 'via...' flows and reducing the incidence of permitted routes, in the process forgetting that their main competitor is the private car and coaches and not other rail operators! Whether it will ever prove possible to write software within the promised new national passenger transport enquiry project to juggle timetables, fares and permitted routes is doubtful but for retailing to become totally impartial nothing less will suffice. In fact, a 'vocal minority' of respondents to the Regulator's consultation[23] argued in favour of separating retailing from operation but the Regulator took the view that retailing is an integral part of customer care and should not be 'hived off'. However, he agreed that different criteria might apply in the case of purchase of advance tickets to purchases for immediate travel![24] The Rail Regulator did, however, instigate a mystery shopping survey to monitor TOCs and National Rail Enquiry System (NRES) compliance with his criteria and pointed both to his powers to enforce this under TOCs' licences and even *in extremis* to re-visit the issue.

Clearly, whilst impartial retailing must be a prerequisite of any seamless and integrated system of public passenger transport, better ticket availability and through-ticketing opportunities are of equal importance and have the benefit also that they vastly simplify the retailing transaction and remove opportunities for partiality!

REGULATION

In the passenger transport industry there already exists an Office of the Rail Regulator (ORR) but deregulated road passenger transport as far as it is regulated at all is overseen by both the Traffic Commissioners and the Office of Fair Trading (OFT). The former clearly have all their resources committed to policing quality (ie, safety) standards and the latter is frequently criticized as not fully understanding the nature of competition in the passenger transport industry and for reacting too late and too ineffectually. In the context of possible deregulation of London Bus services the last government seemed to have accepted the inadequacies of the Commissioner, the OFT and the tendering authority (London Regional Transport) when they suggested as a possible alternative scenario the creation of an OFBUS supremo.

The Railways Act 1993 gives the Rail Regulator what many see as an impossible dual role of promoting competition and protecting consumers. In the latter role he relies heavily on the Rail Users' Consultative Committees (RUCCs) (which he describes as his 'eyes and his ears') and the Central Rail Users' Consultative Committee (CRUCC). The Office of Railway Passenger Franchising (OPRAF) currently has other regulatory powers in respect of fares, participation in network ticketing schemes and minimum level service specification (the so-called Passenger Service Requirements, or PSRs).

It is interesting to note that before rail privatization, the RUCCs were TUCCs (ie, Transport Users Consultative Committees) but were still confined to considering only railway matters! A small crack in this modal apartheid did appear in the Transport Act 1985, which introduced procedures (involving the TUCCs and similar to the original railway closure procedures in the Transport Act 1962) for revoking or varying a bus substitution service. The 1962 procedures have been overtaken now by the 1993 Railways Act except as far as they still relate to some light rail schemes such as the Tyne and Wear Metro and Manchester Metrolink.

At the time of writing, the Secretary of State for Trade and Industry clearly sees Regulators as consumer champions rather than competition facilitators. He sees the old RPI-X pricing formula as having outlived its usefulness with the new utilities (such as British Telecom (BT), water, gas and electricity (both production and transmission) and Railtrack) and prefers controls that would require Regulators to ensure that they share any 'superprofits' with their consumers. However, the Railways Act 1993 has no mechanism to achieve this.

There are stark contrasts between the ways in which road and rail passenger services are regulated. But as Neil Kinnock has already pointed out in his influential 'Citizens' Network'[25] all forms of public transport are complementary and ideally should be procured and controlled as a seamless network with genuine through ticketing and ticket availability. Some kind of transport supremo, be it an OFTRANS or regional government with wide coordinating powers, would be needed to deliver this.

This question has been examined extensively by the House of Commons Environment, Transport and Regional Affairs Committee,[26] which took evidence from, amongst others, the Rail Regulator and the CRUCC. In March 1998, the Committee produced its report, which was a fascinating window on government thinking in the months immediately preceding the integrated transport White Paper that then broadly set out their intentions.

The Committee supported plans for an SRA but although accepting Government's integration objectives did not recommend a Strategic Transport Authority. However, it did see SRA 'in due course' developing into a multi-modal body. It recommended that the SRA should subsume OPRAF's powers and duties as well as the monitoring functions of the Regulator (including dealing with closure proposals and sponsoring RUCCs and CRUCC). It also considers that, just as the Traffic Commissioners do, SRA should have a quality control role and take over safety regulation from Railtrack.

All of these recommendations leave the Rail Regulator with a very slimmed down role as an umpire of competition issues using the powers contained in the Competition Act 1998. Specifically, the Committee singled out regulation of Railtrack's investment regime and of the ROSCO's leasing market. In April 1999 the Secretary of State for Environment, Transport and the Regions appointed a new Rail Regulator and a Franchise Director. However, the 1998 integrated transport White Paper[27] had already promised a Strategic Rail Authority to subsume the latter's responsibilities, the creation of which requires primary legislation. Unable to secure parliamentary time for this and anxious to have at least a shadow SRA in place, the Secretary of State appointed a new Chairman of the British Railways Board,[28] which was then made the shadow authority with the new Franchising Director as its Chief Executive. This creative procedure enables the Secretary of State to pass on to the SRA his objectives, instruction and guidance. The White Paper promises that the SRA will not be constrained by the Franchise Director's current narrow passenger rail focus but will address issues of rail freight, transport planning, sustainable development, passenger network benefits, competition policy, consumer protection and passenger franchising.

COMPETITION LAW

The Transport Act 1985 applied UK competition law to the bus industry,[29] which up to then had operated as a mainly publicly owned oligopoly (NBC, PTEs and municipal operators) protected by a licensing system (road service licences) that granted operators 'route monopolies'. Potential local monopolies, restrictive trade practices and anti-competitive behaviour could all in theory be addressed by this legislation.[30] The Railways Act 1993 gave the Rail Regulator a role joint with the Director General of the Office of Fair Trading of overseeing competition between operators.

References to the OFT have been shown to have been in many cases far too protracted so that any remedies have come too late to help the complainant whose business has often by then been irreparably damaged. This of course was often the anti-competitive intention in the first place, especially where it amounted to predatory pricing or other illegal interference. The gentlemanly practice of securing 'undertakings' from the predators as to their future behaviour often then resulted in a mere pyrrhic victory for the (possibly by now bankrupt) complainant.

The Competition Act 1998, which now applies to transport operators as much as to any trader, is modelled on the EU and USA law under which anti-competitive practices are punished by fines (as in the EU) or exemplary damages (as in the USA), rather than the current UK practice of references to OFT. However, it actually provides only for fines and private rights of action and stops short at the US practice of 'triple' exemplary damages.

Instead of the OFT referring their findings (on complaints relating to anti-competitive practices) to the Monopolies and Merger Commission

(MMC), the Act provides that the Commission's role should be recast. A newly created Competition Commission subsumes this and acts as an appellate body supervising OFT's actions, thus eliminating the current procrastination that can occur with dual references to OFT and the MMC. The situation relating to merger references and potential oligopolies remains substantially unchanged by the Act except that Schedule 10 amends the Fair Trading Act 1973 to strengthen the powers of the Director General for Fair Trading (DGFT), especially his investigatory powers, and increases penalties for not furnishing any information that he requests. It provides for the Utility Regulators, including the Rail Regulator, to exercise their powers concurrently with the DGFT.[31]

The clear intention of the Act is that hostile takeovers should be demonstrably in the public interest. This is an important concept in the context of public passenger transport given its increasingly complex ownership pattern with 75 per cent of bus services now provided by the five largest bus operating groups and 17 of the 25 rail franchises owned fully or in part by bus operating companies (mainly, but not all, in the 'big five' groupings). Arguably, Stagecoach's acquisition of the Rolling Stock Leasing Company (ROSCO) Porterbrook or OPRAF's award of Central Trains' franchise to the National Express Group might not have passed the public interest test. However, both went ahead despite CRUCC's finding that the takeover of a ROSCO by a TOC would almost certainly have far-reaching consequences for passengers and recommending that it should not be permitted.[32]

The accounts given above of the offices of various regulators and commissions show how complex are the issues of regulation and the often associated issue of competition and licensing. These have already been rehearsed in Chapter 3 when licensing was considered. They are essentially political, economic and philosophical and can be summarized as follows:

- For safety and often environmental reasons, some form of quality control or licensing is needed.
- Unless the market is always to dictate what services are provided, some form of quantity licensing will be required to avoid wasteful competition and to secure the provision of socially desirable services where these are unremunerative. Before 1985, for public road passenger services, this took the form of the issue by Traffic Commissioners of road service licences to operators who applied a degree of cross subsidization between their licensed services. After bus deregulation outside London, PTEs and county councils were required to secure by tender those services that the market could not provide to meet the 'requirements' of their areas. In the future, quantity licensing could well be in the form of the franchising system currently working in London.[33]

- Without an explicit quantity-licensing regime, some form of moderation of competition will be essential. The Rail Regulator finds this role sits uncomfortably with his consumer protection role and the bus industry has been highly critical of the misguided attempts by OFT to moderate competition in their industry, which they claim OFT does not understand.
- Who actually regulates/licences is equally as important as how this is done. Debate will continue about the merits of multi-modal models[34] and fragmented uni-modal models like the split of responsibilities for public road passenger regulation between Traffic Commissioners, OFT and tendering authorities or the similar split in the rail industry between ORR and OPRAF.[35] Ultimately, the scope and role of an industry Regulator may be dictated by an over-riding EU directive.
- Whoever regulates, and however it is done, regulators will need to be informed to be effective.

TRANSPORT CONSUMER BODIES

There is no single transport users' consultative body although the transport industry is littered with both legally constituted and voluntary organizations assuming such roles. Examples of the former include the statutory Air Transport User's Consultative Committee[36] and London Regional Passenger Committee (LRPC)[37] plus various PTAs and county councils' Local Transport Groups and Transport Advisory Committees constituted under various powers.[38] Only the LRPC is a truly multi-modal road, rail, underground and light rail (Docklands) committee.

The Air Transport Users' Committee (AUC) assumed its current terms of reference in 1978. These require it to make reports to its parent body, the Civil Aviation Authority (CAA), and recommendations for furthering the interests of air transport users. It can investigate complaints and cooperate with any airport user committees. Perhaps its best-known success has been in obtaining redress for passengers unable to board flights on which they were booked (a practice known in the trade as 'being bumped') because of the widespread practice of airlines overbooking flights in anticipation of some of the passengers not travelling (the so called 'no shows'). The committee has pointed to lack of investment in airport and air traffic control infrastructure to cater for anticipated growth in air travel, supported liberalization and competition, but also complained of the resultant complexity of unregulated fare structures.

The TUCCs that became RUCCs in 1993 are a useful model of user committees to consider. They make a realistic contribution to the work of a regulator, in this case the Rail Regulator (who currently resources and supports them, although this function will pass under the Railways Bill 1999 to the new Strategic Rail Authority – see Chapter 8).

The Railways Act 1993 established eight area RUCCs plus the London Regional Passengers' Committee and a Central RUCC (CRUCC). This, unlike the RUCCs, is established in its own right, not by the Regulator, and the LRPC owes its origin to earlier legislation.[39] The position of the RUCCs for Wales and Scotland following devolution is currently under debate.

Schedules to the 1993 Act describe the administrative and procedural arrangements for the consultative committees. A departure from the arrangements applying to the old TUCCs and CTUCC established in 1962[40] is that their meetings are now open to the public except at times when commercially confidential business or matters relating to the affairs of an individual are to be discussed.

The Committees can take up any matter relating to the provision of railway passenger services and generally but not exclusively are prompted to act where complainants who believe they have not received satisfaction have asked them do so. Where they are not satisfied with an operator's response or if they have reason to believe that the operators are in con-travention of their licences (granted by ORR) they can refer the matter to the Regulator.

The Railways Act 1993[41] enables the Regulator to refer matters relat-ing to the modification of licences to the Monopolies and Mergers Commission (now the Competition Commission[42]), and in so doing to require the Commission to investigate if any matters relating to the pro-vision of a railway service or facility operates or may operate against the public interest and, if so, if such matters might be remedied or prevented by the licence being modified. He may subsequently then vary the rele-vant licence. He must exercise such powers jointly in conjunction with the Director General of the Office of Fair Trading (OFT).[43]

Proposals by OPRAF (or eventually the SRA) or an operator to dis-continue all rail passenger services from stations or along lines or to close rail networks are referred to the Committee, which has a statutory duty to report to the Regulator on any relevant matters and specifically any hardship this may cause. Actual closure decisions are made by the Regulator but there is a procedure for appeals to the Secretary of State.

The 1993 Act also allows RUCCs to consider the question of fares – something that Traffic Commissioners have not been able to do since the Transport Act 1980 (which 'relaxed' road service licensing and deregu-lated long distance express services). However, a weakness of the Act is that RUCCs have no locus in the matter of types of fares that are not named as 'regulated fares', the services provided or the fares charged on what have come to be known as 'open access services' provided by one TOC in competition with another TOC. The second of these matters is to be addressed by the legislation setting up an SRA that will give the RUCCs the locus they seek. Open access agreements can exist where ORR permits them and the operator can successfully 'bid' to Railtrack for a timetable slot or 'path'.

There is a close similarity here to the way in which PTEs and county councils have no control over commercial services that they have not themselves secured by tender, even where these share the same route, other than any control they may have over 'departure slots' at their bus stations and interchanges. Further, PTEs and 'shire' counties, as the statutory transport coordinating authorities, have no locus in respect of the quality of such operations.

The Rail Regulator deliberately held in abeyance the question of 'open access' for passenger service operators during the initial franchising process in order to facilitate this. To a very limited extent the operation of special and charter trains constitutes an exception to this generality. His policy on 'Moderation of Competition for Rail Passenger Services' allows no significant competitive entries before March 1999 and applies substantial restrictions from then until March 2002 whilst providing that these will be reviewed in the year 2001. He proposed that during this latter three years of 'restricted open access' operators should be able to nominate up to 80 per cent of their passenger traffic flows that they would like him to continue to protect, thus allowing him to consider open access bids for the remaining 20 per cent of services. He does not propose, however, to restrain the entry of non-competing services that he defines as those that neither serve the same market as the franchisee nor put his revenue at risk. The policy of the new SRA towards open access is not yet known but will obviously be influenced by the policy they adopt on franchise renegotiations.

In 1998, the Rail Regulator asked the RUCCs and CRUCC to contribute to the DTI's consultation on 'Widening the Scope for Action under the Unfair Terms, Etc Regulations 1994', which proposed *inter alia* that statutory consumer bodies should be able to represent complainants at law and seek injunctions against unfair terms in contracts (in this case, contracts of carriage). Their responses generally welcomed the proposals in principle subject to their being given sufficient personnel, financial and legal resources.

In their 'New Deal for Transport' (1998), the government says it wants the RUCCs to cooperate with bus user representative bodies such as the non-statutory National Federation of Bus Users (NFBUs) and to contribute jointly to the development of Regional Transport Strategies.

There are many voluntary transport user groups. The Rail Regulator has published an excellent little directory listing 168 rail user groups and the National Federation of Bus Users (NFBU) provides a guide for passengers wishing to set up a local bus user group. Their existence often depends on the enthusiasm and commitment of a few individuals yet they are usually well informed. As well as campaigning for better services, they are sometimes forced to be defensive, as for example when faced with proposed line closures or service deregistrations. Often voluntary groups work with and sometimes form local branches of national bodies like Transport 2000 or the Railway Development Society.

The NFBU,[44] in partnership with the Confederation of Passenger Transport (which represents all the large bus operating groups as well as most independents running local services) has recently created a voluntary non-statutory Bus Appeals Body (BAB) under the chairmanship of Professor (now Lord) Bill Bradshaw to arbitrate where passengers have complained to an operator and are dissatisfied with the outcome. The buses 'daughter document'[45] to the government's integrated transport White Paper contains an aspiration to encourage a more effective voice for passengers through both RUCCs and the 'non statutory' NFBU and through 'exploring the scope for new representation involving users and communities'. It goes on to suggest that the BAB, as well as pressurizing recalcitrant operators, will also be able to inform Traffic Commissioners of any persistent failures in services or responses to complaints, and suggests that Commissioners could and should have a wider consumer protection role (as did the Rail Regulator before the transfer of this role to the SRA).

Whilst the government's aspirations in the 'New Deal' for RUCC and Bus User Groups to cooperate are far short of the emergence of any effective statutory Transport User's Consultative Committee mechanism, it might perhaps be a first step towards an eventual truly multimodal form of passenger representation. The growth of bus-rail integration under ATOC's Rail Links initiative and the change of control at Virgin Trains, with Stagecoach Holdings taking 49 per cent of the equity and cooperating in providing bus links, may also speed this process.

FIVE

Managing Human Resources

As already shown, franchised TOCs facing reduced subsidy levels have limited room to manoeuvre. Obviously, they must try to generate more passenger trips and fare revenue but they have little control over their track access or rolling stock leasing charges, which can in total amount to 75 per cent of their costs. What they do have some control over is their labour costs. These can be contained to a limited extent by wage negotiation and productivity bargaining but in many cases operators have taken the more drastic step of 'downsizing', first by cutting administrative staffing levels and then by reducing operative levels.

Thus, following rail privatization, some TOCs reduced driver levels and/or allowed too many drivers to take early retirement or voluntary redundancy, over-optimistically estimating the productivity of their remaining staff, and as a result had to cancel services and face penalty payments under the franchising regime. The knock-on effect of this was a national railway driver shortage that inflated drivers' pay and created a massive training need in the industry.[1] In some cases, conductors have been trained and promoted to driving posts causing a conductor shortage! In parallel, the adoption from BRB days of an open-station policy saw the loss of ticket collector posts and the transmogrification of guards into fare collecting conductors.

In the bus industry, the widespread adoption of one-man operation in the 1960s saw the almost total demise of bus conductors and deregulation was accompanied with similar downsizing and the loss of hundreds of inspector posts. What these examples (and there are similar illustrations in the air and sea ferry passenger industries) demonstrate is the fundamental importance to the passenger transport industry of manpower planning.

MANPOWER PLANNING

Ensuring that operators' staffing needs can always be met by the availability of adequate numbers of competent employees is a key management function. Essentially this is simply a matter of balancing the supply of and demand for labour (see Figure 5.1). The mechanisms for doing so include the selection and recruitment of staff, their training and/or retraining, promotion and sometimes the termination of their employment. However, the factors affecting operators' demand for staff and possible supply of that staff are far from simple. Some of these factors are internal to organizations, within operators' own control, and can be specified in their corporate plans. Others depend on externalities such as the state of the labour market, the economy, technical, social, demographic and political factors and the extent of competition within the operators' market for passengers.

A good manpower plan depends on an understanding of both current and predicted labour needs and an analysis of how well these are now met and likely to be met in the future. Obviously, the current situation can be most easily analyzed by preparing a staff inventory and comparing this to an operator's own organization chart. However, a simple inventory is never sufficient; it needs to be expanded to become an actual audit, not just of numbers of staff in different grades but also their knowledge, skills, competences and qualifications. A succession-planning chart (see Figure 5.2) that identifies known gaps in organizations, for example arising out of anticipated retirement profiles, is a critical part of any audit.

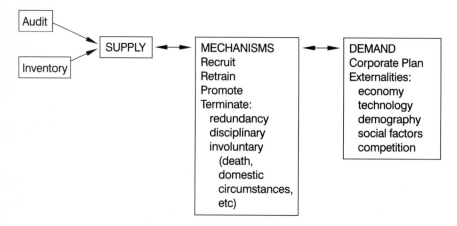

Figure 5.1   Manpower plan

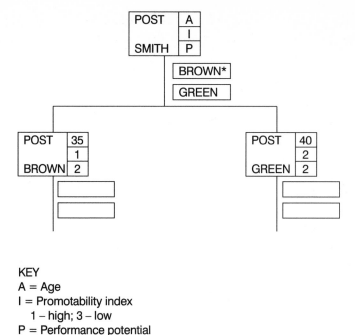

KEY
A = Age
I = Promotability index
   1 – high; 3 – low
P = Performance potential
   1 – high; 3 – low
* = likely promotion to this post

Figure 5.2 Succession plan

So too are survival curves (see Figure 5.3), which show by department, grade or occupation the proportion of staff with different lengths of service, as these give a clue to factors such as workforce retention, renewal and turnover rates. Such data plotting would identify future problems such as a large number of senior managers simultaneously approaching retirement age in a few years time with maybe a lack of suitably qualified junior staff to promote. The same mismatch can occur at any staffing or industry level as was shown by the shakeout of bus and rail drivers after deregulation and privatization, eventually creating severe bus and train driver shortages.

Undoubtedly the most difficult variable to factor into any manpower plan, since it is completely external to any individual operator, is the composition and state of the labour market. This has changed out of all recognition in the last twenty years during which the extractive and manufacturing sectors of the economy have declined and with them over three million jobs in the traditional male dominated and heavily unionized 'smoke stack' industries. Many transport jobs, especially in the railways, depended on these, with concentrated flows of raw materials, fuel (coal in particular) and large workforces located at single sites, some quite often working round the clock shifts. Whilst jobs in the

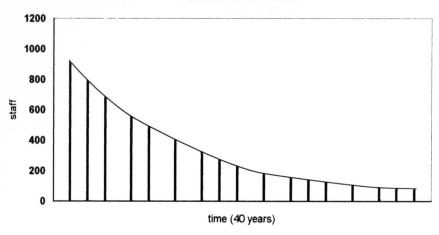

Figure 5.3   Survival curve

Department of Trade and Industry's employment classification 'transport and telecommunications' have remained at about two million, employment in the transport sector has declined whilst that in telecommunications has grown.

However, it is also the nature of employment that has changed. In 1999, for the first time ever, the numbers of males and females in employment were the same, although a much higher proportion of the latter were in part-time employment. Because more jobs are now to be found in the service sector, which includes passenger transport, the amount of unskilled manual labouring work is declining whilst clerical, technical, administrative, managerial and professional work is increasing. Information and communication technology (ICT) is invading every area of work so that there are now fewer and fewer employment opportunities for the unskilled and unqualified. ICT has also delivered impressive productivity gains enabling employers in many cases to 'de-layer', stripping out whole levels of supervisory management. The electronic ticket machine has largely replaced the data collector and bus inspector.

In 1993 Robert Reich, the US Secretary of State for Labor, complained of 'too few good jobs to go round' creating a state of 'jobless prosperity' where large corporations made large profits whilst simultaneously laying-off workers. Professor Charles Handy, one of the most influential commentators of the 1980s and 1990s,[2] has painted a picture of a millennium labour market with half as many employees paid twice as well and producing three times as much. Many trends support this conclusion and whilst space does not allow discussion of these and their likely effect on the labour market, and, it must be remembered, the associated market for passenger transport, it is illuminating to list them here and let readers draw their own, in most cases, fairly obvious conclusions:

- the growth of home working, 'teleworking' and the use of the Internet for e-mail and e-commerce;
- more part-time workers, especially females and married women 'returnees';
- less full-time permanent contracts of employment and a growth of temporary work contracts;
- more flexible working arrangements including flexitime, parental and maternity leave and job sharing;
- growth of agency workers (drivers, secretaries, IT workers, engineers and increasingly professional workers such as nurses and doctors);
- more workers employed by 'franchisees';
- more contracts of employment dependent on the award of contracts by competitive tendering and thus vulnerable on future tender rounds (especially so in road and rail passenger transport);
- a shrinking workforce with entry at a later age after extended education and earlier exit with more premature early retirements as a result of downsizing, delayering or 'work process engineering';[3]
- a sharp reduction in the number of traditional apprenticeships with the decline of engineering industries.[4]

Handy has shown how more and more employers have regressed to employing only those 'core workers' who directly produce their product or deliver their services whilst outsourcing 'peripheral' workers to provide the services on which the core depends such as catering, cleaning, IT, sales, payroll administration and often transport. By the year 2000, he predicts, there will be fewer people working within employers' core activities than serving them from outside. Will Hutton[5] has extended this analysis to describe the results of today's labour market as the '$\frac{1}{3}$rd, $\frac{1}{3}$rd, $\frac{1}{3}$rd' society, with 40 per cent of workers in 'privileged' secure full-time employment, 30 per cent 'marginalized' in part-time, insecure, temporary and often poorly paid work, and 30 per cent unemployed or economically inactive.

Some transport operators have been accused in the past of exploiting this 'marginalized $\frac{1}{3}$rd' by employing part-time drivers, seasonal staff and teleworkers in vast call centres dedicated to timetable enquiries and ticket sales but the situation is not that simple. Just as there are 'work poor households' where no family member is employed, others are 'work rich' where such marginal job opportunities are welcome, just as there is now emerging[6] an army of 'portfolio' workers glad to offer their range of skills to more than one employer. Perhaps a more significant divide in the labour market is opening up between the 'information rich' and the 'information poor'.

What is really crucial in today's labour market is employment protection. The government's signing up to the EU Social Contract and their Fairness at Work legislation covering essentials like minimum wages, working time, unfair dismissal, discrimination, parental leave, etc (all dealt with later in this chapter) will become more important than the actual structure of the market.

STAFF SELECTION AND RECRUITMENT

Passenger transport is both capital and labour intensive. Competent, well-trained and motivated staff are an operators' most valuable resource, much harder to replace than capital equipment and yet often less effort is expended on their procurement than on capital items. The costs associated with recruitment are themselves significant, ranging from advertising, administrative and managerial time to induction, but also including hidden costs such as time lost and overtime worked by existing staff whilst training recruits and the demotivating effects on the workforce of high staff turnover. Passengers can become alienated or even be lost because new staff are not fully competent to assist them and there can be a break in continuity also affecting customer relations.

Whilst many posts in the passenger transport industry are filled by conventional advertising in the trade press,[7] it is also an industry with a tradition of family employment with personal recommendations followed – fathers recommending their children, and employees bringing vacancies to the notice of friends. Employers also often recruit from amongst students on transport studies course in further and higher education or from the ranks of professional bodies like the Institute of Logistics and Transport. Many operators employ or will have employed several generations of the same family. Transport is an industry that 'gets in the blood', with many employees having entered later in their career as a 'stopgap' and then remained to retirement. It appeals to staff with initiative who can take responsibility and enjoy working relatively unsupervised. Conversely, from an operator's point of view, since supervision is usually remote and at a distance it is essential to select such staff. Today's job market also makes use of media such as broadcasting and the Internet in its recruitment drives and some transport operators are seizing these opportunities, especially where skill shortages, such as the driver shortages mentioned earlier, exist. Other well-tried sources of recruitment are agencies, executive search consultancies, Department for Education and Employment (DfEE) job centres and previous applicants.

Personnel professionals recommend a well-tried and tested recruitment procedure that is as applicable to the passenger transport industry as any other. It relies on the maxim that one should first look at the job before looking for the person. It may well be that a 'vacancy' can be absorbed by that person's duties and responsibilities being re-allocated amongst existing staff or that the opportunity can be taken to re-engineer the work of a department. If, however, it is decided that additional staff are needed and a post cannot be filled internally or by promotion, then it is essential that a job description is prepared. This details not only duties and responsibilities but also other factors such as budgets and spending authority, to whom the post holder reports and who reports to him or her, and authority to 'hire and fire'.

From the job description a job analysis can be conducted. This will detail against each task in the description the knowledge and skills that will be required. It can be extended to include desired competences (such as PCV driving entitlement) and even attitudes (such as customer care skills). The knowledge and skills will point to qualifications and experience needed.

The above process allows a personal specification to be drawn up under headings[8] such as attainments, intelligence and aptitudes, which can act as a checklist against which to score candidates during the selection process. The personal specification is effectively the template for recruitment advertisement that will ask applicants to apply either with their curriculum vitae or an application form (in some cases today this can be done on line via the Internet). The employer will want information on education, qualifications and experience, personal details (which should be collected in a non-discriminatory way, discussed below), references and other miscellaneous matters, such as interests, that will help paint pictures of applicants from which a short list can be drawn up.

The interview is still the commonest selection procedure, possibly in tandem with personality or competence tests. Tests of driving competence are not uncommon in the passenger transport industry, as drivers are an operator's front-line staff in daily contact with their 'customers', the passengers whose fares are the operator's main source of revenue. Interviewing is a skill that is not in the remit of this book to investigate, save to point out some of the more obvious pitfalls such as:

- over reliance on a single good point that has created a 'halo' effect;
- over reliance on a single bad point that can prejudice an interviewer or panel;
- the need to guard against racial or sexual discrimination;
- the desirability of taking notes to have a factual record on which to make a decision and not to rely on memory recall after a string of interviews.

Once an appointment has been offered and accepted the employee must be issued with a written statement of his or her terms and conditions within two months[9] but it is also usual before then to provide basic induction training.

TRAINING

The passenger transport industry has a long tradition of employee train-ing. Often there has been a statutory imperative for this – driver training, sea and aircrew training, safety training and the necessary certification of professional competence for licensing purposes are typical examples. The industry also has its own professional institutes that have their specific qualifying examinations, and several industry training organizations (ITOs) that set performance standards for their particular industrial sec-tor and ensure that its training needs are met.

A distinction can be made between transport education and training, although these invariably overlap. Education is broadly focused on knowledge of the industry, its environment and associated subjects such as economics and finance, planning and human resource management. Traditional examinations are used to test educational attainment. Training is more narrowly focused on the skills and competences needed to work in transport, and the achievement of specific competences can be assessed in the workplace by reference to industry specific perform-ance criteria. Such assessment usually leads to a National Vocational Qualification (NVQ) at a defined level in an occupational sector and covering a narrowly defined range of competences. Incorporated in all NVQs is an assessment of candidates' 'underpinning knowledge' with-out which the competences cannot be verified. By contrast, the exami-nations of professional institutes test possession of a broad body of knowledge and understanding and its application. Although the two types of qualification contain the same ingredients, they are mixed in vastly different proportions! Thus, the equation of NVQ levels with specific academic qualifications presents difficulties as they may occupy similar levels in different but parallel hierarchies. They may however be seen as loosely equivalent in terms of career progression and the Further Education Funding Council has attempted to allocate notional NVQ levels to academic qualifications (see Figure 5.4).

Some awarding bodies for transport-related NVQs are also well-known examining bodies – for example, Oxford, Cambridge and RSA Examinations Board (OCR), which also conducts the national Certificate of Professional Competence exams for the DETR, the Open University (OU) and the National Examinations Board in Supervisory Studies (NEBSS). Others, like Automotive Management and Development (ADM),[10] the Rail Industry Training Council (RITC) and Aviation Training Associates (ATA) are also ITOs, in these instances for the road and rail passenger and airline industries respectively. At higher NVQ lev-els,[11] performance criteria tend to be more generic and thus less industry specific[12] and are often based on criteria developed by the Management Charter Initiative (MCI).

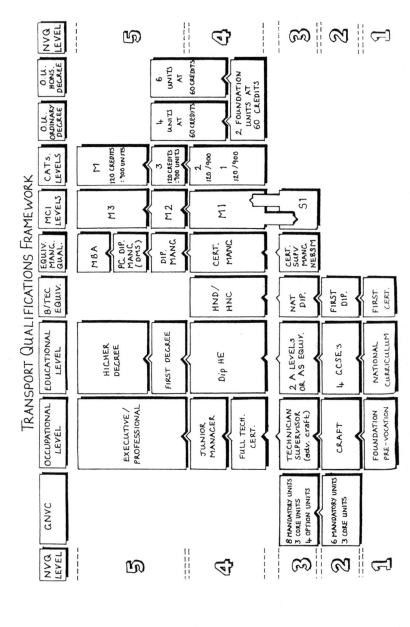

Figure 5.4   Transport qualifications framework

Source: Faculty of Freight, Education Training and Management Development Working Party, Second Survey, Nov 1992
Submission by the author, artwork by Jane Fawcett

In the field of transport education, there are a number of examining bodies, professional and higher education institutions that award qualifications by examination, exemption or Accreditation of Prior Experiential Learning (APEL):

- EDEXAL[13] offers Ordinary/Higher National Diplomas (O/HNDs) with transport options.
- A number of universities offer graduate and postgraduate transport-related degrees.
- Various professional institutes have their own qualifying examinations.[14]

In April 1999, the Chartered Institute of Transport in the UK and the Institute of Logistics merged to form the new Institute of Logistics and Transport (ILT), now the premier multi-modal transport professional body in the UK. ILT are developing from the qualifications of the two parent bodies a new structure based on certificate, diploma and advanced diploma levels.[15] The generic content (economics, finance and human resource management) of the two bodies' certificates is remarkably similar but options (eg, passenger transport and logistics) obviously differed as did the examination (CIT) and assessment (ILog) methodologies. Some appropriate degree level qualifications are accepted by ILT as exempting the holders from their examinations. The new institute is also giving a high priority to the continuous professional development (CPD) of its chartered members. Ultimately the currency of the ILT's qualifications will depend on their recognition by employers as this is what will motivate employees to study for them.

MANAGING AT A DISTANCE – DISCIPLINE AT WORK

Many staff of passenger operators who are in immediate contact with the travelling public are generally, and of necessity, not working under direct supervision. Drivers, conductors and cabin staff have to be self-reliant and dependable. Their performance may be monitored in a number of ways, by electronic ticket sales, radio, global positioning instrumentation, tachograph charts and less frequently by itinerate 'inspectors'. Employers expect their staff to be self-motivated and resourceful when encountering difficulties and indeed it is this freedom from direct supervision that attracts many to jobs in the passenger transport industry. The fact that so much of the production of a passenger transport service is managed at a distance distinguishes it from most other kinds of employment. However well managed the service is there will be times when employees transgress their employers' instructions and have to be held to accounts. Complaints from passengers about individual employees will be logged and investigated and their performance will be measured in other ways. Obviously, operators will have rules that they expect their staffs to obey and the passenger transport industry, because it is so safety critical, is also subject to more than the average level of statutory control. Regulations on drivers' hours, railway safety rule books and airline pilots' flying time are all, rightly, strictly controlled. Nevertheless, because of transgression of statutes or company rules or irregularities such as revenue and ticketing discrepancies, an operator will at times have to resort to disciplinary procedures.

ACAS (the Advisory, Conciliation and Arbitration Service) gives valuable guidance on this matter in a Code of Practice entitled 'Disciplinary Practices and Procedures'. The Code recommends that procedures should be in writing and specify which levels of management can take various forms of disciplinary action. Written procedures should provide for employees to be informed of the complaint against them and to be allowed to state their case, call witnesses, be accompanied by their trade union representative or a friend and be given a right to appeal. Except in cases of gross misconduct it is not recommended that any employee is dismissed for a first breach of discipline but rather that a system of verbal and written warning, culminating in a final written warning be employed. As explained earlier trade union penetration in the passenger transport industry is relatively high and most operators administer a strict disciplinary procedure in compliance with the code and with their unions' approval. The Code does in fact make a specific recommendation that no disciplining of a trade union official should take place without prior discussion with the relevant full-time official.

The Code stresses the importance of good communications and that employees have a right to know the rules and procedures they are expected to follow. It will also respond positively to procedures that clearly ensure fair and consistent treatment of individuals with no overt or covert discriminatory content. Disciplinary procedures should be seen as corrective and only punitive as a last resort.

The first mass passenger transport organizations, the early railway companies, often had a military style management and structure. A tradition of 'uniformed' public service grew in these companies even though they were privately owned initially. There were also formalized disciplinary procedures that even then met most of the rules of natural justice enshrined in the modern Code of Practice. The tradition of uniformed employment with quasi military 'ranks' (eg, Inspector) spread to sea, road and air passenger transport so that today effective disciplinary procedures are accepted as the norm in the industry by employers, employees and trade unions alike, which, considering the safety critical nature of transport employment, is at the very least fortunate.

EMPLOYMENT PROTECTION

The ability of the 'Victorian' employer to hire and fire staff at will is rightly now circumscribed by both UK and EU legislation. The 'New' Labour government of 1997 moved very quickly to adopt both the European 'Social Chapter'[16] and the European Declaration of Human Rights by incorporating these into UK law.[17] The basic human rights of association (which include trade union membership) and freedom of information (which protect, amongst others, 'whistle blowers') have consequences within and beyond transport employment. Just as the previous government's Employment Rights legislation reflected their unitary industrial relations perspective, making no provision, for example, for statutory trade union recognition, the replacement legislation[18] reflects the present government's pluralistic stance and makes such provision.

Other Directives in the Social Chapter concern European works councils, parental leave, part-time employees and the burden of proof in sex discrimination cases. In addition, the government has on its agenda for future regulations on: the cost of staging the ballots required under its 'Fairness at Work' legislation to provide for trade union recognition; rights to time off for family emergencies; and, although this is only marginally an employment protection issue, working family tax credits.

For the first time ever UK legislation provides for a national minimum wage[19] and holidays with pay.[20] Both sets of legislation are already having an effect on operator's costs although by establishing the so called 'level playing field' they are in other ways raising the barriers to entry to the passenger transport industry and creating a more attractive employment regime. However, they will probably have minimum overall impact despite current operative shortages in occupations such as driving and skill shortages (caused by reductions in training budgets) in areas such as scheduling.

UK legislation going back in some cases over at least 25 years attempts to protect employees against various forms of discrimination. This may be in respect of a person's sex or marital status,[21] race or ethnic origin[22] and trade union membership or disability[23] but not yet religion[24] or age. It also provides for equal pay for men and women doing the same or broadly similar work, or work determined by a job evaluation to be of 'equal value'. With the composition of the workforce in the passenger transport industry changing fast and the old male domination being challenged by the appointment of more females, especially in customer care roles, equal opportunities legislation is bound to have a significant effect on the industry. The road passenger transport industry has in the past recruited heavily from ethnic minority communities and has one of the best records of racial harmony of any industry. Disability discrimination legislation is set to have a disproportionate effect on the passenger transport industry, not so much in terms of its employment as its vehicle replacement policies, especially in respect of the requirement for all vehicles on 'journey to work' operations to be eventually made 'accessible'. The provisions in the new Employment Relations legislation[25] relating to maternity and paternity pay and leave also raise important questions not just for society but also for the operators expected to comply!

It is probably in the area of termination of employment where the need for employment protection legislation is most keenly felt. The Transfer of Undertakings and Protection of Employment Regulations 1981 ('TUPE' as it has come to be known) has in theory protected workers since 1981 in any transfer of undertakings situation. This is of particular importance in the passenger transport industry with so many services being provided under service subsidy agreements won by competitive tender or franchised. The UK courts have established that TUPE applies in both the public and private sector.

Employment tribunals deal every year with over 30,000 applications for compensation for redundancy, discrimination, equal pay and unfair dismissal. Later in 2000, a discretionary system of alternative dispute resolution[26] by means of arbitration will be set up in respect of the latter. Regrettably, many unfair dismissal cases arise in the passenger transport industry. Many of these are decided in the employee's favour simply because proper disciplinary procedures (as described earlier) have not been followed. There are certain inadmissible reasons that would make a dismissal automatically unfair such as failure to belong or not belong as the case may be to a trade union or sex or race discrimination. A dismissal is otherwise unfair unless it can be shown to be for one of four fair reasons:

- redundancy (but compensation is still payable);
- misconduct;
- incapability;
- unlawfulness (eg, a driver losing his/her licence).

The law adds, for good measure, as a fifth and highly subjective reason – 'some other substantial cause'! Finally, the qualifying employment period for claims of unfair dismissal was reduced in 1999 from two years to one year.[27]

INDUSTRIAL RELATIONS

The passenger transport industry is highly unionized. Generally, employers have recognized their trade unions and have well-developed systems of collective bargaining and joint negotiation in place. It is unlikely then that the government's intention in their 1998 White Paper 'Fairness at

Work', and now enshrined in legislation,[28] to provide for statutory trade union recognition will have any significant effect in the industry.

Parts of the industry have, however, a tradition of operating a 'closed shop'. Apart from within the engineering sector there are few pre-entry closed shops where union membership is a precondition of employment but the unions often still try to cling on to post-entry closed shops where there is a 'requirement' to belong to continue in employment. Legislation, however, does not recognize the above reality! There exists an enforceable right for individuals to belong to a trade union but since 1993 this has been balanced by a right *not* to belong thus making existing 'de facto' closed shops unenforceable, although they undoubtedly persist by mutual agreement between unions and employers. The government have indicated that they have no intention of turning the clock back to allow enforceable closed shops and over time, as older employees retire or leave, they will probably pass into history[29] as the UK's 'smoke stack' industries are replaced by service industries. However, that does not mean that the strong tradition of trade union solidarity in the passenger transport industry is dying.

SIX

Managing Physical Resources

The most important physical resources of passenger transport operators are the vehicles in which their passengers are carried. Vehicle stock usually represents a significant proportion of the capital employed in the business. Choosing the best vehicle for the different types of passenger transport service to be provided is thus of paramount importance. An inappropriate vehicle in service can result in an unprofitable operation. Unsuitable and unreliable vehicles detract patronage and result in the loss of revenue that might otherwise have been captured. The reverse is true of appropriate and suitable vehicles.

TYPES OF VEHICLE

Passenger carrying vehicles such as buses, trains, ferries or aircraft all have certain characteristics. All require to be propelled by some form of motive power that may or may not be integral to the vehicle. A passenger train provides a good example of this. The traditional and earliest passenger trains consisted of coaches (or rolling stock) hauled by locomotives. Thus, the passenger vehicle and the motive power were separate.

However, the motive power, then steam, was integral with the locomotive. With the advent of electric traction, the motive power became remote generated at some distant power station and delivered to the train via line-side sub-stations and energized rails or conductor wires on overhead catenaries. A further change that took place on suburban lines was the practice of carrying the power pack under the floor of the passenger coaches thus creating what today are described as electric multiple units (EMUs). In the early years of the 20th century, the GWR experimented with railcars, self-propelled passenger coaches with integral internal combustion (petrol) engines, and the dieselization of BR in the 1960s 'modernization' years produced fleets of diesel multiple units with under-slung compression ignition engines (DMUs). The high-speed train (HST) is an express train derivative of the DMU with two power cars (front and rear) incorporated into a fully coupled train of passenger rolling stock.

Thus, rail traction illustrates very well how passenger transport vehicles and motive power may be integral, remote or possess a combination of these attributes. Trams and trolleybuses provide further illustration of this dichotomy. For obvious reasons ships and planes are of integral design and never use a remote power source.[1]

The way over which passenger vehicles operate is also a significant determinant of the type of vehicle to be used. Nearly every passenger's origin and destination is road connected, which makes road transport one of the most flexible and versatile modes of operation and the private car the most significant competitor of passenger transport operators. It also helps to explain why buses were seen as the ideal public transport 'workhorse' to encourage as the spearhead of any government-led public passenger transport revival.[2]

A road is an artificial way to which road vehicles are confined but, as shown earlier, it is extremely flexible since nearly every location is road connected. However, some transport operations for road passengers are not completely flexible. Trolleybuses require overhead wires and guided buses bus ways, and not all large passenger carrying vehicles are suitable to operate on minor rural roads or around housing developments with restricted carriageways. All road transport is to some extent capacity constrained by traffic congestion – there are limits to the number of vehicles that can operate unimpeded over routes where there are heavy demands for passenger movement (such as radial roads into towns congested by commuters) or where there is likely conflict with freight traffic (as on many motorways).[3]

Heavy and light rail, including tramways and light rapid transit systems, are route bound and their operation cannot be quickly transferred to other localities to meet emerging traffic demands or indeed abandoned if patronage falls. Railway closures, for example, have to go through a complicated statutory process involving RUCCs before they can be allowed by the Rail Regulator and the Sheffield Supertram still operates to Herdings Park despite the demolition of the high-rise housing that it was intended to serve! There are limits to the number of guided vehicles that can operate over a stretch of rail and these are dictated by such factors as the signalling systems installed, the speed of the vehicles and their stopping pattern. The passenger upgrade of the West Coast Main line (PUG2/WCML) is an attempt by Railtrack and its partner Virgin Trains to increase the capacity of the main line from London Euston to the West Midlands, Northwest England and Glasgow by the use of high-speed tilting trains and moving block transmission based cab signalling (TBCS).[4] However, it is already being criticized by other TOCs who have formed the Slow Line User Group (SLUG) to lobby against possible capacity constraints on local services sharing the line!

Ships and planes, whilst operating over natural ways, are nevertheless almost as tightly constrained as land transport on many routes because of their dependence on navigational and air traffic control systems, which separate them for good safety reasons but in so doing inevitably create capacity constraints

The number of passengers who can be carried along a given route in a given time will depend not just on the capacity of the vehicles used, but also on the capacity of the route, as described above, and the speed of the vehicles. For example, a single 100-seater Concorde can make two return transatlantic trips in the time it takes for a 300-seater Airbus to make a single return trip but it is nevertheless obvious that the capacity of the Airbus operation exceeds that of Concorde by 50 per cent.[5] However, Concorde's revenue will be greater because of the premium that passengers will be prepared to pay for a faster journey.

Similar examples abound. The 'sprinterization' of Regional Railways in the 1980s, where infrequent long loco-hauled passenger trains were replaced by frequent two-car 'Sprinter' DMUs, generated significant additional traffic.[6] In the same way, the substitution of frequent minibuses for infrequent double-deck bus services that began before bus deregulation as a means of operators attempting to protect their services from competition delivered similar impressive passenger gains.[7]

There is, however, an obvious conflict between vehicle and route capacity. Where there are severe capacity constraints (as for example on London commuter lines and 'Network SE') Railtrack would like operators to run fewer but longer trains whilst the TOCs point out that in many cases platform lengths do not permit such operation. However, in any case they believe that their passengers value frequency as much if not more than comfort and will 'trade off' a degree of overcrowding for an earlier arrival! A compromise being examined on routes into London Waterloo is the provision of double-decker trains.

Bus operators have found that where conversion to operation with 16-seater minibuses has created sufficient demand to enable them to go back to using larger (and thus less frequent) buses, patronage has again declined, which explains the present popularity of the 29–33-seater midibus! In a similar vein, the arguments of those protesting against a second runway at Manchester Airport (since approved by the Secretary of State) hinged on the probable future use of larger aircraft that would mean no additional take off and landing slots would be needed.

The capacity of a route is only as good as that of its most congested element. Thus on a rail network junction capacity is paramount. Railtrack is currently devoting considerable energies and resources to identifying 'pinch points' on its network and devising strategies to freeing these.[8] A bus way will not cause significant congestion if it is terminated before a signalled junction, thus allowing more than one line of queuing traffic at the lights. Nevertheless, the new guidance of the Secretary of State for Transport and the Environment to the Highways Agency, that they should manage better rather than increase road space, means that this will not always be done in future if a continuous bus way can help to reduce the use of private vehicles. In the same way, the capacity of a canal is that of its narrowest lock!

However, one of the single greatest capacity constraints dealt with later in this chapter is the availability of vehicle space at terminals since if a service cannot be accommodated at its origin or destination it cannot operate. The capacity of UK airports dictates the number of transatlantic flights as much if not more than the number of aircraft that air traffic control can accommodate in the air lanes that they control. The number of trains per hour that can run into and out of Birmingham New Street and Leeds City stations dictates the shape not only of the local PTE supported rail networks but also the west and east coast mainlines and Virgin cross country services. In the past, Traffic Commissioners have refused new service registrations where the capacity of a city centre bus station or stands to which they have been registered is fully utilized.[9]

SUITABILITY OF DIFFERENT TRANSPORT MODES

There are no scheduled transatlantic liner services today although cruise vessels regularly cross that ocean. Scheduled air services can make the trip so much faster that sea transport is no longer a competitor. On the other hand, new fast, short-sea crossing vessels such as hovercraft and high-speed ships[10] have re-captured some air traffic across the Channel and Irish Sea. The Channel tunnel with its Le Shuttle 'drive on drive off' services has taken traffic away from the Channel ferries, as has the passenger train service Eurostar, which also challenges some London and continental air services.[11] The French high-speed train (TGV) is competing successfully with domestic air services and it is likely that on some UK rail corridors like the west coast mainline, rail–air competition will increase with the introduction of high-speed tilting trains.

It is very clear from the above that different modes of passenger transport emerge as the preferred option for travellers on different types of journeys. Intercity, regional and commuter railways serve different markets where speed, frequency and capacity are very real factors affecting passenger choice. The leisure passenger visiting friends and relatives and the student, to both of whom price is of more importance than speed or comfort, will happily make a long distance journey by National Express coach, a journey that the business traveller would not contemplate.

In some cases, the actual terrain over which the journey is to be taken dictates the mode and type of vehicle that can be used. Many rural routes use narrow and winding country lanes and the vehicles selected have to negotiate severe gradients. In such cases, a minibus might be the only practical option whereas the same choice may be made in an urban area to be able to increase frequencies whilst offering the same number of seats per hour. The engine, chassis and body of a vehicle will be specified in accordance with a multitude of criteria, such as the terrain to be negotiated, the passenger traffic offering (business, leisure or passengers with disabilities), the desired carrying capacity and legislation relating to driving entitlement. The specification of a motorway coach or intercity train will obviously be quite different to that of a rural bus or commuter train. The degree of comfort that passengers expect will vary according to the length of journey. They will happily stand for a short journey on a light rapid transit vehicle but not for a long journey on an intercity train.

As already pointed out, where capacity on a route is inadequate and existing congestion prohibits more services being provided then the only solution is to operate larger vehicles. However, this may be impractical, for example, where platform lengths are too short to accommodate longer trains or where there are 'route gauge' problems such as low bridges preventing the use of double-decker buses or trains. In such circumstances, passengers may turn to other less suitable modes including in many cases their own private vehicles. An illustration of the sort of problems that might be encountered when attempts are made to introduce higher capacity vehicles is the growing experimentation by the large bus groups in the UK with articulated buses. These have a higher carrying capacity than double-deck vehicles and they can be used on low bridge routes. On the other hand, they have to be driven by PCV drivers with a higher level of driving entitlement,[12] many bus stops and bus station bays are of inadequate length to accommodate them, and they have a much higher proportion of standing to seated passengers than conventional single or double-decker buses. In addition, many bus depots built in some cases to house trams are quite unsuited to articulated buses or are unable to allow these to be maintained under cover. Despite all the above they are clearly popular with passengers in many continental European cities.

PREMISES

The question of operators' premises is one that can only be answered by considering a number of quite complex trade-offs. Vehicles have to be garaged or at least 'stabled' in the open when not in use and they have to be maintained. Operators require office space from which to administer services. Because there will be 'dead mileage' between a garage and the points where vehicles go into or come out of revenue-earning service, it appears superficially attractive to site operating if not administrative premises at the point from which the vehicles work. This is common with airlines that often have a 'home' airport, and used to be quite common with municipal bus operators who could 'afford' premium town centre locations for their depots. The NBC had a long tradition, inherited from its predecessors, of operating out of town-centre bus stations that were wherever possible deliberately constructed with adjacent garages. However, even this did not solve the dead mileage problem as buses had to leave the town-centre garages in the morning to run empty to the suburbs to pick up their first loads. Regrettably, many of these integral garages and bus stations were sold to property developers after bus deregulation and privatization and the new subsidiary companies began operating from out-of-town industrial estates, often with vehicles 'garaged' in the open.

Because the UK rail network was constructed by private companies, albeit under Acts of Parliament, and because assuaging landowners' interests was often of paramount consideration in obtaining statutory powers, rail stations in many places are not optimally sited. Chester, Oxford, Cambridge and Manchester Piccadilly are obvious examples of this. Where it had been possible to build stations in urban centres, the British Rail Property Board has since often sold valuable railway land, which could have been used for car parks, freight terminals or interchanges, on to property developers. The Rail Regulator, though, has now placed a moratorium on such sales pending an investigation of possible uses of railway land. Railway depots at which rolling stock is stabled and serviced are now leased to ROSCOs or rail engineering companies. Indeed the tendency for maintenance and repairs of vehicles to be hived off to outside contractors by road, rail and airline operators has to some extent meant the demise of the prestigious large headquarters and associated depot. Large modern passenger transport companies are today often run from modest out of town offices with vehicle parking and crew 'signing on' facilities being reduced to a minimal functional building, perhaps even remote from the point at which vehicles are 'taken over' by their crews.

Supervision of operations can be accomplished remotely more easily today with radio links, global positioning, electronic ticket machines and smart card technology so that such minimal facilities can be adequate.

Scheduling can be centralized, although there are good arguments for decentralized scheduling offices where staff have expert local knowledge, arguments that can equally be made for local enquiry offices. The march of the regional and national telephone enquiry bureaux and 'intranet', however, working with efficient inter-office telecommunication in the form of shared information technology, militates against this. Schedulers can as easily be in touch with each other via 'the net' as when they once sat at adjacent desks in large scheduling departments in head offices.

TERMINALS

Every passenger's journey has an origin and destination. Sometimes these journeys may be accomplished by a single mode, as for example when passengers hire taxis to their destinations or, more extremely, use their own private transport. Most journeys, however, are multi-modal even if one 'mode' is simply the walk to and from convenient bus stops! Public passenger transport vehicles generally provide a service between two terminating points (termini) or less frequently a circular service to and from a single designated terminus. On route, they may stop to allow passengers to board and/or alight. Some stops may be nothing more than remote locations serving a small population (a country bus stop, for example) whilst others may be important traffic generators such as main line railway stations, large retail, educational or employment developments or locations where it is possible to interchange services or even modes of transport. Termini of a particular mode like airports and the London rail termini may themselves allow interchange with other modes such as taxis and buses. There is thus no clear distinction between termini and terminals although their dictionary definitions, which are not helpful, are respectively, 'boundary' and 'last stage'. What is clear is that the greater the volume of passenger traffic the more likely it will be that some kind of dedicated infrastructure will be necessary together with associated facilities.

Infrastructure and facilities provisions can range from a single bus stop pole and 'flag' to all the paraphernalia associated with a major airport, seaport or large railway station. Provisions for passenger comfort in the form of toilets, cafés and sheltered and/or heated waiting areas are desirable wherever passenger numbers dictate these. Because passengers may often suffer enforced waits or delays at terminals there are often considerable retailing opportunities that the operators or owners of the terminals can exploit in the form of franchises – anything from a McDonalds burger bar to a Tie Rack outlet. Until recently profits and rents from duty-free outlets formed a significant part of the operating revenue of terminals where international journeys commenced or finished.

A prime need of all passengers at busy terminals is information. This need is not only for the schedules of service using the terminal but also for real-time information about their punctuality or reliability (ie, notices of cancellations) displayed on monitors or relayed by way of public address facilities and backed up with enquiry facilities. These latter can also be part of the journey retailing facilities in the form of booking offices where passengers can obtain tickets for onward or future travel. Where passengers are making international journeys there will also be the need for facilities to be provided for the customs and immigration authorities.

Finally, terminals should be designed with adequate passenger circulation areas to avoid crowding and crushing on the arrival or before departure of trains, planes, coaches or boats with large numbers of passengers all embarking or disembarking simultaneously. Passenger dispersal may be on foot (as at large city-centre commuter terminals), by underground, metro, bus or taxi. In addition, many terminals have large car parks to facilitate 'park and ride' journeys and, increasingly, secure cycle storage.

Passenger capacity is not the only constraint facing terminal designers and managers. There will always be a finite number of vehicles that can physically be accommodated at a terminal in any given time. Without major remodelling and re-signalling, Birmingham New Street station can take few if any more trains, although, as described earlier, it would be possible to take longer trains! The terminal operator, in this case Railtrack, thus has a quasi quantity licensing function in allocating train 'slots' to the various TOCs using the station. The same is true of Piccadilly Gardens' bus station in Manchester managed by the Greater Manchester Passenger Transport Executive. Recognizing this, the Transport Act 1985[13] forbad PTEs and local authorities from applying any discrimination in departure charges as between operators. In fact, operators of all modes using busy termini invariably pay charges to the owners whether these are bus station departure charges, airport landing fees, port charges or Railtrack 'track access charges'. However, this provision of the Transport Act was not sufficient to prevent the virtual gridlock in 1991 of Castlegate in Sheffield (a kerb-side bus 'terminal' on the public highway) after deregulation. This had to be addressed by the Traffic Commissioner at the time making a traffic regulation condition[14] and refusing to accept registrations of any further services using the stop.

The most extreme case of 'slot monopoly' is illustrated by the way in which airlines are unwilling to cancel unremunerative services into or out of congested airports for fear of losing a landing or take-off slot that could be transferred to more lucrative flights, such as transatlantic services. It has been suggested that airports should auction slots to maximize the utility of their congested runways and aircraft/passenger handling facilities. Virgin Train's interest in Eurostar services being extended from a new terminal at London St Pancras, either to Heathrow or to connect at St Pancras with an extended Heathrow Express service, is based on sound commercial judgement as this could enable them to transfer slots given to continental flights to transatlantic services. The same logic can be applied to plans by some TOCs to link domestic airports by high-speed trains. For example, National Express, the owners of Midland Main Line would like to see stations at East Midlands and Luton airports. Airports, in fact, are some of the fastest growing passenger (and freight) transport terminals and will now be considered.

SURFACE LINKS TO AIRPORTS

Airports are powerful traffic generators. No one starts or finishes a journey at them but all air travellers journey to and from them. In addition to this movement through airports, passengers' baggage is handled, airfreight and mails are collected and delivered, and passengers are met or seen on their way by friends and relatives ('meeters and greeters' in airport parlance!). For a significant minority of people, a visit to an airport is a leisure experience in itself.

The infrastructure of large airports can resemble that of a sizeable town. Indeed airports are employment generators, it being estimated that for every million passengers per annum throughput, 1,000 staff are directly (by the airport authority) or indirectly (by concessionaries, franchisees and suppliers) employed on site.[15]

Staff must commute to and from their work at the airport. However, much of that work is shift work and no matter how good the local public-transport links to the airport are for passengers, they rarely attempt to serve the 24-hour needs of staff. Many airport authorities are acutely aware of the dilemma of their own staff, employed to provide a public transport service, being dependent on their own private transport to commute and several airports are investigating 'green commuting' plans designed to encourage their employees to reduce their dependence on the private car.

Air transport is the fastest growing sector of the public passenger transport industry and the airports that serve the airlines have always been multi-modal interchanges most typically between private (car) and public (air) transport. The challenge for airport authorities will be how to accommodate this growth in air traffic in a sustainable manner whilst simultaneously managing the inevitable associated growth in surface traffic and avoiding the very real problem of airport sclerosis created by congestion on the ground.

Planning policy guidance emphasizes the imperative of locating traffic generators at locations 'where they can best be served by public transport' such as along radial routes or at existing public transport focal points. There are good examples of airports situated alongside existing public transport corridors (Birmingham International, Gatwick, Amsterdam Schiphol and Frankfurt). The difficulty arises where airports that have historically developed on greenfield sites outside an encroaching urban environment become major traffic generators in their own right.

Whilst new land-use planning decisions can help to arrest the trend towards an unsustainable dispersal of transport generators and the dependence on private transport that this engenders, it can do little to tackle the problems of accommodating predicted growth at existing airports. Planners do, however, possess a legislative instrument under existing town and country planning laws[16] viz the ability to enter into 'section 106' planning agreements with developers. A good example is the 1996 planning agreement made with Birmingham International Airport as part of the outline planning approval for the expansion of their passenger terminal. This stated that 'the Airport Company shall use all reasonable endeavours to achieve a public transport modal share of 20 per cent by 31 December 2005, or when the number of air passengers is at a rate of 10 million per annum, whichever is the later'.

The draft DETR guidance on Local Transport Plans calls for partnership approaches between operators and local authorities including the establishment of Airport Transport Forums with the following objectives:

- to draw up short- and long-term targets for increasing the 'modal split' in favour of public transport journeys;
- to devise a strategy for achieving these targets;
- to oversee the implementation of green commuting plans for all employees based at airports. These might include strategies such as car sharing, walking and cycling, negotiating employee concessions on public transport and perhaps, in view of the shift patterns of work, providing or procuring dedicated employee transport.

A number of recent developments are having the effect of making airports multi-modal public-transport interchanges for passengers who may or may not be 'going airside' in order to travel by air. Instead they may well be taking only a 'surface' trip or making a trip to or from the airport, or between an origin and a destination other than the airport but involving travel and/or interchange at the airport. Such 'surface only' trips obviously add to already existing congestion at the airport, are arguably unsustainable, and should be discouraged. However, this could be a too simplistic a view of the total picture. Congestion at airports occurs both on the ground, on the runway and in the air. Take off and landing 'slots' are, as already described, amongst airline operators' most valuable commercial assets.

A considerable amount of traffic using rail and road approaches to airports is not passengers. Air freight is an even faster growing market than air travel. In a minority of cases, the freight is passenger related – baggage that has been 'checked in off-airport', flight catering supplies and aviation fuel. Some commentators (the writer included) see very little difference between passenger and freight logistics – the processing of passengers and baggage from check-in to aircraft is not that different to the receipt and despatch of consignments into and out of warehouses – as any air traveller will testify!

The parcels market with firms like Royal Mail, UPS and TNT operating their own aircraft is also a major airport user competing with passenger-carrying vehicles for space on already congested surface approaches to airports. The main disincentives to using private cars to access airports are the road congestion surrounding them at peak periods and increasingly throughout most of the working day the availability (or otherwise) of parking at the airport, and the cost of parking where this can be secured.

Traditionally, parking in the immediate vicinity of airports is in high-priced, short-stay car parks. Leaving a car in such locations for any length of time (for example, during the duration of a business or leisure trip) is prohibitively expensive. To overcome this latter disincentive 'off-airport' car park operators provide park-and-ride facilities with more reasonably priced long-stay car parks connected to the airport terminal by frequent courtesy bus services.

It is sometimes suggested that P+R facilities at rail stations might be used by air travellers providing that:

- a realistic long-stay tariff can be offered;
- there is good 24-hour security, for example, with CCTV and patrols;
- the airport is well served from the station by through or connecting services.

More worrying to airports is the 'reverse P+R' that occurs at some airports with more ample parking, especially Gatwick (for London), Dyce (for Aberdeen), Southampton and Birmingham[17] airports' stations, where commuters are known to leave their cars to continue their journey to the city centres by rail.

Once passengers arrive at airports, they may still have considerable distances to travel between different airline terminals or to and from associated bus and rail stations and taxi ranks. Different airports employ different strategies to facilitate such movements. These range from 'travellators' (moving walkways as at Manchester Airport), through frequent circulating free bus services provided by the airport authority or their franchisee bus operator, to the recently defunct 'maglev' rapid transit connecting Birmingham International rail station and the airport (and currently replaced by a bus).

Buses operating franchise services entirely on private roads within airports are not subject to the same legislation as PSVs operating on public roads. Some operators, for example National Express coaches, call at all terminals at large airports such as Heathrow, Gatwick and Manchester, and London Underground's Piccadilly line trains call first at Heathrow Terminal 4 then at Terminals 1–3.

PUBLIC TRANSPORT LINKS WITH AIRPORTS

Most airports have taxis, buses, courtesy buses, coaches or light and heavy rail (both national and international) to provide connecting services;[18] many have all or most of these.

Taxis

Approximately 15 per cent of air travellers start or finish their journeys by taxi. Taxis are an important component of the UK's public transport network. Passengers, especially holiday makers, arriving at airports frequently do so in pre-booked private hire vehicles and indeed may well also pre-book another vehicle from the same operator to meet them on their return. Many private hire operators have in their fleets multi-purpose vehicles (MPVs or 'people movers') with up to eight passenger seats that can be chartered as a whole by holiday groups.

Other air travellers must queue at a taxi rank at the airport, where hackney carriages 'ply for hire' to secure a taxi to take them to their destination. Taxis, unlike public service vehicles, cannot charge separate fares and the cost of a taxi journey can be disproportionately high for a single traveller.

Taxi licensing in the UK is in the hands of local authorities, which often means that a taxi arriving at an airport that is not licensed by the local authority in whose area the airport is situated cannot join the rank to secure a return journey. The taxi licensing regime distinguishes between hackney carriages, which can ply for hire, and private hire vehicles, which must be pre-booked, a distinction that is more and more artificial in today's world of mobile phones except in large city centres, especially London, where trade at ranks is brisk and taxis are still hailed in the street.

The Transport Act 1985[19] provides that private hire and taxi operators can carry pre-booked passengers with their agreement at separate fares. It also provides that licensed taxi (hackney carriage) operators can, again with the agreement of the passengers and provided they board at ranks specially designated for that purpose, carry them at separate fares. So far, very few such ranks have been designated although they exist at some London mainline stations and at Heathrow Airport.

Buses

Most airports are served by local bus operators' registered local services. Many have purpose-built bus stations to accommodate these services. However, journeys to and from an airport using such buses are often protracted, as, unless the service is a dedicated airport link, it will probably observe all stops and cater for intermediate travellers en route who are not making a journey to the airport. Such services usually more closely meet the needs of employees at the airport rather than travellers, although a small number of travellers whose origin or destination is in the suburbs between the airport and city centre will use them. Their reliability is often poor at peak times as they tend to use the congested non-motorway roads.

A number of airports are served by dedicated bus services, either registered local services operating in limited-stop mode or express coaches on which a premium fare can be charged. Heathrow is served by London Regional Transport's A1 and A2 'Airbus', registered local limited-stop half-hourly services from the major main line rail terminals and the National Express operated airport Express Shuttle service from Victoria Coach Station via the M4 (on which a dedicated bus lane has recently been established). There is ticket inter-availability between the two above services. East Midlands Airport (from Derby), Glasgow Airport, Cardiff Airport, Bristol Airport, Luton Airport, Teesside Airport (from Darlington), Stanstead Airport (from Colchester), Nottingham Airport and Leeds/Bradford Airport (from Leeds) are also served by dedicated airport buses.

Coaches

The coach industry has been more successful (than local bus operators) in establishing direct links to major airports (especially Heathrow). Here higher fares can be attracted and substantial growth continues.[20] The National Express Group are the dominant operators of long-distance coach services in England and Wales. The group acquired the Flightlink network of services from Flights travel in 1996. This connects most large population centres with airports at Manchester, Birmingham, Heathrow, Gatwick, Luton and East Midlands. The latter airport is now owned by National Express. Other airports listed in the National Express timetable are Teesside and Speke (Liverpool), the latter being a very recent addition to the network.

Speedlink Airport Services Jetlink service 105 connects Stevenage, Luton Airport, Watford Junction, Heathrow and Gatwick, utilizing the

M25 for much of its journey. There are well-established coach/rail connections to Heathrow, not just at Watford Junction on the west coast main line but also at Reading on Great Western Railways and Woking on the South West Trains network. This network of inter-urban and inter-airport express coach services usually calls at all terminals and bus stations at the airports served, and there are significant interchanges of passengers between services as well as coach passengers flying into and out of the airports. In some cases there are also significant rail/coach interchanges taking place.

National Express are the owners of East Midlands Airport, the Midlands Main Line franchise (operating out of London St Pancras rail station), West Midland Travel, the local operator of bus services around Birmingham International Airport and the Scotrail franchise. The Office of Fair Trading have examined all of these potential distortions of competition and National Express has been required to divest itself of Scottish City Link as a condition of their Scotrail franchise not being disallowed.

With the natural concentration of express coach services on Heathrow it is not surprising that the bus station there is the busiest of all of London Regional Transport's bus stations and that by no means all passengers using it are air travellers.

Light Rapid Transits (LRT)

Plans for the extension of Manchester's Metrolink tramway and West Midland's Metro both include spurs to their respective airports. Newcastle Metro has already been successfully extended to serve Newcastle Airport, and Heathrow Airport is served by an extension to London Underground's Piccadilly line. London City Airport is now served by the Beckton extension to the Docklands Light Railway from where there is a short bus link, as there is also from the North London heavy rail line at Silvertown station.

Whilst LRT links to airports are popular with planners, international experience suggests that they are most useful in promoting employment opportunities at airports and serving the needs of airport employees. Certainly, the provision of the direct, non-stop, heavy rail Heathrow Express link from London Paddington (and possibly in the future from London St Pancras Eurolink terminal also) is expected to produce a decrease in air passengers' use of the Piccadilly line.

Courtesy transport

Hoteliers, 'off-airport' car park providers and travel agents traditionally provide 'free' transport to and from airports. Of course such transport is never free; the payment of a hotel or car park tariff or the purchase of a package holiday confers a right to travel. The operation is thus hire or reward at separate fares and must be covered by the operator having a PSV operator's licence.[21] However, the activities of PSV operators where such operation is ancillary to their main occupation can be carried out under the authority of a restricted PSV operator's licence.[22] The operator may licence a maximum of two vehicles with 16 or less passenger seats in this way and, although still needing to meet the requirements of good repute and financial standing, does not need to demonstrate professional competence. Further, if the vehicle has eight or less passenger seats it is not classed as a passenger-carrying vehicle for which the driver needs a Category D or D1 PCV vocational driving entitlement.

Not surprisingly, a high proportion of courtesy vehicles feeding airports are either minibuses with 9–16 passenger seats or MPVs with eight or less seats operated under Restricted PSV O-licences or, in the latter case, as private hire vehicles on contract to the hotel, travel agency or car-park company. Where larger vehicles are required, it is usual for these to be hired from professional PSV operators with full Standard PSV O-licences. Indeed, contracts to supply courtesy coaches for hotels, car parks, travel agencies and companies, and even the airport authorities themselves (for inter-terminal transfers and 'airside' operations) are fiercely contested for by competitive tender. They often comprise the major part of the activities of coach companies based near airports.[24]

Rail

Manchester, Birmingham, Stanstead, Gatwick, Southampton, Prestwick International (Scotland), Dyce (Aberdeen), Squires Gate (Blackpool) and Teesside airports all have adjacent stations on the UK rail network. The Heathrow Express rail-air link financed by British Airports Authority is now complete and a new station at Luton Airport has been built. Not all of these airport stations are on main lines with frequent services and, even where this is the case, only Manchester and Gatwick have a 24-hour rail service.

The experiences of Manchester are interesting. The train operating companies that have sought to obtain paths to provide regional services to and from the airport are the old regional railways operators. The most notable of these are North West Trains, which provides a frequent flagship service from Windermere, Barrrow, Blackpool and Liverpool to the airport, and Northern Spirit (Regional Railways North East), which provides trans-Pennine services from Newcastle, Middlesborough, Scarborough and Cleethorpes.

Together these services give six trains per hour between Manchester Piccadilly and the airport, two of which observe all stops and three of which are express or semi-fast. Despite this, use of the service every ten minutes from Piccadilly has been disappointing, but has been more than compensated for by the heavy use made of services from further afield in the airport's catchment area, particularly by trans-Pennine passengers who are obviously avoiding using the heavily congested M62.

In 1996, a triangular junction was installed at Heald Green with funding from Greater Manchester PTE, the airport and Cheshire County Council. This enables services from the south to reach the airport but so far only an hourly service runs and only as far as Crewe, with no direct trains to Birmingham. A relatively slow London service was tried by North West Trains and abandoned.

The extent to which passengers at airports might be prepared to substitute a high-speed rail journey to a city-centre station for a connecting flight to a remote airport is the subject of current academic research.[22] In Germany and Holland, there is evidence that passengers at Amsterdam Schipol and Frankfurt airports will transfer to the European high-speed ICE or Thalys trains for quite long journeys to destinations such as Paris, Brussels or Cologne where once they would have 'interlined' on to connecting flights. The same research indicates that connection to high-speed rail services has a significant economic regenerative effect on cities and towns, as too has the provision of new rail infrastructure orbiting (M25 fashion) a city, especially where this connects, as the French TGV Paris bypass does, with a major airport (Charles de Gaulle).[23]

In this context, the reported aspiration of John Prescott[24] for a London orbital railway is quite credible. Long-term thinking is beginning to turn to the almost inevitable demand management of flights as the only realistic strategy for containing growth in airport traffic and effecting a modal shift to alternative high-speed rail links.[25] What is certain is that the growth of traffic in the air is set to be matched by similar traffic generation at and around airports. This will need to be managed in an environmentally sensible and sustainable way, encouraging integration where this is desirable but discouraging non-essential traffic generating activities at what are already heavily congested sites.

SEVEN

Managing the Operating Environment

Whilst vehicles, manpower, information and finance are obvious factors involved in the production of a transport service, land is a less obvious factor. Yet it is clear that any transport service must use land, be it the highway, railway, airport or port, and should pay directly or indirectly for such use. Operators also require depots and offices, also occupying land, to provide ancillary services such as maintenance and management. Apart from the purely commercial costs of land use (which economists refer to as 'private' costs') including items such as rent, track access charges, tolls and licence fees, there are environmental costs (variously referred to as 'public costs' or 'externalities') such as congestion, pollution, noise and accidents. These are not borne directly by the operator but fall on the communities 'hosting' the services. The extent to which the 'commercial' payments (eg, fuel duty) made by operators meet the costs of the externalities attributed to them is the subject of endless debate.[1] Operators need to understand the wider environmental context of their operations to manage their operating environments best.

TRANSPORT AND LAND USE PLANNING

Every land use decision has a transport implication and every provision of transport services and infrastructures has the potential to affect adjacent land use. The 1998 White Paper on Integrated Transport[2] expands the usual definition of integration as being 'within and between different types of transport' to embrace integration with other policies such as environmental, education, health, economic and land use planning. Thus whilst, for example, connecting services and interchanges might help deliver integrated transport at a tactical level, at a more long term strategic level it will be essential to integrate transport planning and land use planning. Although this may seem an obvious 'truism' – what the Deputy Prime Minister referred to at the launch of the Integrated Transport White Paper as 'joined up thinking' – the links between transport and land use planning have been largely ignored in the past. They were, however, specifically recognized by Neil Kinnock in his important EU White Paper in 1996,[3] which proposed the establishment of a hierarchy of transport nodes each with associated permitted land use developments (for example, see Figure 7.1).

The time lapse between a developer obtaining planning consent and completing a development can be considerable but, once complete,

A B C HIERARCHY OF DEVELOPMENT

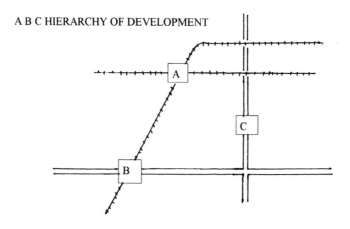

Businesses and services are classified according to their mobility profile, which takes account of employees, visitors and dependency on both road freight and car traffic.

LOCATION	DESCRIPTION	ACTIVITY
A	good access by public transport; car commuting no more than 20%	shops, offices
B	good access by public transport and car; car commuting no more than 33%	shops, offices
C	good access by road, eg alongside motorways; no limit on cars	transport-based facilities NB Out of town retailing not permitted

Figure 7.1   ABC hierarchy of development
Source: Citizens' Network, EU Brussels 1996

many developments have the potential to affect peoples' travel patterns massively. A rash of large out-of-town retail developments was completed in the early 1990s – eg, Meadowhall (Sheffield), Merry Hill (West Midlands), Trafford Centre (Greater Manchester), Metro Centre (Tyneside) and Lakeside and Bluewater Centres (Greater London). They have had an obvious effect on the economy of adjacent city centres and a no less obvious effect on travel, in some cases causing massive congestion on roads in their localities. The presumption in favour of developers in the previous government's planning legislation, albeit reversed by Selwyn Gummer in 1994,[4] seemed to assume almost universal car ownership. This taken together with a myriad of other planning decisions allowing a general migration from urban areas has gradually resulted in a dispersed society with a high dependency on private transport. The preference of developers for out-of-town locations with good motorway links has created a pattern of dispersed trips which public passenger transport operators find difficult to serve. Whilst the timings and routes of some forms of public passenger transport can be quickly altered to satisfy changed demand patterns and serve new developments, others, such as rail transport, are far more route-bound and rely on capturing the value of the land alongside their rapid transit corridors to make these locations attractive to developers. In the early days of town planning, for example, the first new towns at Welwyn Garden City and Letchworth were constructed alongside the East Coast main line, and Milton Keynes today is built astride the West Coast main line.

Whilst Planning Policy Guideline (PPG) 13[5] focused on reducing car dependency and spelt the end of unsustainable land-use decisions conflicting with sensible transport policies, the integrated transport White Paper[6] contained proposals for modernizing the planning system in England by highlighting the importance of planning at the regional level.[7] A key proposal is for Regional Development Agencies to produce Regional Planning Guidances (RPGs)[8] for their regions covering the next 15–20 years and for these RPGs to include 10–15-year Regional Transport Strategies (RTSs). Transport Authorities will be expected to take account of these RTSs in drawing up their five-year Local Transport Plans (LTPs).

Many decisions by central and local government in policy areas other than planning nevertheless can have profound effects on both transport and land use. For example, decisions to centralize health, education and leisure facilities are often accompanied by decisions to re-locate to out-of-town greenfield sites where there is room for expansion and parking. A further ramification is the necessity for travel to be more diversified in order that users can access these centralized facilities. Whilst valuable economies of scale may accrue to the facility provider, the users of the facility will need to substitute greater mobility for their previous accessibility. Where once many facilities were concentrated close to town centres or on busy radial roads into towns, they are now being concentrated and relocated both geographically and administratively in new 'centralized' locations. Thus several old 'infirmaries' and swimming baths are replaced by massive new out-of-town 'super' developments accessible only by private transport, dedicated patient transport services or infrequent bus services. It is rare that all 'centralized' facilities are adjacent. Two supermarkets on opposite sides of town may together have caused the closure of numerous retail outlets in the high street. This has resulted in the substitution of a 'many' (origins) to 'few' (destinations – ie, town centre) travel pattern by a dispersed 'many-to-many' pattern, thus encouraging the use of disaggregated private transport rather than consolidated public transport.

The same pattern of development can be observed in retailing, education and housing. The replacement of 'zoning' policies, where a comprehensive school takes pupils from feeder primary schools in its area, by 'parental choice' has had major transport repercussions. Not only are journeys to school more diverse than ever but also affected are school transport budgets, both the private budgets of parents who ferry their children to school by private transport or pay for longer public transport journeys, and the subsidized child transport budgets of local transport authorities.[9] Zoning also had the effect of distorting the housing market by depressing the price of dwellings in the catchment area of schools perceived to be 'failing' and accelerating the migration of families who could afford to move house to suburbia or greenfield housing developments, often situated beyond the green belt. The consequent 'green belt hopping' in turn increased commuting distances. Wherever an orbital motorway or ring road was completed to relieve town centre congestion caused by through traffic, this created a magnet for developers who wanted their supermarket, leisure facility, campus, office or retail development to be situated where it would be easily 'accessible' by car from the new road. This often created the sort of congestion it was built to overcome!

The above examples serve to illustrate graphically the interdependence between transport policies and land use planning as well as other policies that inevitably all have their own transport and land use implications. Only now, with the embryonic mechanisms for interrelated RPGs, RSTs and LTPs kicking in, is a serious attempt at last being made to address the wider issues.

ENERGY

Mobility requires the consumption of energy, accessibility does not. Thus sensible land use planning integrated with transport policies cannot only reduce both the need to travel and car dependence but can also help to address the issue of the unsustainable depletion of non-renewable sources of energy.

Modern transport is powered predominantly by the combustion of fossil fuels in the form of petroleum products.[10] In 1992, the UK transport sector used more than 43 million tonnes of such products (54 per cent of the UK's total use of petroleum products) – see Figure 7.2. By comparison, in 1962 the sector's use was only 33 per cent of the UK's total use of petroleum products so there has been a steady increase in the relative importance of transport use. Road transport accounts for 80 per cent of that use and the next highest user is air transport, with rail transport accounting for only 1.5 per cent. Transport is a premium user of oil because alternatives are most difficult to find. It accounts for over 50 per cent of all petroleum products used in OECD countries.[11]

Cars are the greatest oil users although haulage, rail and aviation also use significant quantities. How efficiently (measured in passenger or tonne kilometres per litre) the oil is used depends on factors such as the modal split between public and private transport and the energy efficiency of the different vehicles, such as buses and cars, that are used. Countries with dense and concentrated populations such as Japan and Holland offer greatest scope for public transport but conversely less scope for rail freight.

UK annual oil consumption approaches 100 million metric tonnes per annum. About this amount is recovered from the North Sea annually but the UK cannot sustain indefinitely present levels of mobility based on North Sea oil alone as this is fast depleting. If the rest of the world experiences a similar mobility transition, global reserves will deplete even faster. Forecasts of future reserves are coloured by energy prices, which determine the economic viability of more and more expensive extractive processes and the motives of the forecasters, especially oil companies, who need to establish impending crisis as a powerful argument for tax relief to permit more investment in exploration.

Mode	million tonnes used	% transport use	% total UK use
Road	34.99	80.3	43.4
Air	6.69	15.3	8.3
Water	1.26	2.9	1.6
Rail	0.64	1.5	0.8
TOTAL	43.58	100	54.1

Figure 7.2 Transport's use of petroleum products by mode 1992
Source: Table 3.1 Royal Commission for Transport and the
Environment 1994

The rate at which fossil fuels are depleted depends on:

- the extent of society's mobility transition and whether it will 'plateau';
- the demographic transition with world population expected to increase from the present 5 billion to 8–15 billion;
- improvements in energy efficiency delivered by such strategies as more efficient engines, anti-drag devices, weight reduction, higher load factors, electronic controls, variable transmissions and re-generative braking.

Reserves of other fuels (as a multiple of probable oil reserves) are shown in Table 7.1:

Table 7.1   Fuel reserves as multiples of oil reserves

Oil	1.0^{12}
Oil shale	2.7^{13}
Coal	3.0
Uranium 235	8.2^{14}

Some energy resources are renewable, for example hydroelectric, solar, wind, wave and tidal power, and harvests such as rapeseed, which can be converted into 'green' organic fuel, or coppicing, and straw, which can both be burnt by power stations.[15] Geothermal energy can also be harnessed but electricity generated in this way is so costly as to be currently uncompetitive. The same is true, though less so, of nuclear energy, which, apart from radiation risks in the transport and 'burning' of the Uranium (U 235) and problems of disposing of or reprocessing spent fuel, is environmentally much friendlier and less pollutant than other fuels.

Alternative energy sources to oil for transport generally require considerable capital investment. The battery vehicle depends on the development of a lighter than present rechargeable cell and a reliable power pack – so far the sodium sulphur battery is the most promising.

Where remote energy can be utilized, transport can sometimes be powered by electricity that is environmentally more acceptable than oil. Although vehicles driven by electricity may be route-bound, the overheads may be considered unsightly and the electricity itself has to be generated from primary sources of power. Nor should it be forgotten that in the generation, storage and transmission of electrical power there are efficiency losses. Hybrid diesel/electric vehicles able to leave electrified routes, flywheel power storage and thyristor controls are all attempts to replace oil and obtain similar efficiencies from its replacement.

An upward trend in the real price of energy is predictable even though this may vary between sources and may be reversed in the short term. In the past, government policy has been to keep the relativity in prices between all forms of energy stable but privatization of the energy utilities has altered this. The last and current governments are also committed to the 'fuel duty escalator' policy advocated by the Royal Commission on Transport and the Environment under which the real price of petrol and diesel is increased by 3 per cent more than inflation in successive budgets (see, however, Postscript). Even so, some forms of public transport receive fuel-duty rebates and international air transport operators pay no fuel duty at all!

As energy prices rise, investment in alternative sources/uses becomes more urgent. The 1990s 'dash for gas' by the electricity generating industry had implications both for the coal-mining industry and for rail freight. Except for electricity generated by natural means, such as hydro-electric, wind, solar and wave or tidal power, sources are finite. It may even be possible for natural energy to be harnessed directly, eg, the computer-aided sail/oil vessels developed in Japan.

Transport, energy and the environment

Canals and railways in their time had considerable environmental impact during both their construction, operation and in some cases, subsequent abandonment. So too did the industries and land uses they encouraged.[16]

The environmental impact of transport operations includes such factors as:

- land take;
- severance;
- housing loss;
- planning blight;
- visual intrusion;
- noise and vibration – transmitted through both air and ground;
- pollutant emissions;
- energy consumption – both in construction and in operation.

Environmental impact evaluations of all major transport infrastructure proposals are now mandatory.[17]

Pollution

Transport largely depends on the consumption of fossil fuels. The main pollutant by-products of this combustion are:

- Carbon dioxide (CO_2);
- Carbon monoxide (CO);
- Nitrogen oxides (NO_x);
- Partially burnt fuel, volatile organic compounds (VOCs) and hydro-carbons (C_xH_x);

- Sulphur dioxide (SO_2);
- Lead compounds (Pb);
- Particulates.

The amounts and proportions of the above in exhaust gases depend on the design, size, condition, age and maintenance of engines as well as how they are driven and the fuel used. Diesel (compression ignition) engines produce much less carbon monoxide, nitrous oxides and VOCs than petrol (internal combustion) engines but they also produce more harmful particulates, whilst catalytic converters on newer petrol engines can now reduce the above emissions by up to 90 per cent. Thus, the overall desirability of diesel engines in environmental terms is controversial although they are more fuel-efficient and produce less carbon dioxide (the so-called greenhouse gas).

Obviously, the highest concentration of pollutants in the atmosphere is near their point of emission. There is concern about the growing number of young children with asthmatic conditions because they are exposed to high concentrations of pollutants both as pedestrians and as passengers in cars. Perversely, their exposure as passengers can be up to three times that of pedestrians! Some commentators claim to have detected a collective 'societal' guilt connected with unnecessary car usage similar to that associated with smoking in public places, which they claim will swing the electorate in favour of car restraint policies!

In anticyclonic weather conditions pollutants can become trapped at ground level and sunshine can cause the trapped gases to react with one another to form ozone 'smog'. Recent legislation[18] requires local authorities to monitor air quality. Where this falls below 'target', they must declare an air quality management area and draw up an action plan to address this. Cars produce a full 20 per cent of CO_x and 40 per cent of acid rain.

Airborne pollution knows no national boundaries. The Kyoto environmental summit in 1998 committed national governments to contain and reduce their production of 'greenhouse gases'. The UK's Royal Commission on Transport and the Environment (1994) contains 110 recommendations embracing the 'polluter pays principle', the need for transport tax reforms, emission taxes, road pricing and motorway tolls (traffic growth is highest on motorways). The government's fuel duty escalator was an early response to its recommendations and the integrated transport White Paper picks up many of its other suggestions. Anecdotal evidence[19] suggests that the two biggest political issues relating to pollution are noise and greenhouse gas production. A widespread political and societal consensus for the need to reduce car dependency is clearly emerging, a consensus that can only benefit public passenger transport operators.

TRANSPORT PLANNING

The post-Second World War years saw the obvious links between transport and land-use planning either imperfectly understood, not understood or ignored. The Town and Country Planning Act 1947 set up a development control mechanism based on 'zoning' separate residential, industrial, retail and other activities but these 'master plans' paid scant attention to transport links between zones. The Buchanon Report of 1965[20] raised the issue but suggested that in the absence of any consensus for traffic restraint more highway capacity would have to be engineered into the existing infrastructure. The creation of metropolitan counties and PTEs in 1968 created a brief planning window during which some attempts were made to trade off highway and public transport schemes within county-wide structure plans with which district authorities' Local plans were expected to conform. However, this era of system planning was soon overtaken by a much more deregulated planning regime under which the presumption in planning applications was explicitly in favour of developers.[19]

During this era, transport planning became synonymous with highway planning. Forecast traffic growth was accepted as an inevitable consequence of economic growth and the planners' response was to create more highway capacity. During the 1990s, there came a realization amongst planners and in all governments that this 'predict and provide' mechanism was unsustainable, unaffordable and not delivering a solution to the fast-growing problems of congestion and pollution.

Several cumulative events were responsible for cooling this 'lust for tarmac'. The report of the Standing Conference on Trunk Road Assessment (SACTRA) of 1994 queried the Department of Transport's traffic forecasting model and more significantly suggested that the very new road space provided and intended to relieve congestion actually generated extra traffic to compound that congestion! Even more significantly it showed that reducing road space (for example with bus lanes and traffic calming) actually reduced traffic overall rather than, as was believed previously, simply diverting this. Concern over traffic's environmental effects, highlighted by the RCTE report of 1994[22] led to a government White Paper in 1996[23] that clearly pointed to the need to reduce private car dependency, a theme taken up by its successor in their White Paper of 1998.[24] This spelt out in the strongest possible terms the links between transport and land use planning[25] and set out a vision of managing the supply of road and rail space. A common investment appraisal system for both modes was proposed and the Highways Agency was tasked to manage existing highway capacity better (just as Railtrack must do with their assets). The era of 'predict and provide' was superseded with a philosophy of 'predict and prevent'.

The actual details of the transport planner's toolkit have not changed, only the allowable options. Transport planning is essentially an iterative modelling process comprising five stages:

- forecasting;
- trip generation;
- trip distribution;
- modal split;
- assignment.

Forecasting traffic growth superficially appears to be somewhat of a black art and yet it is crucial since the degree of accuracy of this first stage impacts directly on later iterations. The earliest forecasting models[26] were developed by the then Road Research Laboratory and were extrapolative (see, for example, Figure 7.3). Future growth was predicated on past traffic generation patterns. They were essentially aggregated forward projections of trends with an assumed levelling out when 'saturation' (ie, universal car ownership) could be predicted. Later, Sir George Leitch of SACTRA developed a disaggregate forecasting model that compared car ownership with a range of household styles, incomes and expenditure on travel. It was refined to allow cross-sectional analysis of one-, two- and three-car households.

The SACTRA report cited earlier recommended the use of disaggregate forecasting models. However, it is one thing to forecast car ownership, quite another to forecast usage. Germany, for example, has much higher ownership but lower usage than the UK.

Trip generation is the next process that attempts to identify the zones from which the traffic is generated. It makes category analysis assumptions that households with similar characteristics exhibit similar levels of trip generation. In other words, it recognizes that certain land use types

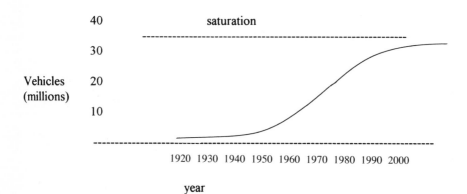

Figure 7.3 An extrapolative forecast model
After Tanner, J (1981), RRL

such as private residential housing and retail centres are associated with similar patterns of trips originating and ending in each zone.

The trip distribution stage is a mathematical model that attempts to allocate all the generated trips to inter-zonal trips (see Figure 7.4). There are in fact a number of such models all of which calculate from the base of today's known inter-zonal trips (t) the predicted number of trips (T) at a defined future date between two representative zones (i and j).

Once the inter-zonal trips are calculated the modal split model attempts to allocate these between public and private transport. It relies on estimating the total trips by car owners and non-car owners, the latter being assumed to be captive to public transport. The extent to which car owners might change modes and use public transport is estimated by comparing the perceived cost of the car trip with the public transport fare. Quarmby's 'logit' model postulates that the proportion of total trips undertaken by a particular mode (car, rail, bus, walk or cycle) is related to the exponential cost of travel.

Modal split targets are often used in planning agreements as a condition of planning consent. Thus, consent to a large development such as a new

MODEL	Notes	Mathematical formula	Key
a) Growth factor	simplest	$T_{ij} = t_{ij} F$	t_{ij} = traffic now between zones i-j; T_{ij} = future traffic; $F = T/t$ (ie growth rate)
b) Avererage growth factor	more sophisticated	$T_{ij} = t_{ij} \left[\dfrac{F_i + F_j}{2} \right]$	F_x = growth factor for zone x
c) Fratar	assumes T will be proportional to t but be affected by growth of zones to which trips attracted	$T_{ij} = \dfrac{T_{i(g)}\, t_{ij}\, F_j}{t_{ij}\, F_j + t_{ik}\, F_k \ldots + t_{in} F_n}$	$T_{i(g)}$ = expected future trips generated from zone i
d) Detroit	variation of b)	$T_{ij} = t_{ij} \left[\dfrac{F_i F_j}{F} \right]$	
e) Gravity		$T_{ij} = kG_i A_j F(C_{ij})$	k = constant F = assumed constant over time G_x = trips generated in zone x A_x = trips attracted to zone x C = generalized cost (measure of separation)

Figure 7.4 Trip distribution models

airport terminal might be given subject to a condition that the developer achieves a modal split of, say, 25 per cent of passengers using public transport. If, as the following table shows, the current modal split is, say, 10 per cent by public transport such a condition could be superficially attractive but if the airport throughput is forecast to rise from, say, 10 million passengers per annum to 20 million per annum, the number of passengers arriving by private car will not be reduced.

Table 7.2   Airport passengers modal split

	Current	Predicted
Airport passengers	10 million	20 million
Modal split	10%	25%
Car	9 million	15 million
Public transport	1 million	5 million

The final model, the assignment model, is then used to estimate which trips (apart from those already pre-assigned like a bus route or rail line) will be made along which highway links. Will drivers, for example, take the longer but quicker (unless congested) motorway route or the shorter but slower A-class road? The model identifies the least-cost routes between zones and utilizes or 'loads' these with the identified traffic that has a choice up to the point where the route is full or congested. It then allocates any remaining traffic to the next optimum route and so on iteratively until all traffic has been 'assigned'. The assignment model can be modified by including multi-route assignments that take account of known congestion and capacity constraints and make allowances for known delays such as traffic lights, tolls or even swing bridges.

Mathematical models are calibrated by testing their robustness with historic figures to see how accurately the result reflects current figures and adjusting their formula accordingly. Transport modelling has the virtue that it embraces the totality of passengers' journeys, from their origin (usually their home) to their destination, be it work, leisure, retail or educational facilities. It is similar to the freight logistics concept of supply chain management where the outputs from one activity (eg, manufacture) become the inputs of another activity (eg, distribution). Freight logisticians also have comparable sophisticated models that enable them to see the effects of a change in one parameter on the entire supply chain.

What is clear is that transport modelling is still a very useful tool. It can enable transport planners to predict, for example, the likely effects of infrastructure changes such as bus lanes. In future, however, the output of such models is more likely to be used to justify management measures for traffic demand than to make a case for any new highway capacity.

EIGHT

Quality Controls

There is evidence that passengers set more store on the reliability of services than on other undoubtedly important factors such as price, frequency, safety and comfort, all of which influence their decision to use public transport.[1] A random sample of the minutes of the Central Rail Users' Consultative Committee between 1949 and 1999 shows that the dominant two issues discussed in the committee's half century of existence have always been punctuality and reliability.

The manager of one TOC recently suggested to his Rail User Consultative Committee that the debate they were having about holding connections would become a sterile debate once he could deliver his company's mission statement to provide a very reliable service. The British Railways Board just before the privatization of their system was embarked on a programme that they called 'Organizing for Quality', which was beginning to deliver impressive results in terms of train reliability that many new TOCs have not yet even matched let alone surpassed.

A good number of passenger transport operators are today committed to implementing such programmes, in some cases describing these in the current vernacular of Total Quality Management (TQM).

TQM

TQM is a process that focuses on the people in an organization and on empowering them to 'get it right first time'. The product of successful TQM is consistent performance to customer expectations. Quality management should never be confused with standards such as BS5750 and ISO 9000 that focus on procedures. Such standards may underpin TQM but their main weakness is that whilst they can deliver consistent performance to set procedures that performance is not necessarily to customer expectations. In other words, if the procedures deliver mediocrity then the standards will ensure consistent mediocrity! Nor is TQM the same as quality control, which is a statistical technique, aimed at identifying when a product is delivered at a standard outside predetermined quality parameters so that corrective action can be taken. The Service Quality Incentive Regimes (SQUIREs) developed by the PTEs may motivate operators to avoid penalties but they do not automatically deliver customer satisfaction. To return to an earlier analogy, the late running penalty connected with making a connection may be greater than the compensation payable under a passenger charter.

Without the absolute commitment of top management, TQM is impossible. The process requires a culture change in many organizations. The public passenger transport industry has become increasingly 'contract led', with public authorities like OPRAF, PTEs and county councils securing services from private operators under tenders and franchise agreements and the operators buying in, again under contracts, support from suppliers and those who maintain vehicles and infrastructure providers, be they Railtrack, airports, ports, the Highways Agency or local highways authorities. Even where such contractual webs can be cemented under the umbrella of 'quality partnerships', there still remains a culture of blame when things go wrong. TQM has to 'drive out fear', allowing staff to admit their mistakes and learn from them. It has been described as the process of moving from management by control to management by commitment.[2]

Another example may help to illustrate the point. After the serious rail accident at Clapham in December 1988, there was an immediate internal inquiry within BRB followed within a year by the Hidden report[3] recommending that within five years the Board install Automatic Train Protection signalling systems across its network and to which BRB then made a commitment (sadly never implemented by Railtrack). That inquiry was essentially inquisitorial, seeking to examine cause rather than apportion blame. In contrast, the inquiry into the Southall disaster, which was the first since rail privatization (Railways Act 1993) to be held under Health and Safety Executive regulations and was even at one point adjourned (for nearly two years until July 1999) under sub judice rules whilst a driver was charged and tried only for the Crown Prosecution Service to eventually offer no evidence, was conducted in an adversarial manner (*Rail Magazine*, February 2000), with the TOC, their driver[4] and Railtrack all legally represented. Obviously such a culture of blame, which thankfully John Prescott's 'Rail Summit' in the spring of 1999 did much to remove and replace with a spirit of cooperation, is anathema to TQM initiatives, which aim to change behaviour and inculcate a commitment to doing the right thing in the right way always so as to 'get it right every time'.

Performance criteria such as passenger complaint levels, telephone enquiry bureaux response times and accuracy of information, punctuality and 'lost mileage' are often expressed as targets or charter standards. Because operations are frequently monitored and reported against targets, and can trigger penalties or compensation, targets are not necessarily the best benchmarks against which to evaluate the effectiveness of TQM, although they can be useful if divorced from such consequences. Perhaps more useful are independently conducted passenger satisfaction surveys or 'mystery shopping' exercises. Whether passengers yet see themselves as customers and respond to 'customer announcements' is a moot point but what is certain is that they react positively to good customer care and when surveyed express their intentions to reuse services with which they have been satisfied.

CUSTOMER CARE

Competition between operators for passengers has grown recently with bus and air deregulation and rail privatization, and the success of some operators in growing their passenger numbers has often been attributed to good customer care. On the other hand consumer representative bodies have reported growing numbers of passenger complaints, which some operators have actually blamed on a culture of complaining engendered by a fast growing societal consumer movement and the active encouragement by private operators to passengers to 'tell us what you think'. Equally, guaranteed compensation in the event of operators not meeting passenger charter figures has had the effect of inflating complaint numbers. Complaints are a negative indication of passenger satisfaction levels whilst surveys, as described above, may give a more objective measure. What is rarely measured is the dissatisfaction of passengers who have changed operator or mode or even used private transport. Competing bus, rail and air operators often fail to see other modes, including private transport, as their real competitors preferring to try to consolidate their presence on a route or in an area or their pre-eminence in meeting the needs of a particular traffic.

In every passenger transport operation there are certain front-line staff whom most passengers meet at some stage of their journey or when arranging this. They are the operators' ambassadors and it is they who need to employ good customer care skills. Most passengers encounter ticket office staff, drivers, conductors, inspectors, guards, cabin staff, check-in clerks and their roles are thus paramount. A smaller number of passengers may also have formed an initial impression of a service from the way they were dealt with when making an enquiry or booking. However, good front-line staff can still reinforce good first impressions or even repair poor impressions. They are exposed to the public like actors on a stage even when relaxed and talking amongst themselves – a situation in which all too often they can forget their ambassador role!

Passengers observe the cleanliness of their vehicle, its ambience (heating, air-conditioning, livery and ride quality), timekeeping and the way in which the bus driver, train conductor/guard, cabin or restaurant car attendant behave. Whilst it is frequently necessary to check or sell tickets during a journey, it is a fact that the payment of a fare represents what psychologists describe as a distress purchase. By this, they mean that passengers are being asked to part with cash (which subconsciously they will equate with its alternative purchasing power, such as a pint of beer, newspaper or ice cream). They do so effectively in exchange not for a ride they do not want particularly (as they might perceive the situation) but for a safe and timely arrival at their intended destination. Not surprisingly then, many passenger/staff confrontations arise at the journey's purchase point. Interestingly, however, the pre-booking of a journey and the 'off vehicle' sale of travel tickets are perceived as a far less stressful event. This is one of the most persuasive arguments for area-wide multi-modal travel cards, apart from the very positive cash flow benefits to operators of payments 'up front'.

Staff/passenger confrontations are often needless and need not arise if the staff concerned had understood better the passenger's needs and anxieties. Many passengers are insecure but try to hide their insecurity in different ways because no one likes to look foolish in public. In another book,[5] the author lists a number of ways in which such insecurity can arise:

- They may not know the correct fare and are afraid to ask because the person selling it looks unfriendly.
- They may be late for an appointment or connection.
- They may be afraid of boarding the wrong vehicle.
- They may be having difficulty disentangling complex information on direction signs, monitors, timetable displays or delivered by inadequate public address systems.
- They may have children or elderly persons 'in tow'.
- They may be young, elderly or disabled themselves.
- They may be separated from their luggage.
- Bus stations, railway stations and air terminals are busy places, scenes of hectic activity, and they may simply be disorientated, confused or insecure.

Good passenger care simply involves recognizing passengers' anxieties, making allowances for their sometimes-irrational behaviour and trying to be helpful and reassuring. A robust knowledge of the operator's services – timetables, fare tables, available ticket types, connections, departure and arrival points, and an obvious willingness to be asked questions and answer these effectively are prerequisites of customer care. Passengers expect staff to be pleasant, calm and concerned, but on occasions they must also be assertive and this incipient conflict of roles is always beneath the surface. Staff need training in how to deal with difficult situations such as drunken or objectionable passengers or exceptional delays. Most passengers will respond positively to being told what the problem is but will react badly to staff who fail to communicate any information as to the nature of a problem.

Sometimes passengers complain directly to front-line staff rather than later to the operator and staff need to be trained on how to handle such situations and pass on complaints. In the same way, the operator's complaint handling procedure must acknowledge complaints and process them in an efficient and timely manner. Ironically, in the early days of rail privatization one of the biggest categories of complaints against TOCs concerned not the primary reason for complaining but their complaint handling procedures!

Operators frequently seek to add value to the total journey experience by providing ancillary services. Examples of such services are toilets, catering, luggage handling and sleeping accommodation (both in transit and/or at terminals), and retailing, including 'duty free' sales (but since 1 July 1999 only now for journeys outside the EU) and 'travel shops' where other journeys or visits can be planned and purchased. More and more of these ancillary services are franchised out to specialist providers but often the passenger is unaware of this. Thus, passengers' impressions of operators can also be coloured by the behaviour of their franchisees. For this reason some large operators, for example Manchester Airport, form partnership with, in this case, their airport tenants to try to deliver a seamless service to their 'customers' – the passengers in transit through the airport. The partnerships embrace such diverse matters as staff training, staff commuting (with partners fully involved in the airport's green commuting plan), health and safety, an airport staffs' newsletter detailing these and other initiatives, and a joint consultative committee in which the partnership is monitored in practice and ideas for its enhancement are discussed. In many ways, this is a true TQM exercise – some would describe it as a huge quality circle – and it has been proved to deliver excellent customer care.

LICENSING

Kipling famously once said 'transport is civilization'. All civil governments seek to some degree or other to control either the supply or operation of public passenger transport and frequently both. Their reasons for doing so depend to some extent on their political ideologies. They may believe for example that wasteful competition exists creating oversupply on 'honeypot' routes whilst failing to provide any unremunerative but socially desirable services. For example, this was the clear rationale behind road service licensing in 1930[6] under which the Traffic Commissioners encouraged cross subsidy between commercial and unremunerative services. If the nationalization of all public passenger transport after the Second World War had been completed it would have meant 100 per cent state control replacing what were already very strict quantity controls.

A licence is nothing more than a permit to own and operate vehicles for reward (ie, commercially) so that passengers may hire them or travel on them for a fare. Because licences thus have a commercial value governments either central or local are able to charge a fee for them and the fees charged are often an important source of revenue. At the very least, licence fees will cover the administrative costs of issuing them. The procedures involved in obtaining a licence mean that governments or the licensing authorities who are their agents have a complete record of the operators, vehicles and facilities that have been licensed. This is not only a bureaucratic necessity if any form of control is to be exercised but it is also useful strategically in times of national emergency. A little-known residual role of the UK's Traffic Commissioners, for example, is to be able to use powers vested in them in the case of national emergencies. Likewise the transport of the UK Task Force to the Falklands would have been much more difficult to arrange if the Maritime Branch of the Department of Trade and Industry had not had a record of UK registered ships.

Some governments use their licensing powers in such a way as to protect their national interests, as for example the UK government has in the past through the Air Transport Licensing Board. However, the belief of the government in a free market for transport was translated into legislation such as bus deregulation in 1986 and rail privatization in 1993. That required licensing authorities to promote actively or at very least prevent the inhibition of competition. In some cases, this duty sits uneasily with others, as instanced by the Rail Regulator's simultaneous dual role[7] of consumer champion and promoter of competition!

Any form of licence that regulates the supply of transport can be described as quantity licensing. The previous licence regime for road services is a good example because by means of this Traffic Commissioners were able to:

- control the incidence and frequency of operation and which operator(s) they would permit to run which service(s);
- control the fares charged;[8]
- control by 'rationing' the number of licensed operators or vehicles.

The rationale behind fares control in any licensing system is usually either to discourage operators from abusing the local monopoly that quantity licensing inevitably bestows, or by the creation of a 'level play-ing field' to prevent strong operators attempting to drive out weaker competitors by 'predatory pricing'.

The ultimate form of quantity licensing is rationing of supply in the way that, for example, local authorities' taxi licensing officers can do by refusing to issue any more hackney carriage licences when they consider that there is 'no unmet demand'[9] in their area. Simply controlling the sup-ply of transport, however, is but one face of licensing. The other side of the licensing coin is what has come to be described as quality licensing. These systems are usually justified on one or both of two grounds – con-sumer protection and safety and environmental considerations.

Even with full-blown quantity controls in road service licences, opera-tors, whilst they are not licensed themselves, had to obtain a PSV licence for every bus that they operated. The bus had to have a certificate of fit-ness issued by a Certifying Officer on the staff of the Traffic Commissioner and the certificate had a finite period of validity or 'life'.[10]

In deregulating road haulage the Transport Act 1968 introduced an 'as of right' goods vehicle operator's licence granted to operators who met quality criteria of competence, repute and financial standing. Providing these criteria are met, Traffic Commissioners have no discretion to refuse the grant of an operator's licence. In 1982,[11] legislation was enacted allowing Traffic Commissioners to impose very strict environmental con-ditions on operators. When buses were similarly deregulated in 1985 there were arguments that equivalent environmental controls should be applied to the very similar PSV operator licensing system that was then allowed to replace the strict road service licensing regime. However, this has not yet happened.

In passenger transport terms a quality licensing system is a guarantee of operators' safety and quality be they taxis, buses, trains or planes. It is their passengers' insurance of a safe arrival that ultimately they purchase through their fare. In some cases too it is the means by which consumers are protected since ultimately they have the option of complaining to the licensing authority if they feel their safety has been compromised or, more usually, the advertised service has not been delivered. The Rail Regulator, as mentioned earlier, was given a consumer protection role by the Railways Act, a role that he performs jointly with the OFT and through the appointment of Rail User Consultative Committee as his 'eyes and ears' and to whom passengers can refer unresolved complaints which they have earlier made to TOCs.

However, it must as well be realized that quality licences are also bar-riers to entry to an industry. If the criteria to be met are set too high, there is even a danger that insufficient operators will come forward to be licensed to meet passenger demand. The suggestion in the buses 'daugh-ter document' to the government's integrated White Paper that Traffic

Commissioners should be able to set quality criteria to be met by operators before they would be prepared to accept their registration to provide services on a Quality Partnership corridor is sensible but nevertheless treads a fine line between quality and quantity! What might in the immediate future be a much greater quality hurdle to PSV operator licensing is the requirement from October 1999 for candidates for the Certificate of Professional Competence (CPC), a prerequisite for the holding of a licence, to sit a much more difficult examination.[12]

That there are differences between the philosophies that underlie quantity and quality licensing is obvious but what is not so obvious is the interaction and inter-relationship between the two. Whilst the former is predicated on a philosophy of protecting 'the public interest' and the latter is more concerned with facilitating competition between all operators 'fit, able and willing'[13] to provide a service, neither extreme can be viable, and passenger transport licensing in its various forms, which will now be considered, will always be essential.

Licensing of public passenger transport vehicles on the highway

A motorcar, defined as a mechanically propelled road vehicle,[14] is a passenger transport vehicle. All motor vehicles, both large and small, are subject to quality controls in the form of annual roadworthiness tests and, in addition, their operation must be covered by 'third party' motor insurance. Unless a motorcar is used as a bus or taxi it remains a private vehicle not subject to any additional form of licensing so long as it is not to be used to carry passengers commercially.

The legislation determining what constitutes the specific kinds of commercial operation for which a licence of one kind or another is required is complex. The Public Passenger Vehicles Act 1981 (PPV Act)[15] defines public service vehicles in the context of how a vehicle is used. In contrast, the legislation relating to driving entitlement is couched in terms of how the vehicle is constructed.

Both sets of legislation divide neatly at eight passenger seats (see Figure 8.1). A vehicle with nine or more passenger seats is defined for driving entitlement purposes[16] as a passenger carrying vehicle (PCV) and can be driven by the holder of a vocational Category D driving entitlement who has passed the PCV driving test. There is a sub category D1 for drivers of minibuses with 9–16 passenger seats.

Whether a PSV operator's licence is also required for the carriage of passengers will depend on how it is used to carry those passengers. If it is a bus used for 'hire or reward' then it will be a PSV. 'Bus' is defined[17] in a similar way to PCV[18] (ie, a motor vehicle adapted to carry nine or more passengers). However, if it is a smaller passenger carrying vehicle (SPCV)

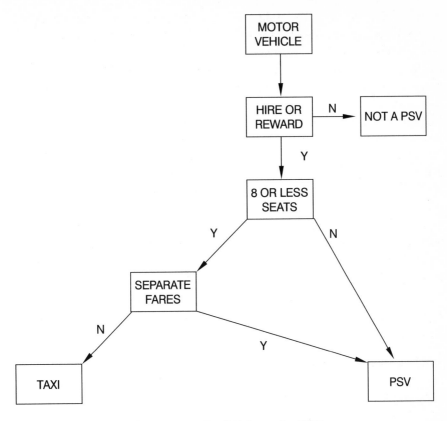

Figure 8.1   Definition of a PSV

than a bus (ie, if it has eight or fewer passenger seats) and is also used for hire or reward it will in addition be a PSV (but not by definition a PCV!) but only if it is used to carry passengers at separate fares. Hire or reward includes not only the fare or the private hire rate for the vehicle but payment made in consideration of other matters (eg, hotel accommodation) that confer a right to be carried (whether or not exercised). Thus, a hotel courtesy bus on which no fares are paid is nevertheless a PSV.[19]

Careful reading of the above paragraph will indicate that a SPCV with eight or fewer seats not used to carry passengers at separate fares is not a PSV. The Public Passenger Vehicles (PPV) Act 1981 excludes such vehicles precisely because they are otherwise licensed under taxi legislation,[20] either as hackney carriages able to ply for hire in the street and on ranks or to carry out pre-booked private hires, or private hire taxis able to perform only the latter function.

Generally, neither kind of taxi is able to charge separate fares. However, at the time of bus deregulation, new legislation[21] was introduced to enable taxis in specific circumstances to carry passengers at separate fares, as it was thought that this flexibility would permit the introduction of innovative new public passenger transport services in rural areas or at times of low demand. Hackney carriages and private hire taxis can now take 'consenting' pre-booked passengers at separate fares. Hackney carriage operators can likewise take passengers, consenting to queue at ranks designated for the purpose, to specific destinations at separate fares (although there are very few such ranks).[22] However, hackney carriage operators can obtain from their Traffic Commissioner, as of right, a special restricted PSV operator's licence that enables the dual use of their vehicle at separate fares as a PSV to operate a registered local service and at a composite fare as a hackney carriage. This was a valuable concession in 1985 as it enabled the use of a taxi as a PSV without the need for the driver to hold a PSV driver's licence. However, the subsequent adoption by the UK of the EC Directive on driving entitlement[23] now means that only a Category B car licence plus a taxi driver's licence is required to drive such a PSV 'taxi-bus'. This is because it is a SPCV and not a PCV with nine or more seats. Thus, taxi bus operation is no more attractive than other licensed ways of running minibuses and SPCVs.

Even before the PPV Act 1981, the widespread practice of running unlicensed small vehicles and charging the occupants was always illegal since the vehicles then became PSVs. However, car sharing for commuting, and institutionalized social car sharing schemes for health, retail and leisure journeys, make economic and environmental sense. Rather than penalize such initiatives the PPV Act regularized them by providing that where the total fares paid are no more than the running costs (including depreciation) and the vehicle has eight or fewer seats it does not become a PSV.

This derogation, however, did not extend to minibuses. It was recognized in 1977 that schools, churches, sports organizations, social clubs and other bodies involved in 'activities of benefit to their community' all ran minibuses with 9–16 passenger seats and frequently made a charge to the passengers. Again this was regularized[24, 25] by the issue of minibus permits allowing such non-commercial operation of what are in effect PSVs but used only by passengers in membership of the appropriate 'community transport' organization without the need for a PSV operator's licence. A specific variation of minibus permits[26] is the community bus permit that allows volunteer drivers of a community transport organization to run registered local services for the public at large. Community buses have been used in a number of instances to provide registered regular rural transport services often assisted by the Rural Transport Development Fund.[27]

Despite all the above unconventional service options, the vast majority of public passenger transport by road is performed under the auspices of PSV operator's licences. A restricted PSV O-licence can be obtained to operate a SPCV that is also a PSV or a minibus provided the main occupation of the operator is not that of an operator of PSVs adapted to carry nine or more passengers. This means that a courtesy minibus can be operated by a hotel, travel agency, car parking company or leisure centre where the cost of the associated accommodation, holiday, parking or leisure activity confers a right to travel on the minibus. Many taxi companies operate a couple of minibuses in their fleet by interpreting 'main activity' in a flexible way. No more than two minibuses may be specified on a restricted licence but the 1985 Act makes an exception to this rule for the Royal Mail who operate over 250 post buses, mostly on restricted PSV operator licences.

Standard PSV O-licence holders are de facto the major providers of public passenger transport services. A PSV O-licence is granted as of right to operators who fulfil the licence criteria that derives from EC legislation.[28] Traffic Commissioners who issue PSV O-licences require operators to fulfil three conditions relating to:

- good repute;
- financial standing;
- professional competence.

However, applicants for a restricted licence do not have to demonstrate professional competence. Good repute relates to the applicant's previous convictions and conduct and minimum financial criteria are laid down in the EC Directive. Whilst these apply only to applicants for standard national and international licences, Commissioners have adopted similar guidelines for all applicants.

An examination, the Certificate of Professional Competence, recently (see above) made more difficult, is proof[29] of the professional competence of either the operators or their designated transport managers. Licences can be revoked for poor maintenance, offences relating to drivers' hours and records, and other quality matters,[30] with operators having the right to a public hearing before the Traffic Commissioner and of appeal to a Transport Tribunal. The PSV O-licence then, whilst in theory purely a quality licence granted as of right, can also be seen to some extent as a quantity restriction since the barriers that it places to entry to the business are not surmountable by just any operator!

Within the framework of PSV operation, there are also other quality controls. The UK[31] and EC[32] Drivers Hours and Records[33] Regulations and the Vehicle Inspectorate's procedures for fleet inspections and roadside checks are examples. These provisions attempt to prevent unsafe driving and the use of mechanically unsafe or overloaded vehicles. Infringements and convictions are noted on operators' records and can result in their receiving a call to a public inquiry to (in the rather quaint words of the PPV Act) 'show reason why their licence should not be suspended, curtailed or revoked'.

The Registration of Local Services[34] can also be seen as a quality control although it is not a licence as such (except in London, which has not been deregulated[35]). This was introduced with deregulation in 1986. Operators must give 42 days notice of services that they wish to provide commercially[36] and similar notice of withdrawal. There are penalties for not running as registered and Traffic Commissioners can make traffic regulation conditions when requested to do so by a transport authority and where it appears to them that they should do so to reduce congestion or prevent danger. The condition may limit the number of vehicles on a road or their frequency of operation. Fuel duty rebate sanctions[37] and conditions attached to O-licences[38] preventing the operation of specific or all registered services can only be described as significant quality controls. These controls could well be ratcheted up when Commissioners are given powers to license quality partnerships.

Rail passenger transport services

The nationalized British Railways Board was a government controlled but self-regulating monopoly of rail passenger services. There was no need for any system of quantity licensing[39] although some 'exit' controls were applied by the Transport User Consultative Committees. The only quality controls were exercised by the Railway Inspectorate (considered later in this chapter).

All that changed in 1993 with rail privatization. The split between infrastructure (Railtrack), operations (TOCs) and rolling stock (ROSCOs) provision created a contractual railway with the various parts of the hitherto homogenous business tied together by commercial agreements. It was obvious that this new restructured railway would require to be regulated. Because of track access limitations, the deregulation model used in the bus industry could never be appropriate. Accordingly, the government, in drafting its legislation in 1993,[40] created an independent Rail Regulator as the industry's licensing authority. Unfortunately, because of the decision to franchise TOCs to private operators, it was necessary to also create a Franchise Director to carry out this process and the powers and duties of the Franchise Director and of the Rail Regulator were often confused. As the process unravelled it also became clear that the Rail Regulator was powerless to intervene in some situations and that some parts of the new industry (notably the ROSCOs) were outside his jurisdiction. For example, the acquisition of the ROSC Porterbrook Leasing by Stagecoach Holdings raised the potential monopoly issue of the vertical integration of TOCs and ROSCOs, and the change of control at Virgin Trains when Stagecoach bought 49 per cent of its shares raised the inevitable competition issues associated with any form of horizontal integration between two modes (bus and rail). To complicate matters further the Act[41] required the

Regulator to exercise certain functions relating to competition law jointly with the Director General of Fair Trading. It is the clear intention of the successor government to address these anomalies and at the time of writing a Transport Bill[42] to create a Strategic Rail Authority is before Parliament. What follows is therefore a description of the current rail-licensing regime with reference to the proposed changes to this. Competition matters are dealt with more thoroughly later in this chapter.

The jurisdiction of the Rail Regulator extends to:

- licensing;
- access agreements;
- closure procedures and adjudication;
- enforcement orders;
- consumer protection; and
- competition law.

He or she is required to license assets, which include passenger and goods trains, networks, stations and light maintenance depots (LMDs). Access agreements focus on infrastructure ownership whilst closure procedures relate to passenger services, networks, stations and LMDs

The jurisdiction of the Franchising Director extends to:

- franchising of passenger services;
- initiating closures;
- securing continued services;
- enforcement orders relating to franchises.

Both the Regulator and Franchise Director are required to:

- protect rail users;
- promote rail use;
- promote network facilities;
- promote efficiency, economy and fair competition; and in so doing
- impose minimum restrictions.

The Franchise Director also has a duty of last resort to secure the continuance of passenger services where the private sector ceases to do so (eg, following the bankruptcy of a TOC) or on being unable to re-let a franchise.[43] The licensing regime is concerned with the licensing of persons to operate railway assets – ie, passenger and goods trains, stations, networks and light maintenance depots. It becomes an offence to provide or operate a railway service for passengers or goods, or to own a railway network, station or light maintenance depot (LMD), or to provide any network, station or light maintenance services unless the operator is authorized by a licence issued by the Rail Regulator.

The Act[44] specifies the procedures for the grant of licences and allows the attachment of conditions to these. Licences may contain a condition requiring the licensee to enter into agreements with other persons for specified purposes. They may also allow a 'qualified person' named in the licence to have a regulatory role under which the licensee is required to comply with his or her requirements. This could be loosely compared to the role of the nominated transport manager in PSV and goods vehicle operator licensing. It is a quality control that can be used by the Rail Regulator to enforce safety standards but it could also encompass the role of Railtrack, the de facto national infrastructure controller, in agreeing operator's safety cases – see below and.[45]

A regulated access agreement may be a:

- track access agreement;
- station access agreement; or a
- depot access agreement.

Obviously, most access agreements are inherited from pre-privatization operations but new agreements and variations require the Regulator's approval and may only be entered into on his or her direction. TOCs may also ask the Regulator for a direction to compel a facility owner to enter into an access agreement.

Although all the above powers appear superficially to enable the Regulator to apply a heavy hand to the railway industry, the reality has been that political constraints, and especially the duties to have regard to value for money criteria and to promote competition, have resulted in a lighter regulatory touch than perhaps the Labour government of 1997 would have wished. However, the Transport Bill 2000 has the potential to strengthen the Regulator's arm whilst at the same time removing some of the anomalies that might hitherto have been repressive.

The Bill establishes a Strategic Rail Authority (SRA). It abolishes the Office of the Director of Passenger Rail Franchising (OPRAF) and the residual British Railways Board, transferring the rights and liabilities of both to the SRA. As well as these transferred functions the Bill confers new functions on the SRA. It will be able, with the approval of the Secretary of State, to secure the provision of services otherwise than by franchising and indeed could become an operator of last resort. Where a franchise is terminated and the SRA considers it cannot be operated as economically or efficiently by tender, it may seek a direction from the Secretary of State to dispense with franchising. ROSCOs are now included amongst the railways 'users' brought within the SRA's scope.

The Regulator's responsibility for consumer protection is transferred to the SRA, which will administer the Rail User Consultative Committees and Central RUCC (C/RUCC). These will also be empowered to investigate any matter relating to any 'open access' operators as well as franchised TOCs. Closure decisions will be taken by the Secretary of State following a simplified procedure conducted by the RUCCs.

The Bill provides the Regulator and SRA with a much tougher enforcement regime, allowing them to impose unlimited[46] fines for licence and franchise agreement contraventions. The Regulator's duty to promote competition is redefined to be for the benefit of railway users.

A shadow SRA is effectively in place with the appointment in July 1999 of Sir Alistaire Morton as Chair of BRB and a new Franchise Director (Mike Grant) who will become the SRA's chief executive. A new regulator[47] appointed at the same time has already warned Railtrack of possible fines if they do not meet their self-imposed target of a 7 per cent reduction in delays attributed to them in 1998–99 (which was not met) and 1999–2000 (effectively setting a 14 per cent target to be met at the end of the two years).

The Bill sets out the SRA's overall objectives, which are less commercial and more social than those of the Regulator and Franchise Director already described. They are:

- to promote the use of the rail network by passengers and freight;
- to secure its development;
- to contribute to the development of an integrated system of passenger and freight transport.

The big issues facing the three 'regulators' charged with these objectives are certain to be investment, re-franchising and open access. The Railways Bill gives them the tools to tackle them; time will tell if they prove to be enough.

Air passenger transport services

The UK's Civil Aviation Authority (CAA) is the regulatory body responsible for all aspects of air passenger transport licensing in respect of economic or quantity controls, safety, environmental and consumer matters or quality controls. Its responsibilities apart from air transport service licensing include air traffic control, air safety and consumer protection. Unusually for a regulatory body it also operates eight airports in Scotland through its subsidiary Highlands and Islands Airports Ltd.

Whilst as the successor of the Air Transport Licensing Board (see Chapter 3) the CAA is able to regulate domestic civil aviation and control services, fares and operators, it must work with other international organizations to license other services to and from the UK. The dominant role of the airlines' own 'trade association', the International Air Transport Association (IATA), in setting fares and tariffs on international services, largely through bilateral intergovernmental air traffic agreements favourable to national 'flag carriers', has declined significantly in the last two decades. This occurred first with the growth of group charter services, then with airline deregulation in the United States and latterly with the introduction of the EU 'open skies' policy (also discussed in Chapter 3). IATA's original 'cartel' role has been unable to survive the challenges of economic liberalization and competition law.[48] Being a trade association with voluntary membership, many airlines remain within it simply to participate in its other activities such as the important role that IATA still has to play[49] in preserving 'network benefits' such as through ticketing.[50]

The CAA has a similar relationship to the Air Transport Users' Committee (discussed in Chapter 4) as that of the SRA to C/RUCCs. Quality control is firmly in the hands of the CAA. Again, there is an international dimension. A United Nation's agency, the International Civil Aviation Organization, encourages cooperation between member states in pursuit of its objectives of ensuring safe civil aviation operation including airports and air navigation systems. Each member state when adopting an ICAO recommendation must use its own legislative machinery to do so (in exactly the same way that EC Directives have to be incorporated into domestic law).

To fly internationally or even on domestic flights, all UK registered aircraft must be operated by the holder of an air transport licence. The licensing criteria are similar to other operator licences (eg, PSV and GV O-licences) in that competence (here defined as experience) and financial standing are prerequisites, and the CAA can suspend, revoke or vary the licence and attach conditions to it.

Pilot licensing and airworthiness certification are also within the CAA's remit. Certificates of airworthiness are issued pursuant to ICAO standards, with the CAA requiring an aircraft type approval certificate and the aircraft to be inspected and flight-tested. The CAA also licenses aerodrome operators through the issue of aerodrome licences and is responsible for air traffic control in the UK, although the Labour government of 1997 is considering whether to carry forward its predecessor's plans to privatize this function[51] (see, however, Postscript).

Sea passenger transport services

Ensuring the safety of ships at sea and the well-being of passengers and crew involves not just shipping companies but also governments and international agencies tasked to set and regulate agreed standards. The International Maritime Organization (IMO) is the most important of these agencies. It also has a pollution control remit. All ships are registered in some country but the registration standards of countries vary enormously and this variation leads to the adoption by some shippers of 'flags of convenience'. In effect, they register their vessels with countries having less exacting standards than the country from which the shipper operates. For example, the 'flag' country may have less generous manning levels applicable to the vessel being registered. Before a ship can be registered, it must be inspected by a recognized classification society such as Lloyd's Register whose purpose is to certify that it is constructed and maintained to the standards laid down by the country of registration. Classification societies are non-governmental, independent organizations set up solely to serve the interests of the shipping industry. The Maritime and Coastguard Agency (MCA) of the DETR is responsible for implementing shipping legislation concerning safety of life at sea. Because the classification societies' standards are so high, some of this work (eg, the issue of load line certificates) is delegated to them. The division surveys passenger vessels, makes random inspections of life-saving appliances (eg, lifeboats and fire-fighting equipment), issues certificates of seaworthiness, examines ships officers and issues Masters, Mates and Engineers' certificates.

The growth of air transport has meant that, apart from cruise liners, most sea passenger transport is on ferries making short sea crossings, but with the increasing use of high-speed vessels such as hovercraft and large catamarans the IMO and MCA are having to adapt rapidly to new operating conditions. A recent example of this was new standards for intermediate bulkheads on roll-on roll-off (RoRo) vessels after the *Herald of Free Enterprise* and *Estonia* tragedies in the 1980s. As with ICAO, discussed above, the effectiveness of IMO depends on the willingness and ability of individual countries to legislate for and enforce the standards established through international conventions and recommendations.[52]

TRANSPORT SAFETY

All the different regulatory bodies and licensing authorities described above are concerned about the safety and security of passengers, crews and the public travelling on, or in other ways coming into contact with, transport operations. However, the approaches that each take to address its concerns differ widely. Some, as shown above, rely on public or even private agencies. For example, the Traffic Commissioners rely on the Police and Vehicle Inspectorate (VI), and the Maritime and Coastguard Agency of the DETR uses classification societies, whilst others like the Railways Inspectorate rely more on their own resources although they delegate some of their work to Railtrack, as described below. There is also a difference between proactive and reactive safety regimes. PSVs are either type approved 'at birth' at the manufacturer's premises or are issued with a Certificate of Initial Fitness (COiF) at a Goods Vehicle (sic) Testing Station or other designated premises by a

Certifying Officer but thereafter must be tested annually by the VI. The three-year 'MOT' test of private cars is franchised to approved garages by the VI. Aircraft are examined after they have flown a specified number of air miles. By contrast ships and trains, whilst subject to random checks, are only formally examined 'at birth', either by the classification society on behalf of the Maritime and Coastguards Agency (which is then responsible for random inspections) or by the Railway Inspectorate, now an agency of the Health and Safety Executive, when a 'safety case' is made for new rolling stock. There is some parallel here with the pre-1981 system of seven-year Certificates of Fitness (COFs) for PSVs, which were then comprehensively stripped, re-examined and rebuilt before a new COF of inevitably shorter duration was issued. The point to note is the absence of proactive annual (or shorter, as is the case with many taxi fleets) testing. However, should an accident occur and should the vehicles be recoverable (not always possible with ships and planes) then the ensuing investigation is extremely thorough and painstaking. Partly this is an attempt to discover the cause of the accident in order to see what lessons can be learnt to prevent future occurrences, and any ensuing inquiry is thus inquisitorial in nature, but, inevitably, if blame is being sought because of issues of compensation then procedures can become more adversarial. The ultimate example of this is prosecutions arising from road accidents. The *sub judice* nature of possible future criminal proceedings can seriously inhibit (or even delay to a point where recall is difficult) a public inquiry into an accident, a consideration that will be considered at the end of this chapter.

The arrangements for ensuring road safety are perhaps the most proactive and complex of those relating to any mode. It is an offence to use a motor vehicle in contravention of a number of statutes and regulations. The following is an indicative, by no means exhaustive, list of these:

- Road Traffic Acts (which also cover requirements for third-party insurance, speeding and parking);
- Construction and Use Regulations (covering, *inter alia*, weights and dimensions, emissions, seat belts and mechanical condition);
- Drivers' Hours and Records Regulations;
- Road Vehicle Lighting Regulations;
- Transport Acts (including licensing of vehicles);
- Finance Acts (in relation to Vehicle Excise Duty);
- The Highway Code (which whilst not statutory may be taken into account by a court hearing a road traffic case).

The 'user' of a vehicle is defined as 'the driver, or person whose servant or agent the driver is'.[53] Observation of the operation of an inspection exercise of vehicles at the roadside is revealing. There can be up to half a dozen inspection agencies in attendance:

- the police, the only authority with power to stop vehicles for inspection;
- The Vehicle Inspectorate, often with two officers, a traffic examiner looking at licences and tachograph charts, and a vehicle examiner checking the condition of the vehicles;
- Customs and Excise, checking for the use of already rebated fuel (red diesel);
- an officer of the Local Authority's Trading Standards branch may be present to weigh vehicles;
- The Driver and Vehicle Licensing Authority may also be checking VED (road tax) discs and driving licences although usually they will delegate that function to the police;
- Officers from the Inland Revenue and Department of Social Security (DSS) may also be present to check on tax paid by casual drivers and benefit frauds.

There are 'fleet inspection and roadside check' procedures for the issue of prohibitions of use of unfit vehicles (PG9s) by police and vehicle examiners (with only the latter being empowered to issue delayed prohibitions) and for prohibitions of use of overloaded vehicles.[54] Such prohibitions are recorded on an operator's licence and may be taken into account by a Traffic Commissioner in a section 17 hearing (see above[55]). The Construction and Use Regulations also provide similar powers for the police to inspect private passenger vehicles. In addition to all the above every road vehicle[56] is subject to its annual 'MOT' test and the Vehicle Certification Agency (VCA) is responsible for the initial certification of new vehicles and components, largely under EU standards.

The Railway Inspectorate became an arm of the Health and Safety Executive after rail privatization. It is responsible for monitoring and enforcing safety and for accident investigation. It accepts a 'safety case' in which Railtrack sets out the operational standards and practices under which it intends to operate to ensure an adequate level of safety. Railtrack thus has a responsibility to accept the safety cases of the TOCs and other users of its infrastructure although these are copied to the Inspectorate who can intervene if they are not satisfied. The Inspectorate also approves new or altered works (eg, signalling) and rolling stock, can take enforcement action and can prosecute for breaches of the Health and Safety at Work Act.

DETR's Aviation Directorate advises ministers on safety although, as described earlier, the CAA is the responsible body. The International Regime for aviation safety stems from the Chicago Convention of 1944 and is formulated by the ICAO which sets minimum standards. There is a proposal for a European Aviation Safety Authority (EASA) to harmonize standards within the EU. DETR's Air Accidents Investigation Branch investigates accidents in the UK and participates in investigations overseas of accidents involving UK registered or manufactured aircraft. The Health and Safety Executive (HSE) has some interest in air transport that focuses on ground activities – refuelling, aircraft towing and baggage handling.

The DETR's Maritime and Coastguard Agency primarily exercises the regulatory and enforcement responsibility for safety and to counter pollution. It coordinates responses to incidents at sea and on the coast involving danger to life or the environment, and its Chief Inspector for Marine Accidents reports directly to the Secretary of State at the DETR. The international regime for safety at sea is developed by the IMO as described earlier. Statutory General Lighthouse Authorities[57] oversee fixed navigational infrastructures. Inshore, responsibility for navigation on most of the canals, rivers and lakes of the UK is in the hands of either the British Waterways Board (BWB) or the Environment Agency (EA). The HSE is unique in the transport field in combining policy development, standard setting, enforcement and investigation and in regulating safety in a wide range of sectors in addition to rail transport where, apart from delegating responsibility for the railway's safety case to Railtrack, it has overall responsibility.

In March 1998, the House of Commons Select Committee on the Environment Transport and Regional Affairs recommended the establishment of a new independent authority for transport safety. Such authorities already exist in some countries notably the USA, New Zealand, Canada, Sweden, the Netherlands and Finland. A DETR 'Consultation Document on Transport Safety'[58] points out that if the recommendation were to be followed consideration could be given to making the HSE the home of a multi-modal transport safety authority. The HSE regulates safety for almost every other commercial activity and widening its remit would avoid the administrative cost of setting up a new body although it would not be without cost itself.

The Select Committee also addressed the thorny question of accident inquiries and legal proceedings. It pointed out that inquiries are necessary to establish what went wrong and how to avoid a recurrence but that if there are indications of a criminal offence investigations may lead to prosecution or there may be a private prosecution. Where death occurs there will be a coroner's inquest and questions of compensation may lead to civil proceedings. The interaction between all the above creates tensions. There is a need to avoid prejudice in criminal proceedings that are sub judice from the findings of parallel public investigations and this can delay an inquiry to the point where recollections are dimmed. Questions of corporate responsibility were also raised after the *Herald of Free*

Enterprise disaster and the Southall railway accident. Following a report by the Law Commission in 1996, the Home Office is looking at the questions of how prosecutions for the offence of corporate manslaughter might be made and how to avoid undue delays on prosecution decisions by the Crown Prosecution Service and the HSE in view of public interest and safety considerations. Were the Select Committee's recommendation for a transport safety authority to be followed, it is interesting to speculate if it would become the precursor for a multi-modal transport regulator with truly multi-modal transport user consultative committees (TUCCs)!

NINE

Communication and Information Management

Nearly 30 per cent of households in the UK have a personal computer (PC) and over half of these are connected to the Internet. Televisions, fibre optic and ISDN telephone lines, satellite communications and mobile phones are all deserting yesterday's analogue communication technology and embracing the new digitized information and communication technology (ICT).

Our global economy is being transformed by the realization that knowledge and information are now significant factors of production and can form an asset base in their own right.[1] Furthermore, knowledge as a product can be resold many times! The emergence of such virtual economies within and alongside such conventional economic activities as the creation and sale of products and services (such as transport) is bound to have profound effects on the future of the passenger transport industry. The process has been vividly described by Charles Leadbeater[2] as a 'weightless economy' that is creating an 'information rich' class of person. The obvious danger from the passenger transport industry's point of view is that by embracing ICT too enthusiastically it could exclude the 'information poor', many of whom have been its most loyal customers. For example, if train-operating companies attempt to imitate airlines by making pre-booking cheaper, more attractive and easier by phone or Internet and penalizing 'walk on' passengers with relatively higher fares, then they can be contributing to the very social exclusion that the New Deal White Paper is trying to tackle! Simply attempting to accelerate the rate of penetration of ICT, whilst desirable, will never be a complete solution; the industry will always have to retain residual conventional means of access.

There is a further threat to the industry in the growth of ICT. The boundaries between the telephone, TV and PC's visual display units (VDUs) are blurring. More people at work, or increasingly at home, will be connected to workstations from which they can shop, video conference and obtain the sort of detailed travel or academic information for which they would only ten years ago have had to visit a travel agent, library or other specialized retail outlet such as a bookshop. Entertainment can be delivered to their screens but increasingly on payment of a fee related to the specific produce (film, sports event or music) rather than as a simple TV licence. (It is after all only a generation ago that a licence was required to receive radio transmissions but the ubiquitous battery powered portable radio made licence enforcement impossible!). Increasingly we are living in a 'pay per' society that is bound to emphasize the problems of social exclusion but, even more, it is certain to reduce the need to travel for employment, leisure or business.[3] Ironically, the New Deal White Paper espouses the need to replace mobility by accessibility but the evidence of the last decade is that passenger miles are increasing. However, within that increase the nature of travel is changing with the number of leisure related journeys now outstripping commuting, retail and education trips.

Perhaps the most significant recent development has been the explosive growth of home working with more people finding it possible to complete the work they are employed to do at home using e-mail, phones and faxes. The savings for employers in terms of office space, heating and lighting and for employees in terms of commuting time gained are both significant, although the downside of isolation from colleagues and loss of opportunity for social interaction at work are only just beginning to be understood. Nor is it just professionals who are exploiting home working as a perhaps superficially more family friendly working environment. Call centres, the fastest growing employment sector in the UK, now with over 2 million operatives employed, are discovering that the workstation of VDU, on-line database and phone can simply and cheaply be installed in an employee's home. The late-night call to a motor breakdown service might well be taken in someone's living room and the stranded motorist would not know this nor care provided the rescue was effected efficiently and promptly.

MANAGEMENT INFORMATION SYSTEMS

Reference has already been made in Chapter 5 to the extent to which information is now routinely captured from such diverse sources as electronic ticket machines, employees' 'smartcard' based passes, global information systems, vehicle monitoring modules (soon to include a new generation of electronic tachographs) and a host of other reporting systems. In some cases this has had the unfortunate effect of creating a data overload that can actually inhibit management performance, but with the kinds of software available today, which can filter data to identify only that relevant to the manager or operative needing it and produce 'exception reports', this is now less of a problem. From a human resource management perspective, however, it has considerable relevance to the transport industry. There is now less and less need to employ staff at supervisory or middle management levels who previously monitored and reported on performance as this function is now automatically carried out by ICT systems. The result has been the demise of posts such as bus inspectors, which as well as having a function now largely redundant as described above, nevertheless also had a considerable customer care dimension. Such a post contributed significantly to passengers' perceptions of personal security, had an ambassadorial role for the operator by their high profile as an information source and discouraged revenue fraud.

There is little doubt that possession of high-integrity data can be of enormous benefit to both the supplier and procurer of transport. In the early 1980s the data obtained by the National Bus Company as a result of their Market Analysis Project, one of the last great market-analysis projects to be carried out by mainly manual as opposed to electronic data-capture methods, proved of enormous value. This was the case in 1986, before their privatization, when their subsidiary companies were required to identify and register commercial services and tender for unregistered non-commercial services so much so that one local authority transport officer, addressing the Association of Transport Coordinating Officers, was prompted to remark 'He who holds the data runs the buses'!

INFORMATION TECHNOLOGY AND LOGISTICS

There can be little doubt that the freight logistics industry has been in the vanguard of the applications of ICT to provide transport solutions. That industry's concept of the supply chain embracing every process from the sourcing of raw materials or components to the warehousing, distribution and retailing of the final product has been fundamental to its success. The passenger transport parallel of the seamless journey from home via appropriate mode or modes of transport to destination has hardly progressed since Neil Kinnock published his 'Citizen's Network' paper in 1996.[4] When a tin of beans is purchased at a supermarket and the bar code scanned, the information captured is relayed back down the supply chain and initiates the procurement by the manufacturer of more beans and tins in order to replenish that sale on the retailer's shelves. By comparison, it is extremely unlikely today that a report by the station master at a seaside resort of crowds of holidaymakers arriving earlier than anticipated (perhaps because of bad weather) and in numbers far in excess of the capacity of scheduled services would trigger the provision of an additional train or rolling stock. Alternatively, closed-circuit television pictures of long queues at bus stops would not automatically result in an operator duplicating a service bus.

Passenger transport operators will doubtless plead that lead times between order and 'stock outs' (the freight equivalent of insufficient supply of capacity or, put more simply, overcrowding) are longer in the freight transport industry. Nor can there be any doubt that freight logisticians were little better than their passenger cousins were at forecasting and meeting demand before they embraced ICT solutions. Today their entire supply chain from manufacture to packaging, trunking, warehousing, distribution and retailing is driven by ICT. Their old systems, known as Materials Requirement Planning,[5] based on forecasting techniques (not unlike the discredited highway authorities' 'predict and provide' models except in time scale!) are now superseded by Manufacturing Resource Planning.[6] This technique is based on consumer demand 'pulling' the product up the supply chain (rather than it being 'pushed' down by forecasts) and uses ICT to integrate the chain's commercial, production and financial aspects. Obviously, without the enormously increased capacity and sophistication of modern hardware, software and communications freight logistics could not have achieved these impressive gains in productivity, efficiency and effectiveness.

Logistics is a military concept and always has embraced passengers (in this case troops) as well as supplies and ammunition but the civilian concept of passenger logistics is relatively new. Yet there are lessons that freight logistics can teach the passenger transport industry as well as the reverse. For example, the logistics concept of just-in-time delivery that can dramatically reduce stock holdings depends on sophisticated vehicle scheduling, a technique at which road, rail and air passenger operators are all extremely competent.

The parallels between passenger and freight logistics are striking and very little appreciated (see Figure 9.1). What else, for example, is an airport departure lounge other than a human warehouse and in what ways do airline reservation systems and boarding cards that passengers receive in exchange for their tickets differ from control systems for freight inventory? Is demand responsive transport in the form of a taxi or dial-a-bus that much different from just-in-time distribution systems or the triggering of production from a bar code reading? Data from electronic ticketing machines are not used in so different a way than that from supermarket checkouts. Freight and passenger transport is making increasing use of global positioning systems. Both dial-a-buses operating on semi-fixed routes with a 'many passengers to few destinations' remit and dial-a-rides offering a totally demand responsive many-to-many' service can benefit from real-time scheduling where a 'dispatcher' has access to global positioning data. The Wiltshire Wigglybus is a dial-a-ride service where ICT is used to advise the driver of impending passengers via an LCD in-cab screen. The haulier or rail freight operator both face similar crew rostering and vehicle scheduling problems to bus or train operator.

A significant difference between the two branches of logistics is that in the UK (although less so in continental Europe) freight logistics companies are increasingly 'retail led'. In other words, retailers specify their requirements usually based on supplying huge regional distribution hubs and transport providers tender to meet these requirements. Whilst there are clear similarities with tendering and franchising the passenger transport industry is still very product led even to the extent that privatized operators are sometimes prepared to raise fares to suppress demand. The concept that the freight logistics industry has embraced of efficient consumer response (ECR) – which translates to integrated passenger transport – is still in many places only an aspiration in a government White Paper. One way of achieving ECR is to look at the entire supply chain in a holistic manner. Thus, some logisticians maintain that there is no reason why the distribution channels by which a product last reached a store

Freight logistics	Passenger logistics
Supply chain	seamless journey
Warehouses	waiting rooms, departure lounges
Out of stock	overcrowding
Retail loyalty cards	airmiles
Retail led distribution	tendering/franchising
Barcodes	computerized reservation systems (CRS)
Hub and spoke	airports
In-cab VDU	taxi cabmaster
Information capture	smart cards, electronic ticket machines
Consignment tracking (AVL)	vehicle positioning (AVL)
Tachograph analysis	tachograph analysis
Routing applications	timetable software
Material Requirement Planning (MRP I) (push factors)	network planning, predict and provide
Manufacturing Resource Planning (MRP II) (pull factors)	demand responsive transport, dial-a-ride
Just in time (JIT)	dial-a-bus
Distribution Requirement Planning (DRP)	Travelcards
	market analysis projects (MAP)
Efficient Consumer Response (ECR)	passenger monitoring (CCTV)
	coordination/integration
Service provision	scheduling; crew allocation, route planning

Figure 9.1 A comparison of passenger and freight logistics

should determine by which alternative channels its replenishment should arrive. Within the chain will be goods in transit that can be viewed as part of the distributor's inventory, warehouses and even slow moving stock at adjacent stores that can be repositioned. By using a technique known as Distribution Requirements Planning these variables can be manipulated to give the most efficient response to consumer demand. Here there are parallels with area-wide travelcards or bus rail inter-available tickets that allow a journey to be made by a variety of different routes and modes at different times.

Depot siting software, which suggests where best to build or acquire vehicle stabling points so as to minimize empty running and maximize revenue earning vehicle deployment, is widely available and used by both passenger and freight operators. For example, a well-known routine in Microsoft's Excel spreadsheet[7] can be employed to decide which depots should serve which retail outlets or equally which bus depots should deploy buses at various terminals to commence early services. Where a charter airline has aircraft deployed at airports abc at the end of the week and requires similar numbers at airports wxyz the following Monday, the programme can suggest how best to reposition these to minimize 'dead' mileage.

SUSTAINABLE TRANSPORT

Many passenger and freight movements are environmentally unsustainable. Sometimes vehicles take inordinately long routes and the use of vehicle routing software[8] can help operators to reduce unnecessary mileage. There is also real concern that in the name of consumer choice, especially the ability to buy 'out of season' produce, food is transported over enormous distances whilst local suppliers are sometimes left with unsold produce. The concept of 'food miles' has been suggested as a means of trying to measure the extent of this problem. Just-in-time distribution, which by definition relies on frequent topping up of stocks at the point of sale or manufacture to avoid costly warehousing, can also be seen as unsustainable, as can the hub-and-spoke distribution systems which require that a parcel from Huddersfield to Halifax will be sorted at a hub in the Midlands. However, there are many hub-and-spoke parallels in passenger transport, most notably at international airports. Out-of-town shopping centres generating enormous additional passenger miles mainly by private car are also less sustainable than town-centre shops where these are accessible by good public transport.

In recent years, there has been much debate about the sustainability of tourism as a passenger transport related activity.[9] In many cases, there are few or no benefits and even some costs to the host region or country.

Tourists can often remain segregated in their coaches and hotels and tour companies are adept at ensuring that they spend most of their money 'up front' before they leave and at repatriating what they spend abroad. In extreme cases, for example on cruise liners, they may even import food from home to ensure a UK menu for their tourists! The 'all inclusive' tour becomes, from the hosts' perspective, all exclusive. However, genuine 'green' tourism can take place within the range of local public transport, cycling and walking and where tourists are encouraged to stay in local homes and guest houses that invest in their local economy. Tourism is not only the fastest growing industry in the world, it is also expected to account for more jobs than any other industry by early in the next millennium and it is an industry almost wholly dependent on public passenger transport.

A similar debate surrounds the benefits and costs of tourism to rural areas. Issues such as footpath erosion, congestion, pollution and second or commuting homes inflating house prices beyond the reach of rural dwellers are cited. Central to the debate, of course, is the part played by both public and private passenger transport. Organizations like the Rural Development Commission (RDC) have viewed tourism from an economic regeneration perspective whilst the Countryside Commission (CoCo) and the Council for the Preservation of Rural England have historically taken an environmental and conservationist view. With the merger of the RDC and CoCo to form the Countryside Agency (CA) in April 1999, there is the prospect of a more holistic approach to rural transport services[10] that can recognize that the bus that takes trippers to the countryside can also carry rural dwellers to the town!

The first part of this chapter has taken an overview of the relevance of freight logistics to passenger logistics, the vital role that ICT plays in both and how each might become more sustainable by exploiting the other's best practice. An obvious example, already discussed at length in Chapter 2, is the provision of hybrid freight/passenger services. The remainder of this chapter will look at specific ICT applications already identified but not fully explained.

REAL-TIME INFORMATION

Research referred to in Chapter 8 positions reliability high if not top of passengers' travel determinants.[11] Unreliability creates uncertainty. Real-time information (RTI) systems, whilst not delivering reliability per se, can at least inform passenger choice and remove the uncertainty that is such a barrier to acceptance of public transport as an attractive and viable alternative.

Passengers require real-time information both before commencing a journey and during the journey itself. Before the journey, it may be delivered to them in a variety of ways:

- Some operators and local authorities make their RTI data available via the Internet. Examples include Northwest Trains and Ipswich Guided Bus (Route 66 – see Figure 9.2 and 9.3).
- Some teletext pages accessed on BBC or ITV broadcasts contain RTI; Manchester Airport transmits a mimic of its arrivals VDU monitor.
- Some telephone enquiry bureaux (TEBx) are able to supply RTI (eg, the National Rail TEBx).
- A few local authorities have installed touch screen interactive VDUs in public places like libraries and post offices and in kiosks at transport interchanges, usually delivering journey planner advice based on published timetables but now more frequently also having a RTI facility. Hotels and retail outlets may also subscribe to such RTI initiatives for the benefit of their customers.

Departures from STOCKPORT

Time	Dest	Exp
2209	Manchester Piccadilly	12 late
2214	Manchester Piccadilly	On Time
2237	Deansgate	1 late
2239	Wigan Wallgate	On Time
2244	Manchester Oxford Road	On Time
2249	Macclesfield	On Time

Figure 9.2   North West Train's Web site contains real-time information

During the journey, monitors, dot matrix and VDU displays, and public announcements both on the vehicle and at stations, bus stops and interchanges can all deliver RTI and in doing so increase passengers' feelings of security. Delays and missed connections are always frustrating but good RTI can help to mitigate their negative effects.

The key to efficient RTI is automatic vehicle location (AVL). Today this can be achieved very reliably by modern global positioning systems (GPS). Because these rely on satellite technology, there is no land-based infrastructure to install and so they are an ideal system to apply where an area-wide RTI is being developed. However, the on-vehicle computing and radio equipment that broadcasts the position of vehicles to the control centre is relatively costly. Land-based systems involve costly road or trackside beacons that have to be linked by cable to the control centre, but the tags or transponders that are fitted to the vehicles to identify them to the control are less expensive. They are ideal where RTI is being installed along a corridor, perhaps a quality partnership route, as the incremental cost of equipping additional vehicles is small although the set up costs are heavy. In some cases, as with Air Traffic Control and Railtrack's signalling systems,[12] the information is already in place and it is only necessary to devise the interfacing software

it's more than just a web site...

BT Laboratories presents real-time travel information for the Superoute 66 buses. The route runs from Ipswich Rail Station to Martlesham Heath, on the edge of the town. The service is run by Suffolk County Council and Eastern Counties.

The following formats are available:

Java

The first version of the site uses Java to display a stylised map of the route with current bus positions and a simulation of a bus stop sign.

The recommended configuration for viewing this page is a Pentium PC with Internet Explorer 3.0, Netscape Navigator 3.0, or above. Due to the vagaries of Java implementations other browsers may experience problems.

Please note that some firewall and proxy server configurations may prevent you from viewing this page in real time.

Key to both pages:
(bus positions and directions)

↓ actual or ↑
   predicted

↓ timetabled ↑

HTML

The second version of the site shows the same information as the Java page, but as a list of the next bus arrivals.

This page is suitable for all machines and browsers, and may be customised to show your own personal selection of stops.

The Superoute 66 Live demonstration is about more than just a web site - find out more how new technology can deliver public transport information!

The bus location equipment and bus stop information systems were supplied by Advanced Communications and Information Systems (ACIS).

Ipswich

Disclaimer. Real time information will be displayed only when it is deemed sufficient data of acceptable quality is available. Otherwise, the bus positions and arrival times shown will be generated from the timetable (dated 11 January 1998). British Telecommunications plc. makes no guarantees as to the availability of the service, or the accuracy and reliability of the information it provides. This service is entirely experimental and content is subject to update or change without notice.

Figure 9.3   Real-time information, Route 66

between this and the RTI system. On part of the Railtrack network, Train Positioning Tracking by Satellite (TPTS) is being developed (see Chapter 8 – safety and signalling) to accommodate high speed trains by a moving block transmission based signalling (TBS) system. On other more rural parts, like the Central Wales and Kyle of Lockalsh lines, radio-based block signalling is used. Both of these could well meld into RTI systems.

Triangulation positioning by beacons is a land-based system that can cope with area-wide AVL requirements. There are also a few systems that rely on measuring a vehicle's progress by means of its odometer along an allocated route. These can trigger displays and announcements on vehicles and in a few cases transmit the location into a wider RTI programme via radio links or even to a chain of transponders at stops that relay the information along the route ahead of the vehicle.[13] Most corridor RTI systems simply rely on positioning beacons en route with transponder tags on vehicles.

RTI systems can be linked to more than just displays and announcements. There can be displays and data capture systems at operator and procurers' premises for the purpose of monitoring compliance or even controlling services. Information from engine management systems (EMSs) and electronic ticket machines can be relayed to the operator in real time, enabling problems such as breakdowns and overcrowding to be anticipated and addressed.

The Transport Research Laboratory[14] in 1998 published a 'review of telematics relevant to public transport' in which over ten UK and five continental European systems were described. The largest of these, the London Transport Countdown system and the high profile Hampshire ROMANSE[15] project, both rely on beacon technology. The latter system is supplemented by odometer readings to enable it to link into the SCOOT traffic management system to provide bus priority at signalled intersections. By contrast, Centrex (WMPTE) considers GPS systems to be more robust and reliable.

Apart from public address systems and pre-journey information on the Internet, teletext or TEBx, RTI systems rely on what have come to be known as variable message signs. Some of these are electromagnetic rotating blocks perhaps just containing three or four short messages such as 'car park full' whilst others may be sophisticated banks of signs such as departure indicators at mainline stations. Yet others are fully variable text message signs based on dot matrix, liquid crystal display (LCD) or laser technology. These can convey information alongside motorways and trunk roads about congestion and road works ahead, weather or other road conditions and are of use to both public and private transport.

Traffic speed monitoring and display systems[16] can transmit both to roadside VMSs and also to in-vehicle navigation systems, enabling drivers to be diverted or in the case of more sophisticated systems to be advised of possible alternative routes. They obviously have most use for operators of long-distance coach services since local services are route bound by their registrations.

Vehicle and traffic telematics is a fast growing industry. Its applications spread beyond what has been described above. It can be an enforcement tool and can be deployed in any dynamic road-pricing scheme that is not just an area-based paper licence system. Issues of data protection and personal privacy have yet to be resolved.[17]

PASSENGER DATA

In theory, operators should be in full possession of data describing the journeys passengers make on their vehicles. In practice this is not always so. In the first place, their ticketing system may not be sufficiently sophisticated to record details such as the type of ticket, origin and actual destination (sometimes simply deduced from the fare paid and taking no account of fraudulent overriding) or even route travelled. This is less so today with so many bus operators using electronic ticket machines (ETMs) and TOCs using similar SPORTIS and APTIS machines. None of these, however, records the use of other operator's inter-available tickets, area-wide travelcards or season tickets (unless the driver or conductor manually does so). Nor are non-paying or overriding passengers accounted for. By comparison, airline and ferry ticketing can act as a complete passenger census because of strict boarding controls.

A complete passenger census would be expensive to conduct although some local transport authorities attempt this from time as a 'snapshot' exercise. More usually, passenger data are obtained by employing random sampling techniques where a representative sample of vehicles is boarded by data collectors and patronage figures are projected from the samples. The sampling frame has to be carefully chosen to avoid bias and distortion. For example, a sample taken on a route passing a lot of old people's homes or schools could not be considered universally representative nor could data collected on Sunday afternoons (although they are representative of Sunday afternoon traffic!). However, statisticians have devised sampling techniques that deliver results within high confidence limits.[18]

Reliable passenger data can be very important to both operators and transport authorities,[19] especially where they form the basis of disbursement of revenue for concessionary fares[20] or travel card schemes. The operator needs to have confidence in the data collection systems used by the transport authority or its agent.

Data downloaded from electronic ticket machines are very robust and capable of being analyzed in many dimensions. They are an invaluable management information tool, especially because of their currency with virtually immediate summaries of the day's patronage and revenue being available. Software capable of exception reporting and of identifying discrepancies between sample figures and reported fares is widely available. If necessary, operators can ask for routes to be resurveyed or sample frames adjusted. There is no doubt, however, that the introduction of smartcard technology will further enhance the reliability of passenger data (see below).

It is the often irrational fear of revenue loss by inaccurate apportionment of pools that has led to the resistance by some operators to participate in ticket inter-availability or area-wide travelcards schemes. Whilst there are also justifiable concerns that some such schemes may fall foul of competition legislation, it is regrettable when other operators rather than the private car are too often perceived as 'the competitor'.

Revenue protection rather than, as was claimed, passenger certainty was clearly the motive behind the creation of a Routing Guide by the Association of Train Operating Companies' (ATOC) in 1995. This purported to identify in respect of any two possible origin and destination stations on the UK rail network a permitted route or routes connecting these. The old BRB rules permitted passengers to travel by any 'reasonable' route but of course all ticket revenue then accrued to a single operator. The Central Rail Users Consultative Committee reported that their members had a 'lingering perception that the guide had been considered necessary only from the TOC's point of view in connection with revenue apportionment rather than from the passengers' point of view in identifying the previous 'any reasonable' route'.[21] The guide is extremely complex, riddled with anomalies and difficult to use, not only by passengers who are bemused by it but also by the TOCs' employees who largely ignore it! In the view of some RUCCs, it can be a disincentive to travel and an erosion of previous network benefits. There is also anecdotal evidence that TOCs are themselves circumventing the guide by issuing more and more tickets via a specified route.[22]

The practice of 'data mining', whereby a supplier of a product or a service attempts to garner as much information as possible about its customers so as to target them with relevant promotions, is not nearly as prevalent in the passenger transport industry as in retailing. Nevertheless, there are parallels with supermarket loyalty cards. Airlines have frequent flyer promotions and Virgin Trains, as might be expected with its parentage, has a loyalty card scheme. ATOC itself has a valuable database of holders of railcards such as those bought by young persons and senior citizens. Transport procurers such as London Regional Transport, PTEs and some 'shire' counties will also have a database of concessionary fare pass and travelcard holders. In some cases, as with Greater Manchester Ticketing Ltd, the promotion of non-statutory travelcards and day tickets has been deliberately handed over to operator consortia to avoid revenue apportionment disputes and complications arising out of competition legislation. Ironically, some of the larger operators in such schemes actually undercut such network tickets with their own day and season tickets priced below them – a practice not far removed from predatory pricing where they are the dominant operator.

As already stated, the more widespread adoption of smartcard ticketing will go some way to addressing operators' suspicions that area-wide inter-availability fails to maximize revenue; two developments anticipated in the New Deal White paper are likely to do the same. These are:

- a national concessionary fare scheme;
- compulsory participation in local authority devised schemes for area travelcards.

VEHICLE DRIVER AND STAFF COMMUNICATIONS

It is taken for granted that ships and aircraft are in radio contact with land. There is a rule in Railtrack's safety case requiring a train driver held at a signal to use the lineside phone to alert the signalman to his position, but in reality most drivers now have in-cab communications, either radio or mobile phone.

Before bus deregulation, most large fleets belonging to PTEs, large municipalities or National Bus Company subsidiaries operating mainly in urban areas had developed radio communication.[23] Some of the local authority and PTE owned systems such as Manchester's 'Metro Comms' survived commercially, selling their services to deregulated newcomers who wished to buy into the system to keep in touch with their vehicles. Others were simply transferred to the dominant operator's depot.

Voice is not the only possible medium on which to base vehicle-to-operator communication channels. The freight logistics industry has developed in-cab faxes and display screens linked to mobile phone channels that enable them to generate and transmit delivery notes for drivers to use to obtain proof of delivery, and this technology is now spilling over into passenger logistics. Calls to the Wiltshire Community Transport's demand responsive dial-a-bus 'Wigglybus' appear on a screen in view of the driver and are accepted by pressing a button on the console. The Coventry taxi fleet is equipped with similar screens using the 'cab master' software. The screens show bookings and drivers can scroll through what are outstanding and accept in a similar manner. With digital phones now superseding the older analogue cell phones there is clear potential for data as well as voice transmission, reception, display and acceptance that is increasingly being exploited.

It is also quite likely today that the vehicle itself is programmed to transmit a variety of data without the intervention of the driver, for example:

- automatic vehicle location;
- engine management systems data;
- electronic ticket machine status and issues;
- traffic priority signals;
- information downloaded from the new generation of electronic tachographs.

THE INFORMED TRAVELLER

Perhaps the most ambitious aspiration in the New Deal White Paper on Integrated Transport (1998) is the intention contained in section 3.74 to seek agreement between operators and local authorities on the format of information and interfaces between different journey planner systems to provide both local and national coverage. The expressed aim is no less than to have a public transport information system systematically extended across the country by 2000.

There are plenty of precedents. The London Transport ROUTES (Rail Omnibus Underground Enquiry System) has not just timetable-based journey planning capabilities but also provides real-time information. Cumbria County Council's Journey Planner now allows enquiries from Cumbria for journeys not only within the county but also to main destinations outside, but would preclude a request for a journey between two points both of which were out of county. Its software contains sophisticated algorithms that factor in walking time where interchanges have to be made between two services that are not co-terminal, for example, by walking from Penrith Rail Station to Penrith Bus Station (5 minutes are allowed).

Railtrack's Internet site allows browsers to specify rail journeys by origin, destination, time and day and will suggest suitable trains and connections. Amusingly it often suggests routes that the routing guide would disallow! Southern Vectis, who helped to design the Cumbria Planner, are devising a journey planner for the whole of Great Britain based on their GB Bus Timetable. Virgin Trains Web-based 'www.thetrainline.co.uk' site gives train times and fares for all TOCs and encourages online booking (see Figure 9.3).

The intention behind ATOC's Bus Links project is to develop a national bus rail timetable containing all the links that have been implemented within the project, including the new Virgin Trains/Stagecoach links. Most of the above are based on different software packages that would probably not run with each other, although actually amalgamating the databases they contain may be less difficult.

SelectYour**Train&Ticket**

The trains that match your plans are shown in the table below.

Valid tickets together with the total price are listed on the left. If you want information on a ticket, just click on its name. If you want to see a breakdown of the price, just click on it.

Train times are listed opposite. Whenever a train is available it is shown as ⊂.

If you want to see a more detailed breakdown of a journey, just click on its departure time.

Please pick the one you'd like to book, by following these steps:
- click on one ⊂ to select your outward train
- continue along and choose a return train by clicking another ⊂
- click on the Go button at the beginning of the row.

MANCHESTER to CAMBRIDGE

	Return Ticket	Total Price (GBP)	Outward Wed 8 Sep 1999					Return Fri 10 Sep 1999				
			Depart 0956	1012	1030	1035	1112	Depart 1004	1027	1034	1105	1127
			Arrive 1353	1421	1434	1506	1523	Arrive 1402	1430	1436	1502	1530
			Changes 2	2	2	3	2	Changes 2	2	1	2	2
Go	Apex	41.00			⊂	⊂			⊂			⊂
Go	Super Advance	46.50			⊂	⊂			⊂			⊂
Go	Saver	50.40	⊂	⊂			⊂			⊂		
Go	Saver	61.00	⊂	⊂	⊂	⊂	⊂		⊂	⊂		⊂
Go	Standard Day	82.20	⊂	⊂			⊂			⊂		
Go	Standard Open	156.00	⊂	⊂	⊂	⊂	⊂		⊂	⊂		⊂
Go	First Open	209.00	⊂	⊂	⊂	⊂	⊂		⊂	⊂		⊂

Return to 'Your Journey Requirements'

In association with

Detailed Journey Breakdown

Outward Journey: Wed 8 Sep 1999

Station:	Arr	Dep	Travel by	Service Provider
MANCHESTER VICTORIA		0956	Train	NORTH WESTERN TRAINS
WAKEFIELD WESTGATE	1109	1118	Train	GREAT NORTH EASTERN RAILWAY
STEVENAGE	1303	1315	Train	WEST ANGLIA GREAT NORTHERN
CAMBRIDGE	1353			

Please use the Back button on your browser to return to the previous page.

In association with

Figure 9.4 Printout from 'thetrainline'

Journey Solutions is a joint initiative between the Confederation of Passenger Transport (CPT) and ATOC to promote inter-modal travel in the UK. RailLinks 'Journey Solutions' logo is to be used as a common branding to identify the initiative, which is currently studying towns with populations over 10,000 that are not already connected by rail, to develop the best inter-modal solutions for each town.

At present, local authorities have a statutory power to publish local passenger information but they are under no obligation to do so although in practice 80 per cent do. The government is considering making this a statutory duty.[24] They are also proposing that operators should have an obligation to supply route registration details to the Traffic Commissioners that they are required to copy to the local transport authority concerned. They would be in a standard electronic format that would facilitate both the authorities' publication and input into their proposed national public-transport information system.

The ultimate intention, the New Deal White Paper says, is for passengers to be able to access the system through one enquiry point although it also refers to access through teletext and the Internet. ATOC's National Rail Enquiry Bureau, which is on a local 0845 number,[25] had an inauspicious start. The Rail Regulator levied fines because when it was monitored as a result of a flood of complaints to RUCCs it was found not to be performing up to agreed charter standards in terms of response times and times engaged tones were heard. Those aspects of the performance of the National rail TEBx are now broadly satisfactory but there is concern in some quarters about the quality and reliability of the information given, especially when services are disrupted by delays or even planned engineering work. A problem identified by the RUCCs is that calls to the 0845 local number are routed to whichever call centre has the capacity to receive them so that the operator answering might not have the same local knowledge as the passenger making the enquiry. The reverse, of course, may be true where the operator has good knowledge of the destination. Equally, neither may be the case! This shortcoming can be remedied by additional operator training and better software that can be interrogated in different ways. A further criticism voiced is that operators are call-centre staff and not 'rail persons' with inbred railway knowledge as they were when BRB ran local TEBxs. Mention has been made of the phenomenal growth of call centres, and ATOCs TEBxs are all operated on franchises won by centres operated by mainly non-rail undertakings such as BT Connections in Business or Serco, but Southwest Trains also share the TEBx load with these two. Staff turnover in call centres is also high as the stress levels can be wearing but there is also evidence that the growth has slowed and may even be reversed as people begin to prefer interrogating timetable and fare databases themselves via the Internet.[26] At the time of writing, there is abundant evidence that the largest operators are striving to build up timetable and journey planning systems that can eventually be 'joined up' under the government's informed traveller initiative. Arriva, the third largest bus operator in the UK, now has a Web site that will ultimately provide timetables of all their services by building on their plans for electronic submission of service registrations and amendments.[27]

OTHER ICT APPLICATIONS

The brochure of the transport consultant MVA offers software applications for bus registration, scheduling and timetabling, and ETM data analysis. It is a typical consultant's menu. Others, such as Omnibus systems, offer software compatible with their timetabling algorithms for preparing driver allocations and duty rosters (see Chapter 2). The transport trade press such as *Modern Railways* and *Bus and Coach Weekly* advertise timetabling packages for train operating companies[28] – see, for example, Figures 9.4(i–v) – and computer reservation systems for coach operators.[29]

Specialized software has been written for almost all types of passenger transport operation. Reference has already been made to the taxi booking acceptance applications used in Coventry. The community transport

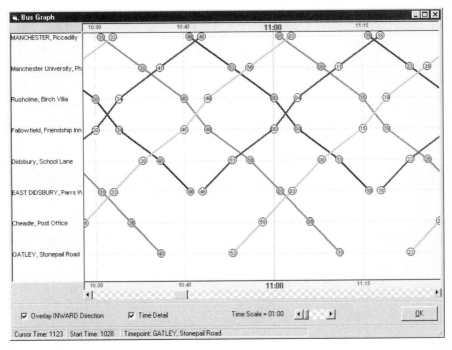

Figure 9.5(i)   Print outs from scheduling and allocation software – timetable graphs
Source: Omnibus Systems

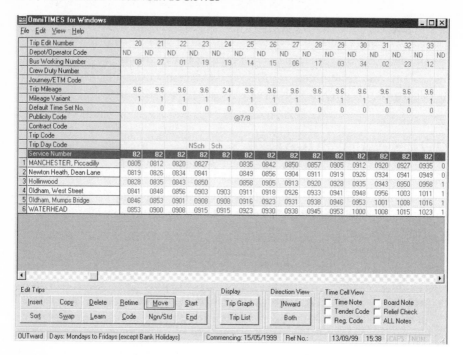

Figure 9.5(ii)   Working timetable
Source: Omnibus Systems

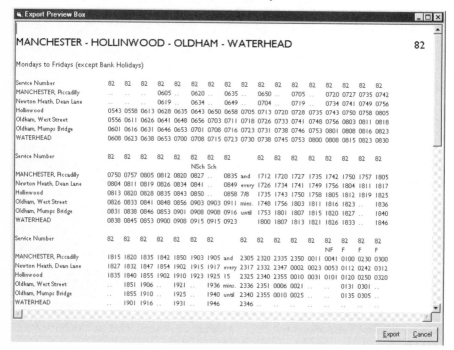

Figure 9.5(iii)   Software generated public timetable
Source: Omnibus Systems

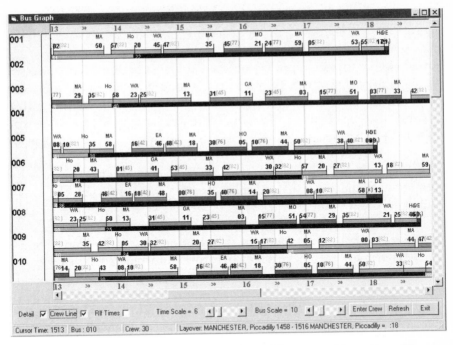

Figure 9.5(iv) Crew duties generated from working timetable
Source: Omnibus Systems

Figure 9.5(v) Duty roster
Source: Omnibus Systems

sector has a particular difficulty devising the most efficient way of meeting the 'many (requests) to many (destinations)' for its dial-a-ride services. Even the dial-a-bus type many (requests) to few (destinations) are not all simple to accommodate on the day (see the references above to the Wiltshire Wigglybus). In the past, the procedure has been to require 24-hours notice of bookings, but with today's software it is now often possible to accept bookings for which there is capacity even after departure of the minibus, with the software 'tweaking' the journey plan to accommodate them.

ATOC are developing an automatic teller machine (ATM) of the kind commonly found today in multiplex cinemas that can match the credit card details of pre-booked tickets with a card swipe. The machine issues the tickets thus reducing the congestion at ticket office windows caused by passengers collecting tickets at their station before they travel. Some widely available software, such as Microsoft Autoroute 2000 that runs on a standard PC with a Windows 98 operating system, can be of great value to operators even if it is only used to measure route mileage for the purpose of claims for a fuel duty debate (see, for example, Figure 9.5).

Finally, suites of software such as Microsoft Office or Lotus Smartsuite that combine databases, word processing, spreadsheets and financial packages are nowadays almost an essential requirement for all but the smallest businesses, including most passenger transport operators. Larger operators will probably have their software installed on a central server with their staff able to access this via an internal intranet. The intranet itself could well contain the company's Web site, which could be accessed from outside via the Internet. Such arrangements allow internal and external communication by e-mail that is cheaper than fax and as quick if not quicker.

More than most industries, passenger transport has embraced the Internet. It is, as discussed above, an excellent medium for travel enquiries, selling tickets and confirming reservations. Suppliers can be included by means of hyperlinks so that users 'browsing the net' can see where connections can be made (see, for example, Figure 9.6) or added value packages can be purchased perhaps in the form of accommodation or admission to events. For anyone with a lively interest in the passenger transport industry there is a plethora of sites, many of which contain hyperlinks to one another and further related sites. Travel bargains can often be picked up almost right up to the advertised departure of the coach, train or plane. However, operators must beware of concentrating too much on these new media to the exclusion of conventional and 'walk on and pay' passengers, who are often either the undecided, who therefore cannot book ahead, or the 'information poor', who have neither the necessary hardware/software or competence. They should none the less still be seen as valued customers.

England, United Kingdom
Oldham to Manchester
106.8 miles, 2 hours, 21 minutes

09:00 0.0 Mile	1	Depart Oldham on A671 (South) For 0.3 mi
09:01 0.3 Mile		Bear RIGHT (South-West) onto A62 For 1.9 mi
09:05 2.2 Mile		At junction, turn RIGHT (West) onto M66 For 8.4 mi
09:13 10.7 Mile		At M66 J2, turn LEFT (West) onto A58 For 0.7 mi Towards Bolton
09:14 11.4 Mile		Continue (West) on A56 For 0.3 mi Towards Limefield
09:15 11.7 Mile	2	At Bury, return South on A56 For 0.3 mi
09:16 11.9 Mile		Continue (East) on A58 For 0.7 mi Towards Rochdale
09:18 12.7 Mile		At M66 J2, turn RIGHT (South) onto M66 For 2.9 mi Towards Manchester
09:21 15.6 Mile		At M62 J18/M66 J4, turn RIGHT (West) onto M62 For 4.2 mi Towards Manchester
09:26 19.7 Mile		At M61 J1, continue (West) on M61 For 19.5 mi Towards Bolton
09:43 39.2 Mile		At M61 J9/M65 J2, turn LEFT (West) onto A6 For 4.6 mi
09:49 43.8 Mile	3	At Preston, stay on A6 For 0.8 mi
09:51 44.6 Mile		Bear LEFT (West) onto A59 For 8.9 mi
10:04 53.6 Mile		Continue (West) on A565 For 9.4 mi Towards Southport
10:20 63.0 Mile		Turn RIGHT (North-West) onto Local road(s) For 0.4 mi Towards Southport
10:22 63.4 Mile	4	At Southport, return South-East on Local road(s) For 0.4 mi
10:24 63.9 Mile		Turn LEFT (North-East) onto A565 For 0.9 mi
10:27 64.8 Mile		Turn RIGHT (South-East) onto A570 For 17.1 mi Towards Skelmersdale
10:51 81.9 Mile	5	At St Helens, return North on A570 For 0.2 mi Towards Skelmersdale
10:52 82.1 Mile		Turn RIGHT (East) onto A580 For 5.5 mi Towards Trafford Park
10:58 87.6 Mile		At M6 J23, bear RIGHT (South-East) onto M6 For 4.4 mi Towards Newcastle-under-Lyme
11:03 92.0 Mile		At M6 J21a/M62 J10, bear LEFT (East) onto M62 For 9.1 mi Towards Trafford Park
11:11 101.1 Mile		At M62 J12/M63 J1, bear RIGHT (East) onto M602 For 4.1 mi Towards Manchester
11:17 105.2 Mile		Bear LEFT (East) onto A57 For 0.6 mi
11:18 105.8 Mile		Turn LEFT (North) onto A5066 For 1.1 mi Towards Manchester
11:21 106.8 Mile	6	Arrive Manchester

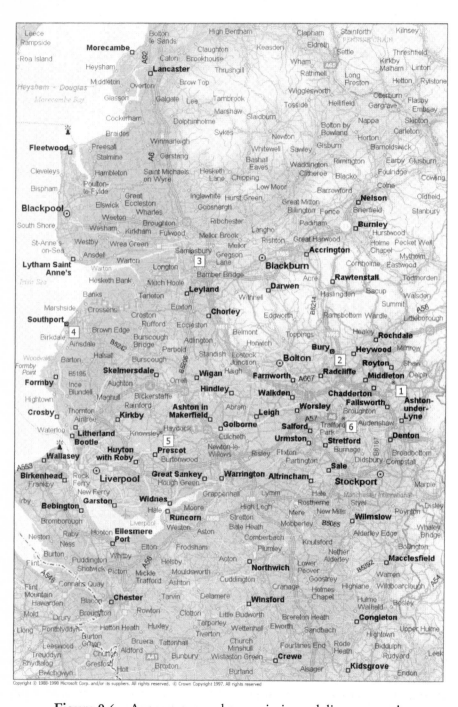

Figure 9.6 Autoroute used to optimize a delivery round

SMARTCARDS

Perhaps the most exciting development in information technology in the last decade for the passenger transport industry has been the invention of the Smartcard. Smartcards are similar to the ordinary plastic credit and debit cards but they also incorporate an embedded microchip that can be read (like the magnetic stripe on credit cards) either in a machine by means of the contacts on the surface of the card or more usefully by means of a signal to an aerial that is also embedded. These 'contactless' smartcards have the greatest potential for the transport industry. The chips can store far more information about the cardholder than the magnetic stripe and can, again most usefully, be written to as well as read. It is thus possible to use them as a holder's account on which the value of cash credited to that account can be written and from which the cost of transactions can be debited. They have been aptly described as 'electronic purses' or 'stored value tickets' (SVTs).[28] They are similar to but 'smarter' than a BT phone card!

The different 'fields' within the card's database can be used to hold not only a monetary value but also information about the holder such as concessionary travel entitlement. Not all the fields need be used in connection with travel; the card could double as a Mondex[29] card to permit small purchases like a newspaper or taxi fare from participating outlets. Even more exciting in view of the New Deal's commitment to road pricing schemes is the possibility of using the technology to abstract congestion charges from smartcards displayed in windscreens.

Not every transport operator or authority is entirely enthusiastic about the possibilities of Smartcards. Some point out that because the technology decrements, with the card having been charged with a cash value, losing its value with travel being purchased, passengers will still experience some 'distress' when paying a fare, even though they have already parted with the cash 'up front'. This could be a positive disincentive to car dependency if the motorist sees the card lose value when in congestion! However, this 'distress' need not be programmed to apply in every case; the card could be used to purchase a travelcard or season ticket entitlement, the only difference being that the entitlement would be stored on the card, allowing unlimited travel in the time frame bought, rather than printed on a ticket needing to be shown (or read). Concessionary fare entitlement could also be written on to a Smartcard as could railcard discounts, staff privilege travel and indeed any other holder attribute. A particular benefit is the ability to buy a number of trips that are not time constrained. The concept is similar to a carnet or multi-journey clippercard like the Dutch Strippenkarten, valid on bus, train and taxi anywhere in Holland. With fewer people employed on a simple five-day week pattern, this feature is likely to be highly valued by those 'commuters' who sometimes travel off-peak or only two or three times per week and for whom the traditional season ticket offers no savings. Off-peak discounts can be given simply by decrementing different fares at different times.

The largest single SVT experiment in the UK is London Regional Transport's (LRT) Prestige project. This will use contactless smartcards that will open barriers for fare-paid passengers. It will be an integrated revenue collection and protection system that Transys has been tasked to deliver by 2002 under a private finance initiative (PFI). Whilst initially covering bus and underground, it has potential to expand to cover the TOCs running commuter services into London and indeed one TOC, London Tilbury and Southend, is already installing barriers in connection with its own revenue protection system and these will be Prestige compatible. Other potential uses are linked promotions (eg, a student card), frequent user discounts and road pricing.

The geographical availability of a smartcard is limited only by the scope of the scheme, not by artificial travelcard boundaries. Thus, the holder of a Prestige card may one day be able to use this to travel within Greater Manchester if it uses the same protocol as any future GMPTE scheme. It is this transferability that interests the DETR, which has set up a smartcard forum to bring together suppliers, operators and transport authorities developing systems. There is also an integrated smartcard foundation (ISCO) that has appointed consultants MVA to develop a UK transport smartcard standard.

LRT were motivated to commission Prestige by a number of factors:

- Their existing fare collection equipment is life-expired and its limited capabilities constrain ticketing initiatives.
- Ticket office queues are unacceptably long and one-person operator bus boarding times are slow.
- Fare evasion was estimated at £43 million per annum.
- There is a lack of high quality management information.

There was a perception that Prestige would run in parallel with Countdown to provide a more secure passenger environment and indeed a possibility of redeploying existing revenue protection, control and monitoring staff of LRT on to more customer care related activities. There is also a realization of passengers' apprehension of losing a SVT on which a high value is stored, but Prestige is reassuring in that once a lost or stolen smartcard is reported it can be placed on a 'hot list' and becomes invalid. The software is also able to deliver a report showing how much has been spent on the card so that a new card to the value of the unspent lost card can be issued.

CONCLUSIONS

Public passenger transport is at a crossroads. The New Deal offers some solutions, with the possibility of revenues from road pricing and work-place parking being 'hypothecated' and used to fund public transport. However, this requires legislation and the 'stick' of charges alone is unlikely to effect a significant modal shift. If it did, public transport could have insufficient capacity to cope. Immediate improvements are urgent and perhaps these can only come if transport authorities are pre-pared and allowed to borrow by mortgaging future revenue streams from road pricing and congestion charging. If this opportunity is lost, the stick will still be wielded but the beatings will be self-inflicted and the pain will come from congestion, gridlock and pollution. The Holy Grail of the 1968 Transport Act may finally be in sight and we could see 'a properly coordinated and integrated public passenger transport system to meet the needs of the area' at last.

Postscript – the Transport Bill

The Bill was introduced in the House of Commons after this book was written. It is in four parts:

I.   Air traffic control.
II.   Local transport.
III. Road user and workplace parking charges.
IV.   Railways.

There is a Part V with supplementary provisions, amendments and repeals. Part IV follows closely the Railways Bill 1993 that ran out of parliamentary time.

Safety

Nothing in the Bill gives effect to the suggestion by the Select Committee on Transport of the creation of an overarching Transport Safety Authority. However, in both Part I (air traffic control) and Part IV (railways) it makes a clear separation between economic and safety regulation.

In the case of air traffic, it leaves the CAA with responsibility only for economic regulation of air traffic, including the allocation of airspace by creating a licensing regime for all air traffic control services (beyond airport approaches) with the Secretary of State as the licensing authority. A separate National Air Traffic Services (NATS) licensed in this way is to be provided by means of a public–private partnership between the

Secretary of State for Transport, NATS employees and a strategic partner from the private sector.

The Bill is silent on safety issues although it also makes the same clear separation (as with civil aviation) between economic regulation (by the Rail Regulator), safety regulation by the Railway Inspectorate (HMI Railways) of the Health and Safety Executive, and consumer protection (including fares) by the Strategic Rail Authority. It does not, as was widely predicted after the Paddington rail crash, strip Railtrack of its safety function of agreeing and accepting operators' safety cases.

PART I – AIR TRAFFIC CONTROL

This part of the Bill is the only part to apply to all of the UK. It will separate National Air Traffic Services (NATS) from the Civil Aviation Authority (CAA) as described above.

PART II – LOCAL TRANSPORT

Local transport plans

Part II is applicable in England and Wales and relates to local transport plans and bus strategies. Every Local Transport Authority (LTA) (ie, county councils, unitary authorities and PTEs) will be required to prepare and publish local transport plans containing their bus strategies to replace their current transport policies and programmes (TPPs) and public transport plans (PTPs). These LTPs are to be prepared for a maximum of five years (rather than the present 'rolling' annual TPP 'bids') although they can be reviewed annually. The plans must have regard to the needs of the elderly and disabled.

Bus quality partnerships

LTAs, jointly or alone, will be able as now to enter into quality partnerships (QPs) with operators of regular local services, under which they set standards and provide facilities including, where they have not already been determined, information facilities but excluding frequencies or times, for reasons of possible conflict with competition law. They will also require operators to observe these standards as a legally enforceable condition of using the facilities. Consultation is required with bus operators, users, the Traffic Commissioner and, if the QP uses trunk roads, the Secretary of State or National Assembly for Wales.

Bus quality contracts

Where LTAs are satisfied that what is effectively an area-wide franchising scheme similar to London Regional Transport is the only way to implement their bus strategies, they may enter into quality contracts (QCs) in default of QPs. Tendering processes for awarding such exclusive rights are prescribed. LTAs must obtain best value for money (BVM) and their duty to cooperate with LEAs and Social Services is suspended in QC areas, as too are any requirements as to local service registration. Thus, the LTA becomes the enforcing authority. There will be a 21-month lead in time to allow operators to redeploy their resources and adjust services, a five-year maximum tendering horizon, and provision for short duration contracts to be made in emergencies.

Integrated bus ticketing

LTAs will be able to require bus operators to agree to accept each other's tickets or to participate in an integrated ticketing system to which 'add on' rail travel can be negotiated. They (LTAs) will have a duty to determine what local bus information is needed and to ensure it is made available, if necessary recovering their reasonable costs from operators who do not provide this voluntarily.

Traffic regulation conditions

They may ask the Traffic Commissioner to make traffic regulation conditions not just to avoid congestion but also to limit or reduce noise and pollution.

Concessionary bus travel

All elderly people will have a right to at least half fare bus travel at defined off-peak times. Their eligibility will be established by the issue of passes at a cost of not more than £5 per annum. These concessionary fares can later be extended by order of the Secretary of State or the National Assembly for Wales to include other classes of person (eg, young persons) or of travel (rail, permit minibus or taxi). The basis for reimbursing operators for their compulsory participation will be equivalent to the current rules in the Transport Act 1985 under which they are no better or worse off having regard to new revenue from any additional generated traffic.

Tendering

New best value for money (BVM) criteria for tendering will replace those in the Transport Act 1985, and the current requirement for LTAs not to inhibit competition will be replaced by a new duty to have regard to the interests of the public and operators. This will make it easier to supplement existing commercial services by tender.

Fuel duty rebate

Fuel duty rebate (FDR) will be phased out and replaced by a more flexible grant to reflect the environmental effects of different types of vehicles and fuels. The present sanction that Traffic Commissioners can, but rarely do, impose on erring operators of registered local services (comprising 20 per cent claw back of FDR) is temporarily replaced by a discretionary 1 per cent to 20 per cent claw back and will eventually be replaced by fines reflecting the operator's fleet size.

Financial

Grants to LTAs such as the current infrastructure grant in the Transport Act 1968, transport supplementary grants, metropolitan railways grants and rural bus grants will be subsumed into a more permanent statutory grant structure.

PART III – ROAD USER AND WORKPLACE PARKING CHARGES

Road user charges

LTAs alone or jointly may make road user charging schemes for the purposes of fulfilling their LTPs. So too may the Secretary of State (SS) or the National Assembly for Wales (NAW) in relation to trunk roads, motorways and bridges, and tunnels, but only where requested to do so by LTAs to complement their schemes. All schemes have to be approved by the SS or the NAW who have made it clear that LTAs must first demonstrate substantial improvements to their public transport networks.

Workplace parking charges

LTAs alone or jointly (but not the SS or the NAW) will be able to license the parking of a maximum number of vehicles at workplaces within a workplace parking scheme's area and charge a levy based on the number of 'licensed units'. Schemes must support their LTPs. They can cover employees, employers, suppliers and business customers' vehicles but not those of retail customers, thus misapplying the schemes to out-of-town retail developments although there is an option retained to apply these later by subsidiary legislation.

Provisions are made about content, prior consultation, public inquiry, enforcement, appeal and adjudication relating to both road user and workplace parking charging schemes.

A Schedule applying to both road user and work place parking charges provides for periods of up to ten years' hypothecation of revenues to public transport. This will be additional revenue and not replace existing central funding. The SS has powers to extend the ten-year horizon.

PART IV – RAILWAYS

Strategic Rail Authority

The de facto creation of a shadow SRA from the old BRB (Chairman Sir Alistaire Morton) and the Office of the Passenger Franchising Director (Mike Grant) is given statutory effect. It will be funded and given objectives, instructions and guidance by the SS but will have its own borrowing limits and will be able to set up wholly owned subsidiary companies, an essential power if it is to be able to act in extremis as an operator of last resort. The Bill is silent about any consumer representation on the SRA.

The SRA is established for three purposes:

- to promote the use of the network for passengers and freight;
- to secure its development;
- to contribute to the development of an integrated transport system.

It is expected to aim to:

- protect user interests;
- achieve sustainable development;
- promote efficiency and economy in the provision of services;
- promote network benefits;
- enable providers to plan with a reasonable degree of assurance and impose minimum restrictions consistent with the performance of its functions.

In so doing, it must consult with the Rail Regulator and have regard to:

- safety;
- the protection of the environment;
- the interests of disabled passenger.

Some of its above powers and duties are broadly inherited from the Regulator's duties under the Railways Act 1993, especially the SRA's consumer protection remit. References to 'users' now include passengers, freight customers, ROSCOs, TOCs and railway facility providers.

The SRA will be able to make grants to secure the development of railway services and assets including:

- freight facility grants (which however fall within the remit of the Scottish Ministers in Scotland);
- grants to local authorities and PTEs including, in the case of PTEs, section 20 (Transport Act 1968) grants to support PTE rail services and the metropolitan railways grant intended to compensate PTEs for their rail franchisees' track access charges. This means that in any tri-partite franchise agreement involving a TOC, PTE and SRA the latter would be both party and fund holder!
- grants to fund the integration of heavy rail and LRT systems;
- grants to enhance rail infrastructure where this is uncommercial but socially desirable.

Where there are no acceptable private bidders for a terminated franchise, the SRA (see above) becomes the de facto operator of last resort. Complicated re-tendering provisions apply, however, and closure procedures are not excluded. The SRA may designate services that ought to be franchised thus facilitating their current franchise replacement initiative.

The SRA also inherits the Disabled Persons' Protection Policy (DPPP), the British Transport Police (BTP) and any residual rights, duties, liabilities and staff of the BRB. It will be able to promote or oppose Railways Bills and orders under the Transport and Works Act 1992.

Rail replacement services needed during temporary disruptions to rail services can be secured by tender by the SRA.

Consumer protection

The consumer protection matters that the SRA inherits from the Rail Regulator (RR) include the following and the SRA becomes responsible with the RR for any licence provisions relating to these:

- telephone enquiries;
- through ticketing;
- security;
- the interests of disabled passengers;

- penalty fares;
- insurance;
- conditions relating to fares (except penalty fares) and to liaison with RUCCs.

User Consultative Committees

The central and regional Rail User Consultative Committees (C/RUCCs) are renamed Rail Passenger Council/Committees (RPCs) and the SRA becomes their sponsor. The multi-modal London Regional Passenger Committee (LRPC), though, will come under the new London mayor and the Greater London Authority (GLA), and the Scottish and Welsh Committees may be devolved to their regional assemblies.

RPCs' functions are extended to include review of open access services not provided under a franchise. They can create sub-committees, remunerate members and collect whatever information they require. Their new wider duty is now to keep under review matters affecting the interest of the public in relation to the passenger railway and to cooperate with other bodies representing the interests of users of public passenger transport services.

Closure procedures

RUCC powers in the Railways Act 1993 relating to closures and the holding of Public Hearings to establish hardship are amended. The Regulator's function is transferred to the Secretary of State thus removing an appellate stage in the proceedings. The Franchise Director as an officer of the SRA will still initiate closure proceedings but the simplified provisions for minor closures are expanded to include track doing no more than serve an already served station or depot.

The procedures akin to the Transport Act 1962 relating to closures of experimental, non-franchised or excluded services are consolidated.

The Rail Regulator

The Regulator is required to facilitate the SRA's strategies rather than facilitating privatization, and when promoting competition must do so for the benefit of users. He or she gets new powers of direction, including the ability to require the provision (at market values) of new facilities, and may impose unlimited fines for contravention of franchise agreements and licence conditions. The Regulator can also make, approve, amend or revoke access agreements including those relating to facilities proposed or under construction.

Passenger Transport Executives

PTEs may state their desired Passenger Service Requirements (PSRs) to the SRA but the SRA must not implement them without a direction from the SS if:

- this would prevent or seriously hinder them (the SRA) from complying with the OIG received from the SS or Scottish Ministers;
- or if this would have an adverse effect on the provision of any railway passenger or goods service;
- or if this would increase the amounts that the SRA would have to pay to the franchise holder.

The Bill concludes with miscellaneous provisions relating to:

- devolution;
- the joint exercise of some of their powers by the RR and the Director General of the OFT;
- pensions;
- Schedules relating to and expanding specific clauses and covering, *inter alia*, consequential amendments and revocations.

There is little in the Bill not already trailed in the 1998 White Paper 'A New Deal for Transport', or the daughter documents 'From Workhorse to Thoroughbred' (buses), 'Breaking the Log Jam' (road user pricing) or 'New Deal for Railways', nor is there much in these papers requiring primary legislation that the Bill has not addressed.

CONCLUSIONS

However, the government's most recent reactions to the sentiments expressed in these documents in terms of their expressed national transport policies is worryingly ambivalent. It is becoming clear that the priority promised for public transport is not yet being delivered to the extent indicated and that targets for traffic reduction are unlikely to be achieved. No doubt ministers will argue that any meaningful progress must be predicated on the necessary primary legislation, and that results will follow after the enactment of the enabling clauses in the Transport Bill. Be that as it may, some recent happenings give cause for concern, whilst others, however, may be viewed as mildly optimistic.

John Prescott MP, the Deputy Prime Minister (DPM) and Minister for the Environment, Transport and the Regions, has had to contend with a press largely hostile to his perceived anti-roads and pro-public-transport stance, and there has been speculation that his transport role has been deliberately downgraded by the appointment of Transport Minister Lord Gus McDonald as minister in 'day to day' charge of transport matters. The DPM refutes this, claiming to remain in overall control and to have secured an £80bn ten-year transport investment package (although this clearly includes both 'new' and 'old' moneys – such as Rural Bus Grants) which will 'provide the long-term stability to achieve large-scale capital investment' in transport, including investment in rail and public transport (Institute of Public Policy Research, London, January 2000). He has asked Gus McDonald to develop detailed plans in partnership with the public and private sectors and local government and report to him in the summer of 2000. In the same statement, he promised to make life easier for motorists by tackling congestion bottlenecks and increasing the number of by-passes to be constructed, a promise which sits uneasily with the tenor of the New Deal, but may reassure the motorized voter in what is now the run up to the next general election! In a similar vein is Lord McDonald's remark that government transport policy now favours 'widening car ownership to the socially excluded' and accepting that 'we cannot beat the car culture' (*TR&IN Times* Issue 18, TR&IN, Huddersfield, January 2000).

The abandonment of the fuel duty escalator promoted by the Royal Commission on Transport and the Environment, under which fuel duty has been increased year on year by 3 per cent above inflation, is yet another sop to voters, especially aimed at rural motorists who have less choice of alternative public transport, but it has been tempered by the Chancellor's announcement that any additional tax from fuel duty increases above inflation will be appropriated for transport schemes (always provided they are not road schemes!).

There appears to be a softening of the government's (and DPM's) perception that Light Rapid Transit schemes are 'gold plated' and unaffordable in comparison with their more 'silver plated' bus-based schemes which are perceived as being able to deliver similar benefits over wider areas at less cost. Following the opening by the Prime Minister of the extension of Manchester's Metrolink to Salford Quays, the government has asked GMPTE to discuss using the special additional funding from the fuel duty fund, which can now be made available to authorities bidding to pilot new road charging schemes, specifically to help them to first of all undertake major public transport improvements. This approach has now been endorsed by a £250m grant to the GMPTE for the Metrolink extensions in the March 2000 budget, the largest grant to any LRT scheme outside London. It will enable the network to be completed as a single contract rather than piecemeal and aligns well with the provisions in the Transport Bill both requiring that Local Transport Authorities demonstrate improvements to their transport infrastructure before levying motorists and that the SRA facilitate the dual use of heavy and light rail.

There has been disappointment at the report by the Commission for Integrated Transport which accepts that overall traffic reduction targets as envisaged in the Road Traffic Reduction and Road Traffic Reduction (Targets) Acts 1997/8 are unachievable in the context of the UK's fast-growing economy and that these should be replaced by more realistic individual area targets aimed primarily at combating local congestion.

It is too early to guess whether the SRA's ambitious franchise replacement programme will allow the 'investment, investment, investment' which its Chairman wants, or whether the DETR's clear preference for bus Quality partnerships, and their lack of enthusiasm for wholesale bus re-regulation in the shape of Quality Contracts, will produce sufficient changes in modal splits to significantly combat the capacity constraints on the UK's transport network which are producing ever greater congestion and sclerosis.

On a more upbeat note, however, there can be little doubt that the introduction of the tighter discipline of Local Transport Plans and the emergence of Regional Transport Strategies is profoundly affecting the way in which local government now thinks about transport. 'Predict and Provide' policies are giving way to 'Manage and Prevent' strategies.

The 20th century was the century of the car, will we now move away from a culture of mobility dependence, or will the next millennium be no different?

References

CHAPTER 1

1 Scottish Office (1996) 'Rural Transport Action Guide'.
2 Nathaniel Lichfield and Partners for the Greater Manchester Public Transport Executive in 1984.
3 TAS of Preston.
4 Department of the Environment, Transport and the Regions (DETR) (1998) 'Rural Bus Service Grants'.
5 Transport Act 1985 s 88.
6 Confederation of Passenger Transport 'Facts 98'.
7 eg, Manchester Minibuses.
8 Education Act 1996 s 56.
9 DETR (1993) 'PPG13'.
10 Buchanon, C (1963) 'Traffic in towns'.
11 DETR (1998a) 'New Deal for Transport'.
12 Apart from road space, the retail motor industry occupies considerable land areas with showrooms and workshops.
13 DETR (1998).
14 Cleary, J and Hillman, M (1992), in *Travel Sickness*, ed Roberts, Lawrence and Wishart, London.
15 DETR (1998a).
16 Greater London Council 'Abercrombie Report'.
17 Buchanon (1963).
18 Ernest Marples.
19 A remit extended to other local authorities by the Local Government Act 1972.

20 DETR (1998a).
21 Rural Development Commission, Salisbury.
22 British Railways Board (1963) 'Reshaping British Railways'.
23 The Rural, Uplands and Countryside Commission for Northwest England (1997) Annual Report.
24 Rural Development Commission (1997) Rural Services Survey, Salisbury.
25 Department of the Environment and the Ministry of Agriculture, Forestry and Fisheries (1995) 'Rural England'.
26 In 1999, the RDC merged with the Countryside Commission to become the Countryside Agency.
27 The Countryside Agency (1999) 'The State of the Countryside'.

CHAPTER 2

1 Transport Act 1985 s 63(10)(a).
2 County (or 'shire') councils when the Act was passed, but now including unitary authorities created since then.
3 Under a minibus permit – Transport Act 1985 s 19.
4 Transport Act 1968 s 20 and Railways Act 1993 s 32.
5 Goods Vehicle (Licensing of Operators) Act 1995.
6 Public Passenger Vehicles Act 1981 s 13.
7 With the exception of Royal Mail, the maximum number of vehicles that can be operated on a Restricted licence is two.
8 These fares are 'protected' by s 28 of the Railways Act 1993.
9 Sharing of taxis and taxi buses at separate fares, Transport Act 1985 ss 10–12.
10 This provision in the Public Passenger Vehicles Act 1981 section 1 and schedule 1 effectively distinguishes PSVs from taxis.
11 Rout v Swallow Hotels Ltd 1992.
12 Public Passenger Vehicles Act 1981 s 1.
13 A passenger carrying vehicle with nine or more passenger seats is defined as a bus – Road Vehicles (Construction and Use) Regulations 1984 SI 1188.
14 One of the exceptional circumstances under which a hackney carriage operator can carry at separate fares is when the holder of that licence obtains 'as of right' a special restricted PSV O-licence from the Traffic Commissioner enabling the additional use of the vehicle at separate fares as a taxi bus.
15 English, Welsh and Scottish Railways, the major UK rail freight operator, also has a licence from the rail regulator to provide passenger excursion trains on behalf of other operators.
16 Minibus Act 1977, now section 19 of the Transport Act 1985.

17 The Railways Act 1993 section 5 used the words 'based on' but as a result of a judicial review instigated in January 1996 by 'Save Our Railways' of the PSRs issued in respect of the first franchises, PSRs are now to be 'broadly similar' to the then current timetable.

18 Office of the Passenger Rail Franchise Director (OPRAF) (1996) 'Passenger Rail Industry Overview'.

19 PSV (Registration of Local Services)(Amendment) Regulations 1994.

20 Transport Act 1968, EC Driver's Hours Regulations 3820/85, Railway (Safety Critical Work) Regulations 1994, the Air Navigation Order 1989 and the EC Working Time Directive 1998.

21 Savage, C (1959) *An Economic History of Transport*, Hutchinson, London.

22 Turnpike Acts 1663 and 1773.

23 Public Passenger Vehicles Act 1981 s1.

24 Transport Act 1985 section 11, the so-called 'taxi bus' licence – see Chapters 3 and 8.

25 Refer to Chapter 1 – 'Understanding passengers'.

26 The Disability Discrimination Act 1965.

CHAPTER 3

1 The Bridgewater Canal, 1763, was quickly followed by a network of other canals connecting most parts of the country.

2 Savage, C (1959).

3 Although steam traction was used for freight trains on the earlier Stockton to Darlington Railway (1825), passenger trains on that line were still horse drawn.

4 Gladstone's Railways Act 1844 even provided for a daily statutory 'Parliamentary train' in each direction at a maximum prescribed fare of one penny per mile.

5 Despite a series of Railway and Canal Traffic Acts in 1854/73/88 attempting to protect canal traffic by controlling railway rates and charges through a powerful Railway Commission.

6 Local Government Act 1888.

7 Operated by a Mr Shillibeer.

8 Vanguard Motors. In 1912, the 'General' came under the control of the Underground under Albert Stanley (later Lord Ashfield).

9 Principally the Thomas Tilling Group, which agreed to concentrate further activities outside London, mainly in the Home Counties, East Anglia and the West Country.

10 Led in 1926 by the 'Chocolate Express' buses and followed by many others.

11 The London Passenger Transport Board.

12 Savage, C (1959).

13 Railways (Road Transport) Act 1927. The major groups were Tilling and British Automobile Traction Co. (BAT), National Omnibus and Traction Co. Ltd, Red and White and Scottish Motor Traction.

14 Town Police Clauses Acts (a mechanism loosely applicable to horse buses and quite inappropriate for controlling motor bus operation).

15 Proposed by the Royal Commission on Transport 1928 – the Thesiger Committee.

16 Other large operators and groups were National Omnibus and Traction Co., Red and White, Lancashire United Transport and Bartons of Nottingham.

17 In order to facilitate the development of its bus interests BET had formed a subsidiary, British Automobile Traction Co. Ltd (BAT), that had been a subsidiary of the Tilling Company until the split of 1942. The split was accompanied by a significant exchange of assets, whole companies, fleets and depots to rationalize the groups' operating areas with Tilling emerging as the predominantly rural operator.

18 Notably County Durham, where a number of acquisitions eventually became Durham District Services, which intended to become a pilot Area Board scheme.

19 Midland General, Nottinghamshire and Derby, Llanelli and District.

20 The Road Haulage Disposals Board was created in 1953 to privatize British Road Services by selling off its operating units.

21 The 1962 Act did however create a statutory railway closures procedure overseen by the Transport User Consultative Committees to report to the Secretary of State for Transport on any hardship that closures made for commercial reasons might cause.

22 Tyneside, Merseyside, Greater Manchester (SELNEC) and West Midlands, to which were added in 1969 Strathclyde and, after local government reorganization in 1972 that created Metropolitan Counties, South and West Yorkshire. The Transport (London) Act 1969 gave London Transport Executive (LTE) a similar relationship to Greater London Council.

23 There were exceptions. The residual BRB interests in the Halifax, Huddersfield, Todmorden and Sheffield municipal undertakings passed to the two Yorkshire PTEs and in Scotland the Scottish Transport Group acquired the National Bus Company's (NBC) buses north of the border.

24 The other 'Boards' were British Transport Docks, British Waterways, Scottish Transport Group (including McBraynes Ferry Services) and the National Freight Corporation.

25 Local Government Act 1972.

26 District councils can augment county council concessionary fares schemes.

27 Transport Act 1980. This also set up licence-free 'trial areas' to test the concept of deregulation.

28 Initially the PTE's bus operations were 'hived off' as separate companies operating at arms length from their owners, the PTAs, but eventually these too were privatized.

29 Complemented by its other half, London Underground.

30 The foregoing account of the history of road passenger transport draws heavily on a paper prepared by J Hulme for his students at Huddersfield University in 1993 entitled *The Development of Public Ownership and Control in Inland Transport*.

31 Dyos and Aldcroft (1969) *British Transport*, Pelican.

32 US Deregulation Act 1978.

33 Shaw, S (1993) *Transport Policy and Strategy*, Blackwell.

34 Even where the local authority is still the sole shareholder of a previous municipal undertaking, the 1985 Act requires the Board of Directors (including elected councillors) to operate at 'arms length' from the company.

35 Transport Act 1968 s 20, now Railways Act 1993 ss 33 and 34. After the imposition of track access charges following rail privatization in 1993, a Metropolitan Rail Grant was added to keep the section 20 funding at broadly its former level.

36 Railtrack's capital was converted to shares on the stock exchange despite the Railways Act 1993 never envisaging this and indeed never actually containing the word Railtrack!

37 Directive 1998/76.

38 Application by Southern Motorways to SE Traffic Commissioners opposed by Surrey County Council May 1986.

39 DETR (1998a).

40 DETR (1999) 'A New Deal for Buses – from Workhorse to Thoroughbred'.

41 DETR (1998b) 'Building Partnerships for Prosperity'.

42 Local Government (Planning and Land) Act 1980.

43 Wistrich, E (1983) *The Politics of Transport*, Longman, London.

44 SACTRA's study of 1998 illustrated that additional roads simply generated more traffic rather than displacing congestion on to them, but, more importantly, that the reverse is true and road-calming measures can actually reduce overall traffic levels.

45 Local Government (Planning and Land) Act 1980.

46 DETR (1998a).

47 Part II of UDPs equates to the old local plans whilst Part I equates to more strategic structure plans.

48 Local Government and Rating Act 1997.

49 DETR (1998a).

CHAPTER 4

1 NBC's Market Analysis Project – MAP.
2 Tyson (1992), GMPTE.
3 The Service Subsidy Agreements (Tendering Regulations) 1985.
4 Directive 92/50.
5 Over 400,000 ECUs over the life of the tender.
6 Hibbs, J (1985) *Bus and Coach Management*, Chapman Hall.
7 Glaister, S (1986) Deregulation and Competition, *Journal of Transport Economics and Policy*, May.
8 Fawcett, P (1989) *Minibus Services*, Croners.
9 *Logistics Management*, Croners, London. Loose-leaf, updated.
10 CIPFA (1983) 'Passenger Vehicle Costs'.
11 *Operational Costing for Transport Management*, Croners, London. Loose-leaf, updated.
12 Doganis, R (1991) *Flying off course*, Harper.
13 Transport Act 1980.
14 The Service Subsidy Agreements and Tendering Regulations 1985.
15 Despite this, a well-publicized experiment in South Manchester has shown impressive traffic generation by using buses with advertised lower fares although in this case the more expensive buses were also run by the same operator.
16 The Penalty Fares Rules 1997 made by the Rail Regulator to replace similar earlier legislation applicable to BRB.
17 The Contracts (Unfair Terms) Act 1977.
18 Office of the Rail Regulator (ORR) (1997) 'Accurate and Impartial Retailing'.
19 www.rail.co.uk.
20 www.thetrainline.co.uk.
21 DETR (1998a).
22 C/RUCCs.
23 ORR (1997).
24 By comparison, in the travel trade the Monopolies and Mergers Commission (MMC) was currently investigating certain travel agents owned by tour companies to ensure that package holidays were sold impartially.
25 EU (1995) Green Paper.
26 House of Commons (1998) Third Report, Vol 1, HMSO.
27 DETR (1998a).
28 Sir Alistaire Morton.
29 Excluding LRT and Northern Ireland Transport, neither of which was deregulated.
30 Fair Trading Act 1973, Restrictive Trade Practices Act 1979, Competition Act 1980 and Transport Act 1985.

31 A provision already substantially contained in section 67 of the Railways Act 1993.
32 CRUCC Annual Report 1997 p 30.
33 'Quality Contracts' as envisaged in the buses 'daughter' document – DETR (1999) 'Workhorse to Thoroughbred'.
34 The so-called OFTRANS model.
35 To be addressed by the creation of a shadow SRA.
36 Civil Aviation Act 1971.
37 Created by the London Passenger Transport Act 1984.
38 Transport Act 1962.
39 Fawcett, P (1989).
40 Transport Act 1962.
41 Section 38, Competition Act 1999.
42 Competition Act 1999.
43 Section 67.
44 National Federation of Bus Users, PO Box 320, Portsmouth PO5 3SD 01705 814493.
45 DETR (1999), s 10.10.

CHAPTER 5

1 Virgin Trains and ASLEF addressed this training need in an innovative way by the creation of 'millennium trains', a jointly owned driver training operation.
2 Inside Organisations, 1985; The Empty Raincoat, 1993.
3 57 per cent of males over the age of 55 were 'economically inactive' in 1993!
4 The Department for Education and Employment's 'New Deal' for unemployed youths and long term unemployed adults is intended to address this trend.
5 Hutton, W (1995) The State We're In, Mackays, Chatham.
6 Inside Organisations; The Empty Raincoat.
7 For example, Bus and Coach Week, Professional Transport Management, Local Transport Today, Modern Railways and Flight.
8 The best known of these, the National Institute of Industrial Psychology's 'Seven Point Plan' lists physique, attainment, intelligence, aptitudes, interests, disposition and circumstances.
9 Employment Rights Act 1996.
10 This body subsumed bus and coach training as well as automotive training for the motor retail industry.
11 Levels 3 (supervisory management), 4 (middle management) and 5 (senior management).
12 Such as managing people, resources, information and finances.

13 Previously the Business and Technician Education Council B/TEC.
14 For example, the Institute of Road Transport Engineers and the Institute of Transport Administration.
15 Roughly equivalent to NVQ levels 3,4 and 5 or ONC/A level, HNC and degree.
16 Articles 117/8 of the Treaty of Rome.
17 Employment Relations Act 1999; Human Rights Act 1998.
18 The Employment Relations Act 1999.
19 Minimum Wage Act 1998.
20 Directive 93/104.
21 Sex Discrimination Acts 1975 and 1986.
22 Race Relations Act 1976.
23 Disability Discrimination Act 1995.
24 Except in Northern Ireland.
25 The Employment Relations Act 1999.
26 Employment Rights (Dispute Resolutions) Act 1998.
27 It is still two years for claims for redundancy payments.
28 The Employment Relations Act 1999.
29 In 1971 there were 12 million trade unionists including 5 million in closed shops. Today these figures are 9 million and 2 million respectively although trade union membership is beginning to show signs of increased penetration.

CHAPTER 6

1 With the hypothetical exception of balloons, gliders and yachts!
2 DETR (1998a), (1999).
3 25 per cent of M62 traffic is road freight and over 50 per cent of 'passenger' traffic can be accounted for by company cars!
4 TBCS does not rely on line side signals, which partition routes into 'blocks' that are then only allowed to be occupied by one train at a time, but uses global positioning systems that allow trains to occupy a moving block or 'envelope' but not enter the preceding moving block.
5 That is 200 Concorde passengers and 300 Airbus passengers.
6 On the north trans-Pennine route between Manchester and Leeds the replacement of an hourly service by a train every 20 minutes increased patronage from 2,000 to 6,000 journeys per day.
7 Fawcett, P (1989). See also Chapter 4 for generation factors.
8 Railtrack (1999) 'Network Management Statement'.
9 As in Sheffield in 1991–92.
10 For example, the catamaran hulled vessels on Irish Sea crossings.
11 Especially to Paris and Brussels.

12 PCV (passenger carrying vehicle) class D+E, irrespective of whether the vehicle is or is not a PSV (passenger service vehicle used for hire or reward).

13 Section 82.

14 Section 8.

15 Shaw, S (1993).

16 Section 106 of the Planning Act 1990.

17 Birmingham International Airport (1996) 'Vision 2005, Public Transport Plan'.

18 New Rails for London, *Modern Railways*, Spring 1997; Airport Rail Links, *Rail Professional*, Edition 8, 1997; *Making Tracks*, Heathrow Airport Transport Policy; GB Rail Timetable, Summer 1999, p 47, Railtrack; Britain's Coach Network, Winter Timetable 1997, National Express Group; Great Britain Bus Timetable, Southern Vectis, 1996.

19 Transport Act 1985 s 10.

20 White, P (1996) *The Experience of the UK Bus and Coach Industries – Privatisation and deregulation of transport*, Hertford College, Oxford.

21 Public Passenger Vehicles Act 1981 s 1.

22 Transport Act 1985 s13.

23 Whitelegg, J et al (1993) *High Speed Trains*, Leading Edge.

24 Secretary of State for Environment, Transport and the Regions.

25 Airport access strategies. *Local Transport Today*, 3 December 1998.

CHAPTER 7

1 A New Approach to Appraisal (NATA) at section 4.195, DETR 1998.

2 DETR (1998) section 1.22.

3 Kinnock, N (1996) *A Citizen's Network*, European Union.

4 DETR (1993).

5 DETR (1993).

6 DETR (1998).

7 Parallel Welsh and Scottish White Papers preceding devolution were similar.

8 PPG11 – Regional Planning.

9 A comparison by GMPTE of child concessionary fares in two comparable towns, Bolton and Bury, in 1990 showed a threefold difference in Bury (where there was parental choice) compared to Bolton (which had not then implemented this policy).

10 Royal Commission on Transport and the Environment (1994), OUP.

11 Adams (1981) *Transport Planning – vision and practice*, Routledge.

12 Over 50 per cent in the Middle East; the USA is no longer self-sufficient.
13 Mainly in Canada. Processing requires energy and water and the volume of waste produced is greater than that of the shale used!
14 Sources geographically well distributed.
15 White, N A (1977) quoted in Adams (1981).
16 Hoyle and Knowles (1992) *Farrington in Modern Transport Geography*, Belhaven.
17 EC Directive 85/337.
18 Road Traffic Reduction Act 1997; Road Traffic Reduction (Targets) Act 1998.
19 NW RDA Draft Regional Transport Strategy Task Group, 21 June 1999.
20 Buchanon, C (1963).
21 Local Government Planning and Land Act 1980 and Planning and Compensation Act 1991.
22 Royal Commission on Transport and the Environment.
23 'Transport, The Way Forward', 1996.
24 DETR (1998a).
25 See DETR (1993).
26 Tanner, J (1981).

CHAPTER 8

1 Glaister, S (1985) Competition on Urban Bus Routes, *Journal of Transport Economics*, January.
2 The same person (Hertzberg) is said to have reflected when breakfasting on his bacon and eggs that the hen was involved but the pig was committed!
3 DTP (1989), Cmmd 820, HMSO, London.
4 Because the driver faces criminal proceedings any earlier inquiry could not proceed because of the rule of sub judice.
5 *Croner's Coach and Bus Drivers' Handbook* (1993), 3rd edn, Croner Publications, Kingston upon Thames.
6 Road Traffic Act 1930 – see Chapter 3 for a full discussion.
7 Railways Act 1993 s 4. It is anticipated that the proposed Strategic Rail Authority (SRA) will take over the Regulator's consumer protection role.
8 It has been argued (Hibbs (1968) *History of British Bus Services*) that by conducting 'fares hearings' they over enthusiastically interpreted their remit in the Transport Act 1930 to 'ensure that fares were not unreasonable'.
9 Transport Act 1985 s 16.

10 Usually the first Certificate of Fitness (COF) was for seven years with subsequent COFs issued on full re-examination for a six and then a period of one or more years. At the time of PSV licences there were no annual MOT tests for buses.

11 The Transport Act 1982, which followed the report in 1980 of the Armitage Committee on Lorries, People and the Environment.

12 EC Directive 25/98 replaces the current CPC exam composed of objective test questions with an exam that comprises both these and a written case study.

13 Gubbins, E (1996) *Managing Transport Operations*, 2nd edn.

14 Road Vehicles (Construction and Use Regulations) 1986 SI 1078.

15 PPV Act 1981 s 1.

16 The Motor Vehicles (Driving Licences) Regulations 1996 SI 2824.

17 Road Vehicles (Construction and Use Regulations) 1986.

18 Rout v Swallow Hotels Ltd 1992.

19 Rout v Swallow Hotels Ltd 1992.

20 Town Police Clauses Act 1847; Local Government (Miscellaneous Provisions) Act 1976; Metropolitan Public Carriage Act 1869; Private Hire Vehicles (London) Act 1998 – the last named most recently licensed London 'minicabs'.

21 Transport Act 1985 ss 10–12.

22 Only London Waterloo, Heathrow Airport and Blackpool Promenade (the last named as a result of a petition of 10 per cent of the licensed hackney operators, as provided for in the Act, forcing the local authority to designate the ranks) are known to the author.

23 The Motor Vehicles (Driving Licences) Regulations 1996.

24 Transport Act 1985 ss 19–22.

25 Minibus Act 1977.

26 Minibus Act 1977.

27 Administered by the Countryside Agency, originally the Rural Development Commission.

28 EC Directive 25/98 on access to the profession of passenger transport operator.

29 Together with other recognized qualifications.

30 PPV Act 1981 s 17.

31 Transport Act 1968 relating to the hours of domestic drivers performing in the main regular timetabled work.

32 Relating to private hire and international work.

33 EC Regulation 3821/85.

34 PSV (Registration of Local Services) Regulations 1986 SI 1671.

35 The London Local Service Licence is in effect a variant of the Road Service Licensing system that existed from 1930 to 1985.

36 A fast track procedure applies to subsidized services won by tender from local transport authorities who support a registration.

37 Transport Act 1985 s 111.

38 Transport Act 1985 s 26.

39 However, before the formation of the British Transport Executive with nationalization in 1947, there was some control by the Railway Rates Tribunal over passenger fares (see Chapter 3).

40 The Railways Act 1993.

41 The Railways Act 1993 s 67.

42 The Transport Bill 2000.

43 Franchising policy is a creature of the Secretary of State and the Franchise Director does not have the same degree of independence as the Rail Regulator. The duty to secure continuance of a service can in some ways be compared to the duty of PTEs and 'shire' counties to secure by tender those services that the market cannot provide – Transport Act 1985.

44 The Railways Act 1993 ss 8 and 9.

45 Fawcett, P (1997) *The Railways Act in Practice*, TR&IN, Huddersfield.

46 Clauses 19 and 20 only require fines to be reasonable.

47 Tom Windsor is the new Rail Regulator appointed on 1 July 1999.

48 The UK's Competition Act 1999 is the most recent, based on EU Competition Directives, but US 'anti-trust' laws were an earlier challenge.

49 The Computer Reservation Systems of 'alliances' of powerful airlines like the 'One World Alliance' that includes British Airways have the potential to erode even this function.

50 The Association of Train Operating Companies (ATOC) has an almost identical role but this has not prevented the creation of an array of rail fares every bit as confusing as are now found on airlines.

51 When the previous government proposed the privatization of the Vehicle Inspectorate, and the passenger and freight transport trade associations opposed the idea, there was nevertheless some support for a direct sale to a recognized body such as Lloyds, the RAC or the AA.

52 Shaw, S (1993) and Gubbins, E (1996) *Managing Transport Operations*, 2nd edn, Kogan Page.

53 Transport Act 1968 s 92.

54 Road Traffic Act 1991 s 13.

55 PPV Act 1981.

56 With the exception of vehicles with eight or fewer passenger seats that are not tested until the third anniversary of their registration.

57 Statutory bodies replacing Trinity House.

58 DETR (1999).

CHAPTER 9

1 Consider for example the stock market's inflated valuation of 'cyber shares' in companies such as Amazon.com (the world's largest book retailer, which sells only via the Internet).

2 Leadbeater, C (1999) *Living on Thin Air*, Viking.

3 Hepworth, M and Dukasis, K (1992) *Transport in the Information Age*, Wheels and Wires, Belhaven.

4 European Union (1996) *Citizen's Network*, Brussels.

5 MRP I.

6 MRP II.

7 Solver, an Excel 'macro' routine.

8 For example, Autoroute (discussed later in this chapter) and Paragon (a collection/delivery routing algorithm).

9 Mombiot, G (1999) An unfair exchange, *The Guardian*, 15 May.

10 CA administers the Rural Transport Development Fund in England.

11 Glaister, S (1985) Competition on Urban Bus Routes, *Journal of Transport Economics*, January.

12 A system known as TRUST is used by Railtrack to report train movements and compare these to timetables for compliance monitoring purposes. ATOC is developing software (REALITY) within its Rail Journey Information system (RJIS) used by NRES that will give real-time information about the positioning of every train and can be interrogated by TEBx (telephone enquiry bureaux) operatives and passengers' mobile phones using PDA (personal data assistance software).

13 Rossendale Transport's route 264 is a proposal with such a 'Buslink' system. As the bus passes the vehicle detection unit, the transceiver communicates with this and a signal passes to the first stop, which relays this to each forward stop. As these are passed, revised running times are computed and displayed along the route.

14 TRL report 342 1998.

15 ROMANSE (Road Management System for Europe) Winchester STOPWATCH project.

16 For example, Trafficmaster.

17 The Hong Kong electronic road pricing scheme collapsed because of privacy fears in the run up to hand over to China!

18 There is a simple algebraic relationship between the size and standard deviation of a sample and the probability that the sample mean will be within defined confidence limits. Sample sizes delivering 95 per cent probabilities based on two standard deviations are common.

19 There are procedures for operators to appeal against compulsory participation in concessionary fares schemes because the basis of reimbursement is inappropriate either to their service or to services in general.

20 Travel Concession Schemes 1986.

21 Minutes of CRUCC July 1996.

22 Annual Report of RUCC for the Northwest 1997/8.

23 Band III transmission giving bus to base, bus to inspector and group call capability was the most commonly chosen system.

24 DETR (1999), paragraph 8.3.

25 0345 484950.

26 *The Guardian*, 26 July 1999.

27 www.arriva.co.uk.

28 ISO 1443 applies.

29 A 'cashless society' experiment in Swindon is aiming to increase the number of everyday transactions in the district by smartcard.

Bibliography

Fawcett, P (1989) *Minibus Services*, Croners, London
Fawcett, McLeish and Ogden (1992) *Logistics Management*, M+E
Glaister, S et al (1998) *Transport Policy in Britain*, Macmillan, London
Hibbs, J (1985) *Bus and Coach Management*, Chapman Hall, London
Simpson, B (1994) *Urban Public Transport Today*, E and FN Spon, London
Truelove, P (1992) *Decision Making in Transport Planning*, Longmans, London
Whyte, P (1992) *Public Transport Planning*, 3rd edn, Hutchinson, London

Index